MOTHER
TERESA

An authorized biography

Kathryn Spink

Fount
An Imprint of HarperCollinsPublishers

Fount Paperbacks is an Imprint
of HarperCollins*Religious*
Part of HarperCollins*Publishers*
77-85 Fulham Palace Road, London w6 8jb

First published in the Great Britain in 1997
by HarperCollins*Publishers*
This edition 1998

1 3 5 7 9 10 8 6 4 2

A catalogue record for this book
is available from the British Library

ISBN 0 00 628104 4

Printed and bound in Great Britain by
Caledonian International Book Manufacturing Ltd, Glasgow

This book is dedicated to the memory of Mother Teresa, Ann Blaikie, Bunty Watts and Father Van Exem, to all of whom I owe an immeasurable debt of gratitude. I would also like to express my appreciation to the many others – Sisters, Brothers, Co-Workers and priests – throughout the world who have given of their time, talents, hospitality and insight in the preparation of this book. To Cherry Fisher, to John Pawsey my agent, and to all the friends and companions of my journey too numerous to mention individually here, my warmest thanks. To one of them in particular I can pay no more appropriate tribute than to say that she sought at great personal cost to create, as Mother Teresa would have wished, 'something beautiful for God'.

ACKNOWLEDGEMENTS

The author and publisher wish to acknowledge with thanks reference to the following books:

Something Beautiful for God, Malcolm Muggeridge, Collins, London, 1971.

Madre Teresa – Prima Biografia Completa, Lush Gjergji, Milan, Editoriale Jaca Books, 1983 (italic text on pages 13, 14, 15 and 17).

Such a Vision of the Street: Mother Teresa, the Spirit and the Work, Eileen Egan, New York, Doubleday Image, 1985; London, Sidgewick & Jackson, 1985.

CONTENTS

PREFACE

My first contact with Mother Teresa was in 1980, via a crackling telephone line from London to Calcutta. I had discovered, in a battered tin trunk belonging to one of her earliest lay helpers, the unofficial archives of her international mission. By then that mission consisted of the Missionary Sisters of Charity, a similar Order for men, contemplative branches of the two Congregations, spiritual links with over four hundred enclosed Orders of different denominations, and an association of several thousand helpers or "Co-Workers" scattered over five continents. The records then of what Mother Teresa had on more than one occasion referred to with a certain satisfaction as the "most disorganized organization in the world" consisted of already yellowing letters, articles and snippets of paper thrown together by a stroke of vague foresight. Yet they reflected, it seemed to me, at very least a story of extraordinary growth in the thirty-two years since a solitary woman had stepped out into the slums of Calcutta to live amongst the poorest of the poor as one of them.

For three nights in succession I sat up into the early hours of the morning, trying to make contact with Mother Teresa. On the third attempt she answered the telephone herself, as was her general practice at night when she was at the mother house in Calcutta. By then Malcolm Muggeridge had written *Something Beautiful for God*, the book which was to open the eyes of the world to the work of Mother Teresa and her Missionaries of Charity, and there had been a few others. It was enough, Mother Teresa told me. There was no more material. But with all the irritability of one who has lost too much sleep, I presumed to argue. Unwilling perhaps to be unkind, she conceded that we could meet when next she came to London. We did so and in the sparsely furnished parlour of the Sisters' London home I experienced for the first time her gift for giving her whole attention to the person she encountered. She gave me her permission to write, telling me that I did not have to ask, and adding that she hoped that I was not putting any of my own money into the venture. Apparently, Nobel laureate though she was, she had no inkling that her consent to that, my first "real" book with all its defects and limitations, would be enough to launch my career as a writer. I did not know it then but would afterwards discover that precisely those qualities which in this world's terms might well have counted against me were what contributed to the favourable outcome of our encounter: my youth, my inexperience, my sense of inadequacy and uncertainty.

During the years that followed we would meet on numerous other occasions in India, England, France, Rome, in a coloured township outside Cape Town, in just a few of those locations which her own distinctive geography of compassion had determined as places where the abandoned poor needed the particular care of the Missionaries of Charity. I witnessed not only the love and the luminous smile for which she became increasingly internationally renowned but also her practical abilities, the way in which she liked to rearrange the furniture in the Sisters' houses, the efficiency which meant that somehow everything was perfectly organized and administered without any organization or administration, the lack of sentimentality and the immense shrewdness that went hand in hand with intuitive understanding, the earthy qualities which did not detract from her spirituality but which were somehow moulded by it. I came to know her humour and her toughness. She was, I discovered, not only humble and small but also strong-willed, resolute, determined and totally fearless, because God was on her side. This assumed union of intention was not one with which everybody easily came to terms. "What Mother wants, she gets" was a truism widely accepted amongst those who knew her. It was accepted because the strength of her conviction had so manifestly been instrumental in the achievement of extraordinary results, because of the love she both gave and inspired, and because her own heart, which saw and knew everything, forgave everything also. In some mysterious way she lit up everyone and everything she encountered.

Even a ride in a transit van through the dusty, congested streets of Calcutta in the company of one who was widely known there simply as "Ma" or "Mother" could be a transforming experience.

Always it would begin and end with communal prayer, the saying of the rosary. There were unaffected gestures of greeting for those passers-by who, recognizing the distinctive white sari with the blue border and the well-known stooping shoulders, would pause to look. At intervals the furrows of her face would dissolve into an all-embracing smile in response to their smiles or at some humorous thought, at the possibility, for example, that in the company of both her and her Sisters I might be taken for a postulant. All the time the strong, disproportionately large hands would continue to work their way silently through the rosary beads. For Hindus simply to be in the presence of a holy person brings with it a *darshan*, a form of blessing. For this reason crowds struggled miles during the life time of Mahatma Gandhi to catch a distant glimpse of India's "Great Soul", and for this reason now rich and poor alike sought the company or merely the presence of Mother Teresa. I came to respect this concept of *darshan* for, sceptic that I potentially was, I never left her presence without feeling better, uplifted, somehow blessed. Like the lepers on the pavements of Calcutta, somehow I too walked more sure-footedly beneath her gaze.

Her dedication moved both the materially poor and the powerful, irrespective of race or religious creed. I have seen people weep at her leaving though they have "met" her only at a distance across a crowded room. India's late premier, Jawaharlal Nehru, inaugurating Mother Teresa's first children's home in Delhi in 1961, could not conceal the emotion in his voice as he told her: "Believe me, Mother, we need you just as the poor do." American Senator Edward Kennedy, who saw her work in Calcutta during the 1971 Bangladesh war, shed public tears. When Lord Runcie, then Archbishop of Canterbury, visited the Missionaries of Charity in Calcutta in December 1986, he was reported to have wanted "to kneel and kiss Mother Teresa's feet". It had been, he said, "the most humbling and uplifting experience of my life". He was by no means alone in expressing such sentiments.

In February 1991 I went to Calcutta once again to ask Mother Teresa's permission to write. On the bench outside the chapel overlooking the courtyard of the mother house I waited and watched as a procession of people from all over the world packed the corridor and stairway in the hope of speaking to her or simply of touching her feet. Mother Teresa was eighty years old. Her five-foot frame was severely bent. Her health was far from robust, and a pacemaker had been fitted to counteract a heart condition. She looked frail and her voice was weaker. The blue-grey eyes had lost a little of their penetration. Yet the influence of this tiny woman was still very much in evidence. Small notes written by hand and signed "Mother", gave directives relating to the most ordinary of practical details. The central courtyard of the mother house contained two tanks of water. "Sisters, please do not keep anything on top of the tank", a carefully handwritten note appealed, "Thank you, Mother." It was during a period of intense international tension which preceded the Gulf War. Outside the chapel the copy of a letter Mother Teresa had written to Presidents George Bush and Saddam Hussein, appealing to them to "choose the way of peace", bore witness to the role she was still playing on the world scene:

Dear President George Bush and President Saddam Hussein,

I come to you with tears in my eyes and God's love in my heart to plead to you for the poor and those who will become poor if the war that we all dread and fear happens. I beg you with my whole heart to work for, to labour for God's peace and to be reconciled with one another.

You both have your cases to make and your people to care for but first please listen to the One who came into the world to teach us peace. You have the power and the strength to destroy God's presence and image, his men, his women and his children. Please listen to the will of God. God has created us to be loved by his love and not destroyed by our hatred.

In the short term there may be winners and losers in this war that we all dread, but that never can, nor ever will justify the suffering, pain and loss of life which your weapons will cause.

The letter went on to explain that she begged on behalf of the innocent ones, the poor of the world and of those who would become poor because of the war. She pleaded for those who would be orphaned and widowed and left alone, and for those who would have "the most precious thing that God could give us, Life, taken away from them".

I appeal to you – to your love, your love of God and your fellow man. In the name of God and in the name of those you will make poor, do not destroy life and peace. Let the love and peace triumph and let your names be remembered for the good you have done, the joy you have spread and the love you have shared.

Please pray for me and my sisters as we try to love and serve the Poor because they belong to God and are loved in his eyes, as we and our Poor are praying for you. We pray that you will love and nourish what God has so lovingly entrusted to your care.

The letter was signed, as always, "God bless you. M. Teresa, MC." She had already dispatched the deputy secretary general of the charity Refugee Year and a priest, Father Kevin Doheny, as her personal ambassadors in a bid to break the deadlock in Baghdad. History would show such efforts to be abortive, but their author was manifestly determined that if the peace of the world was to be destroyed it would not be for want of her energetic and even-handed intervention. The same energy was poured into the multitude of encounters brought by each and every day, into appeasing a weeping woman whose husband had left her and taken their children with him, or into addressing a symposium on Women and the Bible held at Loreto House courtesy of the Congregation to which Mother Teresa had belonged before she founded her own. When a man ran amok in the courtyard and parlour of the mother house, tearing the curtains and shouting for Mother Teresa, it was she who managed to calm him down. When the telephone calls came in the night from her Sisters throughout the world it was still she who went to answer them. The night before my arrival she had fallen over in the dark on her way to respond to such a call. Yet as I watched her meeting the apparently endless procession of visitors, there was still a certain strength and rustic efficiency in her body and movements. In a brief space of time she managed to greet each one and hand to most a holy medal or a prayer card. Inevitably the question arose as to whether this was just the religious equivalent of a superstar meting out autographs, but the impact of those encounters, albeit brief, was unmistakable. Manifestly very much more had passed between Mother Teresa and those whose hands she grasped than mere words or the sentimental religious pictures which even the most sophisticated would subsequently treasure. For her every individual mattered. "I believe", she once said, "in person to person contact. Every person is Christ for me and since there is only one Jesus, the person I am meeting is the one person in the world at that moment." Thus each person went away revitalized by the conviction that for a while at least they had been the only one in the world who really mattered. Mother Teresa's secret, she herself maintained, was prayer and the centrality of Christ: Christ present and hungry and thirsty in the poor, whatever form that poverty might take, Christ given in the broken bread of the Eucharist. Similarly the achievements, the work, she would insist with wonder in her voice, was not her work but God's work. She and those who laboured with her were but channels, instruments of his love.

The reaction to my request was predictably the surrender of the suggestion to prayer. The humility and simplicity of her attitude towards her life had remained conspicuously unaltered by the fact that so many had been prepared to proclaim her a saint in her own lifetime. In April 1990 Pope John Paul II had, at her request, accepted her resignation as head of the Missionaries of Charity. Her private aspiration, she had confided to one who was exceptionally close to her, was to return to Nirmal Hriday, the home for the dying in Calcutta, there to work as she had in the very earliest days, quietly bringing love and care to those who most needed it, to Christ in his most distressing disguise. Apparently it had not entered into her thinking that the hundreds who flocked each day to the mother house on Acharya J. Chandra Bose Road would follow her now wherever she went, that her life was public property, and that the public attention, with which she had come to terms for the sake of the poor of the world but which had undoubtedly represented one of her greatest personal trials, would pursue her relentlessly to the end of her days.

For several days she prayed. Then, quite suddenly, I received the summons to see her and the decision: Yes, I must write but I must do it "for the glory of God". I must write about "the spirit and the joy of loving Jesus in the poorest of the poor and each other", and about the deep life of prayer which alone could make that love possible. As always the focus was deflected from herself. Over the years she had been consistently terse in her response to questions which endeavoured to probe her personal life and motivation. "No one thinks of the pen while reading a letter," she once wrote, stressing the unimportance of such considerations, "they only want to know the mind of the person who wrote the letter. That's exactly what I am in God's hand – a little pencil. God is writing his love letter to the world in this way, through works of love."

Those who have sought to find in Mother Teresa's life complex psychological explanations have been consistently frustrated. Hers is a life not devoid of controversy – perversely it is not unheard of for church men and women to be the ones who do not want to hear talk of Mother Teresa – but it is a life of extreme simplicity as far as questions of motivation are concerned. Unsatisfying though it may seem to some in the century of Freud, her life is full of areas which do not admit of rational enquiry, and the answer to such questions is almost invariably "for Jesus", "for love of God". "If you remove Jesus from my life," she once told a group of reporters, "my life is reduced to a mere nothing." A Hindu observer on the edge of this mystery, a man who said he was not very religious but who had known and helped Mother Teresa for years, endorsed her claim without wanting to. He said that he saw the amazing extent and fruits of the work, and he saw how the Missionaries of Charity and Mother Teresa were not extraordinary in any way, and he could not add it up.

To Mother Teresa the only acceptable reason for writing about her life would be to show what she had never questioned as the missing factor in that equation. For her the only tolerable pretext for describing the lights that guided her in her vocation would be in order that they might be a light to others; the only justification for showing the more recent developments of the work might be to show how what was actually done and the spirit in which it was undertaken was the same throughout the world. The spirit of the Missionaries of Charity was one of "Loving trust, total surrender and cheerfulness as lived by Jesus and his mother". The mainten-ance of that spirit ensured that the work was not their work but God's work, and only if it was God's work would it, indeed should it, continue.

As the Missionaries of Charity continued to grow in number and spread throughout the world, and as the burden of her own advancing years became more pressing, the spirit of the Order was a matter which she raised on more than one occasion. She told me that I must write something beautiful about the joy and about the interior life upon which the life of action depended. "By the life of the soul," Mother Teresa once wrote, "Jesus Christ imparts to me his Spirit. He becomes the principle of a higher activity which prompts me, if I do not put any obstacle in the way, to think, judge, love, suffer and work with him, by him and like him. . . . If we learn this interior life, the words of our Lord will be fulfilled in our regard: 'He that abideth in me, and I in him, the same bringeth forth much fruit.'" So completely had she made that "principle of higher activity" the guiding principle of every aspect of a life which had so indisputably "brought forth fruit" that to write of the Spirit and to write of Mother Teresa were virtually one and the same thing.

Yet to deny Mother Teresa her "ordinariness", the humanity that was richly hers, is to render her life and the "principle" that governed it inaccessible to the remainder of humanity. She did not want to be raised aloft, any more than she liked the idea of people perceiving the poverty to which she had spent her life responding as being confined to the tolerably distant reaches of some "Third World" country. She knew that to enshrine Mother Teresa in Calcutta was potentially a means by which people could absolve themselves from their own immediate and daily responsibility. Like sending a cheque from the comfort of an armchair, applauding the unattainable virtues of Mother Teresa was potentially a buffer against real personal commitment. So it was that she was the principal exponent of her own weakness. "Holiness", she would insist when people acclaimed her as a living saint, "is not the luxury of the few. It is a simple duty for you and for me." "If there are poor in the world it is because you and I don't give enough."

Mother Teresa's strong-jawed face was earthy not ethereal. For people repelled by pale piety there was a toughness and vitality about it. If the quality which redeemed the wrinkles of time and weather was frequently referred to as "luminosity", it could, extraordinarily, equally well be described as merriment. It was a face which spoke, as she did, of a sense of the mystery of God very much in the world. She believed in a God who dwelt among us, fully God and fully human, and so she despised nothing human. Rather, she gloried in the life in us, our world and universe. In her seventies she wrote her own resumé of her philosophy of life:

> *Life is an opportunity, avail it.*
> *Life is a beauty, admire it.*
> *Life is bliss, taste it.*
> *Life is a dream, realize it.*
> *Life is a challenge, meet it.*
> *Life is a duty, complete it.*
> *Life is a game, play it.*
> *Life is costly, care for it.*
> *Life is a wealth, keep it.*
> *Life is love, enjoy it.*
> *Life is mystery, know it.*
> *Life is a promise, fulfil it.*
> *Life is sorrow, overcome it.*
> *Life is a song, sing it.*
> *Life is a struggle, accept it.*
> *Life is a tragedy, brace it.*
> *Life is an adventure, dare it.*
> *Life is life, save it!*
> *Life is luck, make it.*
> *Life is too precious, do not destroy it.*

The words are inscribed on a poster hanging in a home for AIDS sufferers which she and her Sisters opened at Christmas 1985, in the very heart of New York City. She called the home "Gift of Love".

MOTHER TERESA

CHAPTER ONE

The Hidden Treasure

"Mine was a happy family. I had one brother and one sister, but I do not like to talk about it. It is not important now. The important thing is to follow God's way, the way he leads us to do something beautiful for him."

Mother Teresa's constant insistence on the insignificance of her personal life meant that she spoke little about her early years. When she did so it was to stress that hers had been a childhood rendered harmonious by small, everyday things and the support of a loving family. Time and time again in later years, she would insist upon the importance of the hidden and the ordinary life, pointing out that the carpenter's son from Nazareth had spent thirty years doing humble work in a carpenter's workshop before assuming his public role, and using this as an illustration of the exemplary humility of Jesus. So unconcerned was she about accuracy in relation to the chronicling of her own life, and so disinclined actually to read anything written about her, that for many years and in a succession of books her birthdate was erroneously recorded as 27 August 1910. It even appeared in the Indian Loreto Entrance Book as her date of birth. In fact, as she confided to her friend, co-worker and American author, Eileen Egan, that was the date on which she was christened Agnes Gonxha Bojaxhiu. The date which marked the beginning of her Christian life was undoubtedly the more important to Mother Teresa, but she was none the less actually born in Skopje, Serbia, on the previous day.

Her background was, according to the insights provided by her brother, Lazar, and a cousin, Lush Gjergji, indeed essentially "ordinary". She was the youngest of the three children born to Nikola and Dranafile Bojaxhiu, both of whom were Albanian but who had come originally from Prizren, a city which during their daughter's childhood was part of Yugoslavia but had belonged at one time to the kingdom of Serbia. Nikola was descended from a large and prosperous family with a long tradition of trade. He was a merchant and entrepreneur drawn to the town of Skopje by its role as a commercial centre. According to the local parish priest, immediately on his arrival in Skopje, Nikola bought a house and gradually, thanks to involvement through a friend in a successful building firm, came to own a number of properties, in one of which the Bojaxhiu family lived. Initially Nikola supplied medicines for one of Skopje's leading doctors. Later he went into partnership with a rich Italian merchant who traded in a wide variety of goods, including oil, sugar, cloth and leather, and he began to travel to different parts of Europe on business. A capable man who sat on the town council and became a leading figure in Skopje's civic life, a supporter of the arts and of the local church, and a gifted linguist who spoke not only Albanian and Serbo-Croat, but also Turkish, Italian and French, Nikola was a strict disciplinarian who took a keen interest in his children's education. He was stern at times and expected high standards of them, reminding them that they must not forget whose children they were. Yet his homecomings were always eagerly awaited, partly because he was invariably the bearer of gifts, but primarily because he was also a talented story-teller who kept his young audience amused with enthralling tales of his travels.

In later life Mother Teresa would carry with her very traditional ideas about the function of the woman in the home, ideas for which Drana Bojaxhiu provided the role model. In one of the infrequent references the adult Mother Teresa made to her family background, she remembered how, while her father was away working, her mother busied herself about the house, cooking, mending and performing other domestic tasks, but as soon as her father returned, all work stopped. Her mother would put on a clean dress and comb her hair and ensure that the children were fresh and tidy to greet him.

Lazar, who was three years older than Agnes, recalled those early events as being "peaceful and pleasant". Yet they took place against a background of political turbulence of the kind that engendered strong patriotic feelings and a deep sense of national identity. The year in which Agnes was born (1910) witnessed the first Albanian uprising. Two years later the first Balkan war broke out as part of the unrest in the Balkan States which could contribute to the outbreak of the First World War. Internal fighting went on in both Serbia and neighbouring Albania. Albania won its independence in November 1912, thus depriving Serbia of the coastline to which it aspired and which it would only acquire with the creation of Yugoslavia as a federation of Serbia and five other States. An atmosphere of hostility prevailed between Albania and Serbia and, rooted as it was in both races, the Bojaxhiu family could hardly remain unaffected by the conflict. Nikola Bojaxhiu, with his extensive and well-established business interests, was a man not without political interests also, who showed his sympathy for the Albanian freedom fighters by providing them not only with financial support but also with hospitality.

On 28 November 1912 the proclamation of Albanian independence by its national leaders was marked in the Bojaxhiu household with revelry and celebrations. Nikola was by nature a sociable man whose home provided a warm welcome for guests ranging from the poor of Skopje to the town's Archbishop. On that particular night the house was filled with leading Albanian patriots who talked and sang to the accompaniment of mandolin playing into the early hours. Their host made no secret of his commitment to the Albanian nationalist cause. That same commitment involved him in a movement established after the First World War to have the province of Kosovo, with its predominantly Albanian population, joined to a greater Albania. It was in pursuit of this objective that in 1919 Nikola Bojaxhiu travelled some 160 miles to a political gathering in Belgrade. He left home, together with his fellow city councillors, apparently in the best of health. He returned in a carriage with the Italian consul, on the brink of death. Haemorrhaging severely, he was taken to the local hospital where emergency surgery failed to save his life. Nikola Bojaxhiu was only forty-five when he died. A question mark still lingers over the circumstances of his death, but there were those among his family and the medical profession who were convinced that he was poisoned.

The shock of the sudden loss of her husband was a devastating one for Drana Bojaxhiu, compounded by the fact that following

Nikola's death, his Italian business partner appropriated the assets of the business. Drana's own relatives were merchants and land-owners with large estates in Novo Selo to which she had some claim, but she possessed no documents to establish her rights and was in any case disinclined to pursue the matter. Consequently she and her children were left with little but the roof over their heads. For the first time the Bojaxhiu children experienced what it was to be without financial security. Drana did not, however, allow it to detract from their happiness. She went through an initial period of grief, during which she leaned heavily on the support of her eldest child Aga, who was fifteen at the time, but afterwards she assumed her new role as provider with all the strength of character of which she was undoubtedly possessed. Thus it was very largely under the influence of her devout mother, and her insistence on the value of the non-material riches of kindness, generosity and compassion for the poor and weak, that the foundations for Agnes's future apostolate were laid. Agnes was only eight years old when her father died. "Home", she would assert in later life, "is where the mother is." In old age particularly the physical attributes which Mother Teresa shared with her mother became strikingly apparent but they undoubtedly shared other characteristics also, to a point where some of the adult Mother Teresa's very distinctive sayings were almost a word for word echo of her mother's spiritual directives. Hence, for example, the often repeated instruction: "Be only all for God."

If the Bojaxhiu home had always been open to all, there had invariably been a special welcome for the poor. An elderly woman had come regularly to the house for meals. "Welcome her warmly, with love", Nikola instructed them. "My child, never eat a single mouthful unless you are sharing it with others." It was an approach to people and to possessions which Drana Bojaxhiu, serious, highly disciplined and deeply religious as she was, both shared and comple-mented. She took to sewing and embroidery and selling cloth to provide not only for the material needs of her children but also for those of people who were even less fortunate. The family table continued to be a gathering place for the poor for whom she cared with a gentle warmth. Years later Lazar would recall questioning his mother as to who the people who shared his meals were. "Some of them are our relations," was the response, "but all of them are our people." No one ever left empty-handed.

At least once a week Drana would visit an old woman who had been abandoned by her family, to take her food and clean her house. She washed and fed and cared for File, an alcoholic woman covered with sores, as if she was a small child. The six children of a poor widow became part of Drana's own family when their mother died. Agnes would sometimes accompany her mother on her errands of mercy, for Drana was eager that the lessons of love in action and the importance of leading a Christian life, albeit without deliberately attracting attention to one's own virtue, should be communicated to her children. "When you do good," she instructed them, "do it quietly, as if you were throwing a stone into the sea." Such lessons were instilled by solid example. One story recounted by Mother Teresa, more because it contained a spiritual lesson than because it provided an insight into her own background, recorded how one day her mother brought home a basket of good apples. Calling her three children to inspect for themselves how perfect and unflawed each apple was, she then placed a rotten apple in the middle of them and left the basket covered. Next day the children were again summoned to examine the state of the apples. Many of them had begun to rot. The process was used to demonstrate the corrupting influence of mixing in the wrong kind of company.

"The family that prays together, stays together", was one of the adult Mother Teresa's much used axioms. The Bojaxhiu family had been Catholic for many generations. Prayer was an integral part of their family life. Every evening they assembled to pray together, and regular attendance at the local Catholic church was a source of considerable support to them. In Albania the Catholic population, even during the years preceding the wars, was never more than ten per cent, the majority of the population being Muslim. In Serbia for centuries the majority faith had been Orthodox. Neighbouring Croatia was largely Roman Catholic, but there was a long history of hostility between Croatia and Serbia. As the focal point of worship for Albanians representing a minority religion, therefore, the parish church of the Sacred Heart in Skopje performed not only a spiritual role but also one of preserving a culture and sense of identity. At the same time the coexistence of different religions in the increasingly atheistic population of Skopje called forth a certain tolerance. Drana was an active member of the Sacred Heart congregation, and her younger daughter followed in her footsteps. Agnes was, in Lazar's recollection, a naturally obedient and thoughtful child, whose example her mother tended to cite to her two other children. From a very early age she went readily to church services. She was educated first at a convent-run primary school but then went on to a state school, and so it was from her home and from the church that she received her religious instruction. The Bojaxhiu family was musical. Singing, playing instruments and even composition was an accepted part of family life. Learning to play the mandolin presented Agnes with no particular difficulties and, again, her musical gifts found an outlet at the church of the Sacred Heart. Like her sister, Aga, she joined the church choir, where together in time they would become known as the church's two "nightingales" who were frequently singled out for solo parts.

By the age of twelve Agnes felt herself called to the religious life, an intensely personal experience on which she would not elaborate, other than to say that it did not take the form of any supernatural or prophetic apparition: "It is a private matter. It was not a vision. I've never had a vision." Until Agnes went away to become a nun herself she had never even seen one. Yet the possibility of her youngest child being called to the religious life did not come as a total surprise to Drana, who intimated on more than one occasion to her other children that she did not feel that Agnes would be with them for long, either because of her poor health, for Agnes had a weak chest and was prone to chronic coughs, or because she would be called to give herself to God. For six years Agnes thought and prayed about it. By her own admission there were times when she doubted whether she had a vocation but in the end she was convinced that she was being called to "belong completely to God". "Our Lady of the Black Mountain at Letnice helped me to see this."

The annual pilgrimage to the chapel of the Madonna of Letnice on the slopes of Skopje's Black Mountain was the highlight of the parish year. The Bojaxhiu family would go in a horse-drawn carriage to join groups of pilgrims, both Catholic and non-Catholic, who made their way, singing and praying, up the hillside as an act of faith. There were times, however, when in the interests of Agnes's delicate health, Drana would arrange for her to visit the shrine when there were not quite so many other people present. Agnes was fond of praying alone in the chapel, and the periods spent there appear to have been a source of both physical and spiritual sustenance to her for the remainder of the year. They also gave her the confirmation of her vocation that she sought.

It was a Croatian Jesuit priest, Father Jambrekovic, who provided her with a litmus test during periods of doubt. He had become the priest at the Sacred Heart in May 1925 and introduced the young people of the parish to many things, teaching them about medicine, science, poetry, drama and even orchestral conducting. It was he who set up in Skopje a Sodality of Children of Mary, a Christian society for girls, of which Agnes became an active member. She was a popular child with an appealing sense of fun and plenty of female friends, although shy with boys and inclined at times to be somewhat withdrawn and introverted. The sodality introduced her to, among other things, the challenges of St Ignatius Loyola's Spiritual Exercises: "What have I done for Christ? What am I doing for Christ? What will I do for Christ?" Agnes was fond of reading. A library initiated by Father Jambrekovic kept her supplied with books. He also established a mixed Catholic youth group with a programme of walks, parties, concerts and other outings, and in general he had a profound effect upon the spiritual and cultural life of his young parishioners. His response to Agnes's question as to how she could know whether God was really calling her was that joy was the proof of the rightness of any endeavour. Joy, he maintained, was the compass which pointed the direction in life.

As a Jesuit, Father Jambrekovic passed on to his parishioners news of the missionary work undertaken by the Society of Jesus as part of a widespread wave of enthusiasm for the missions encouraged by the writings of Pope Pius XI and prevalent at the time. In 1924 a number of Yugoslavian priests had left for India to undertake missionary work in Bengal, in the archdiocese of Calcutta. Sent first to the seminary at Kurseong and subsequently allocated to the district of 24-Parganas on the outskirts of Calcutta, and to the Sunderbans, from India they wrote fervent and inspiring letters about the work of missionaries among the poor and the sick. Their writing, the occasional visits of missionaries to Skopje, and Father Jambrekovic's own enthusiasm for the work gave a focus to Agnes' vocation. As a very small child she had dreamed of serving the poor of Africa. Although it had been Africa which first captured her imagination, the letters which came through from India drew her attention in a different direction. Agnes impressed all those around her with her detailed knowledge of the activities undertaken by different missions. She spent longer periods of retreat at Cesnagore, and by the time she was eighteen she was convinced that her own calling was to be a missionary, to "go out and give the life of Christ to the people".

By then the generally exemplary if occasionally mischievous child had grown into an attractive young woman whose active contribution to the life of the community was much valued. She was a born organizer and something of a driving force in all the activities she undertook. At school she had done well, although not quite as well as her elder sister Aga, and she had already discovered a certain gift for communicating her knowledge to others. Some of her own classmates came to her for extra tuition. At various junctures she had harboured hopes of a career in music or writing. A passionate lover of poetry, she composed poems herself. Two articles she wrote were published in the local newspaper, and there were those about her who felt that she had a talent in that direction which should be pursued. The decision to become a missionary nun was not an easy one. It was undoubtedly a struggle, for there is every reason to believe that Agnes was a young girl deeply attached to her family and one who relished the prospect of having her own home and children. When in October 1981 an Australian journalist asked whether the mother of thousands had missed having her own child, Mother Teresa's response was, "Naturally, naturally, of course. That is the sacrifice we make. That is the gift we give to God." She was quick to point out the many compensations and rewards of her life of chastity. By then her immensely extended family had provided her with thousands of children, men and women to love. The sacrifice was none the less real. To join a missionary order as she did in the 1920s entailed not only the commitment to chastity but most likely also the prospect of a lifetime of total separation from her blood relatives, friends and homeland. At that time there was little opportunity for home visits, or travel by family members to distant lands. Yet Agnes applied to join the Loreto Sisters, the Irish branch of the Institute of the Blessed Virgin Mary, about whose work the Yugoslav priests in Bengal had written with a fervour which she found compelling.

When first Agnes informed her mother of her intention, Drana initially refused her consent, not because she was surprised or dis-approved but because she wanted to test the strength of her daugh-ter's conviction. When it became apparent that Agnes would not be swayed from her decision, Drana went to her room, closed the door and remained there for twenty-four hours. Eventually, not without an element of considerable personal sacrifice, she gave her daughter her blessing, but with the warning that she must give herself totally and faithfully to God. Years later, looking back on that crucial decision, Mother Teresa recalled how her mother had reminded her that she must be "only, all for God and Jesus". "If I had not been true to my vocation she would have judged me as God would judge me. One day she will ask me: 'My child, have you lived only, all for God?'"

By 1928 Lazar had already been away from home for several years. He had first won a scholarship to study in Austria, and then joined Albania's Military Academy. On 1 September 1928 Albania became a monarchy under King Zog I, and the young Second Lieutenant Bojaxhiu enlisted in the army of the newly crowned king. Although later Lazar would comment on how very like his deeply religious mother Mother Teresa was, at the time the news of Agnes's vocation came as a surprise to him. He wrote her a somewhat imperious letter enquiring whether she really knew what she was doing. "You think you are important," was Agnes's defiant response, "because you are an officer serving a king with two million subjects. But I am serving the King of the whole world."

On the Feast of the Assumption 1928, Agnes joined the pilgrim-age to Letnice for the last time, and on the evening of 26 September she boarded a train for Zagreb. Katoličke misije, *Catholic Missions*, a Zagreb periodical which, with its regular reports of Catholic missionary work undertaken by Croatian and Slovene missionaries in India, had contributed to the shaping of Agnes's vocation, reported how about a hundred tearful people were present to wave her off on her journey from Skopje to an unknown land. Agnes's hope was that she was destined for the mother house of the Loreto Sisters in Rathfarnham, Dublin. For some time she waited with her mother and Aga in Zagreb to be joined by Betika Kajnc, another young woman wanting to join the Loreto Order. Then finally, on 13 October she parted from her mother and sister, and together with her new companion set off on a long and gruelling train journey across Europe. At the time the Loreto Sisters had a hostel in Paris and it was in Paris that, with the assistance of an interpreter from the Yugoslavian Embassy, the two girls were interviewed by Mother Eugene MacAvin, the Sister in charge at Loreto House, Auteuil. On the strength of the meeting, Mother Eugene MacAvin recommended them to the Mother General of the Order, Mother M. Raphael Deasy at Rathfarnham, Dublin.

The two girls received their postulant's caps at Loreto Abbey, Rathfarnham on 12 October 1928 but they spent only six weeks there, during which time they concentrated primarily on learning English, the language in which their spiritual studies would be conducted. Understandably in view of its brevity, their stay left only the impression of two quiet young women, dutifully struggling with a new life in a language which was completely strange to them. Agnes Bojaxhiu spoke not a word of English on her arrival but she had inherited something of her father's gift for languages and she was further helped in her efforts by Mother Mary Emmanuel McDermott who was a postulant with her at Rathfarnham. It was none the less no easy task, and in order to facilitate their progress, the two postulants from Yugoslavia were asked never to speak to each other in their own language, a directive to which they were both consistently faithful. On 1 December 1928, they set sail for India and a new world of separation and service. By then Gonxha Agnes Bojaxhiu had chosen the name of Sister Mary Teresa of the Child Jesus – after Teresa of Lisieux, the "Little Flower" who had pointed the way to holiness through fidelity in small things, Mother Teresa was at pains to emphasize, not the great Teresa of Avila. Her travelling companion had taken the name of Mary Magdalene.

The long voyage through the Suez canal, the Red Sea, the Indian Ocean and, finally, the Bay of Bengal can only have heightened the girls' sense of isolation from all that was familiar. Christmas was celebrated at sea. Together with three Franciscan missionary nuns who were also on board, they sang Christmas carols round a small improvised paper crib beneath a canopy of glittering stars. Their primary regret, Teresa's first contribution to *Catholic Missions* on 6 January 1929 recorded, was that there was no Catholic priest on board to celebrate Mass.

Her first landfall close to the "land of dreams" was at Colombo, where the tall, fruit-laden palms and the beauty of nature in general left her astonished. She observed the life in the city with "strange feelings". Half-naked Sri-Lankans, their skin and hair glistening in the hot sun, the men who like human horses pulled their little carts through the congested streets, her own journey in one of those carts against her natural inclinations and praying all the time that her weight would not be too heavy for the puller to bear – all these experiences left a powerful impression and were set down on paper. So too was the fact from which she evidently derived much comfort, that a Catholic priest would be a fellow passenger for the final stages of the voyage:

So now we had Mass daily, and life on board no longer seemed so desolate to us. We did not have a very solemn New Year's Eve but all the same we sang the Te Deum *in our hearts. Thanks be to God, we began the new year well – with a sung Mass which seemed a little more majestic to us.*

Madras was the next port of call and there the "indescribable" poverty and strange customs of the people shocked her profoundly. Her contact with the poor of Skopje had by no means immunized her against the extremity of the need she encountered there.

Many families live in the streets, along the city walls, even in places thronged with people. Day and night they live out in the open on mats they have made from large palm leaves – or frequently on the bare ground. They are all virtually naked, wearing at best a ragged loincloth. . . . As we went along the street we chanced upon one family gathered around a dead relation, wrapped in worn red rags, strewn with yellow flowers, his face painted in coloured stripes. It was a horrifying scene. If our people could only

*see all this, they would stop grumbling about their own misfortunes and offer
thanks to God for blessing them with such abundance.*

The two young women from Yugoslavia arrived in Calcutta on 6 January 1929 but their first encounter with Kipling's "city of dreadful night" was a brief one. Only one week later they were sent to begin their novitiate in earnest in Darjeeling, a hill station some 7,000 feet up in the foothills of the Himalayas. On 23 May 1929 Teresa of the Child Jesus was formally made a Loreto novice. An entry in the Indian Loreto Entrance Book records that on that date she "received the holy habit". Monsignor Ferdinand Périer, the Archbishop of Calcutta who, many years later, would play a vital role in her initiation to another form of religious life, was present at the ceremony at which her change of name and commencement of two years of intensive training in the spirituality and work of Loreto was officially confirmed. The novitiate was a period of preparation and probation for the religious life. For Loreto nuns it also involved preparation for their particular apostolate of teaching, an apostolate which suited Sister Teresa's talents and fulfilled some of the early aspirations which the religious life might otherwise have required her to relinquish. Dressed in the cumbersome black habit and veil which, with scant regard for the Indian climate, the Loreto novices wore in those days, she embarked upon the new life, which also involved the learning of Hindi and Bengali, with industry and good cheer.

In 1991 at Loreto House, Calcutta, Sister Marie Thérèse, a Loreto nun who had come out to India one year ahead of Sister Teresa, remembered the young novice as having been a "great girl, very jolly and bright, full of fun". "She didn't know much English in those days but it was marvellous how she picked it up. She was always a great worker too. Very hard working. She was also a very kind and charitable sort of person even as a young nun."

Following her first temporary vows on 24 May 1931, Teresa began teaching in the Loreto convent school in the relatively privileged environs of Darjeeling. She also worked for a brief period helping the nursing staff in a small medical station. Again the November 1931 issue of *Catholic Missions* provided a record of her first experience of close proximity with the suffering poor of India:

Many have come from a distance, walking for as much as three hours. What a state they are in! Their ears and feet are covered in sores. They have lumps and lesions on their backs, among the numerous ulcers. Many stay at home because they are too debilitated by tropical fever to come. One is in the terminal stage of tuberculosis. Some need medicine. It takes a long time to treat them all and give the advice that is needed. You have to explain to them at least three times how to take a particular medicine, and answer the same question three times.

On one occasion a man arrived with a bundle from which protruded what the young novice at first took to be two dry twigs, but which proved to be the emaciated legs of a boy so weak he was on the point of death:

The man is afraid we will not take the child, and says, "If you do not want him, I will throw him into the grass. The jackals will not turn up their noses at him." My heart freezes. The poor child! Weak, and blind – totally blind. With much pity and love I take the little one into my arms, and fold him in my apron. The child has found a second mother.

Already for her there was an intimate and mysterious relationship between the vulnerable Christ and the suffering people she encountered. In the hospital pharmacy hung a picture of Christ the Redeemer surrounded by a throng of suffering people on whose faces were engraved the torments of their lives. Each morning before she opened the door to a veranda packed with desperately sick people she would look at that picture:

In it is concentrated everything that I feel. I think, "Jesus, it is for you and for souls!"

So it was that the incident of the tiny blind child she held enfolded in her apron became the "crowning point" of her working day:

"Who so receives a child, receives me", said the divine Friend of all little ones.

Sister Teresa's deeply spiritual attitude to suffering, and indeed to all other aspects of the religious life, did not pass unnoticed. Sister Marie Thérèse remembered her prayerfulness being a source of amicable teasing which was taken in good part. In other respects she was for the most part unremarkable, not particularly educated, not particularly intelligent. In fact it was for her ineptitude at lighting the candles for Benediction that some remembered her best.

*

From Darjeeling she was sent to Loreto Entally, one of six schools run by the Loreto Sisters in Calcutta. There, in one of the eastern districts of Calcutta, she taught first geography and then history in an impressive collection of buildings sited in a sizeable compound enclosed by high walls. She held no formal qualifications to do so but in those days, as Sister Marie Thérèse pointed out, not so much store was set by formal qualifications. Those who could teach were simply given the opportunity to do so, and Sister Teresa proved to be more than competent in the classroom. Inside the imposing classical style gateway to Loreto Entally, stood a boarding school catering especially for girls from broken homes, for orphans and children with only one parent. Here English was the first language used. In the same compound, however, was St Mary's high school for Bengali girls, where lessons were conducted in Bengali and English was taught as a second language. It was run by a sister Order affiliated to the Loreto Sisters whose members, known as the Daughters of St Anne, were Bengali women. They dressed in saris and taught in their own tongue. It was in this Bengali high school that Sister Teresa was to teach and gradually to become known as "the Bengali Teresa" to distinguish her from the Irish Sister Marie Thérèse.

During her earliest days in Calcutta the "Bengali Teresa" also taught at St Teresa's primary school, some distance from the confines of Loreto Entally. To suggest that the walls of Loreto divorced their occupants from the poverty that coexisted so uneasily with all the grandeur of a colonial city of key importance, is to do the Order an injustice. The particular vocation of the Loreto nuns, to which over the years they have been faithful with great effect, was to tackle the problems of poverty through education. In 1935 Sister Teresa found herself brought into direct contact with the realities of deprivation among the pupils at St Teresa's. So poverty-stricken were the conditions in which she found herself teaching that she was obliged to begin lessons by rolling up the sleeves of her habit, finding water and a broom and sweeping the floor, an act which occasioned much amazement among children accustomed to seeing people of only the lowest castes undertake such menial tasks. The room in question had once been a long chapel but was now divided up to accommodate five classes. At other times she was required to teach in what she pronounced was something more like a stable, or simply outside in a courtyard. When first she saw where the children slept and ate she was, to use her own expression, "full of anguish". "It is not possible to find worse poverty", she wrote. Yet the discovery of this poverty was accompanied by a lesson concerning the compensatory capacity for happiness. The mere act of placing her hand on each dirty little head occasioned, she discovered, extraordinary joy. "From that day onwards they called me 'Ma', which means 'Mother'. How little it takes to make simple souls happy!"

On 24 May 1937 in Darjeeling Sister Teresa committed herself to her vows of poverty, chastity and obedience for life, and in doing so became, as was then usual for Loreto nuns, "Mother Teresa".

Shortly before she did so one of the slum children she had come to know came to her looking pale and sad:

He asked whether I would be coming back to them, because he had heard that I was going to become "Mother". He began to cry, and through his tears he said, "Oh, don't become Mother!" I held him to me and asked him, "What is the matter? Do not worry. I will be back. I will always be your Ma."

Every Sunday she went to visit the poor in the *bustees*, the slum areas of Calcutta. She had nothing to give them by way of material assistance, for poverty both of spirit and fact was a mark of her own life. Somehow she invariably managed to come by the shabbiest things in the community, those things which no one else wanted. There were more patches and darns in her sheets than there was original material. The mis-shapen, deformed feet of her later years were the consequences of the concealed but persistent wearing of second-hand shoes that did not fit her properly, but the experience of mixing with India's poor was already reinforcing the lesson of her childhood: that the absence of material things did not necessarily impair the capacity for happiness. It showed her that her presence alone was frequently enough to bring them joy. "Oh God, how easy it is to spread happiness in that place", she wrote after one visit to a woman who possessed so desperately little but who greeted her arrival with an overwhelming display of happiness. "Give me the strength to be ever the light of their lives, so that I may lead them at last to you!"

At Entally there was a Sodality of Mary which operated in a very similar fashion to the sodality to which Mother Teresa herself had belonged as a girl in Skopje. Under the spiritual directorship of a Belgian priest, Father Julien Henry, and with Mother Teresa's encouragement, its members visited patients in a local hospital and went into the slum of Motijhil which sprawled, with its improvised shacks and its mud alleyways teeming with life, just the other side of the walls of the Entally compound. These visits to the bustees became the subject of subsequent discussion and were constantly related to the Gospel message. "Mother Teresa", one of her pupils – who would later join her in her work as a Missionary Sister of Charity – recalled, "was not only our teacher, she was all the time drawing us to Christ. Whether we were Christian, Hindu or Muslim, she used to talk to us about Jesus. Especially she would tell the story of the Samaritan woman. How Christ was thirsting for water and how he is thirsting for love, and about the visitation, how Our Lady went in haste because charity cannot wait, and we must not lose time or pass by."

Throughout the war years the need in Calcutta mounted. Bengal suffered devastatingly from the disruption occasioned by the demands of a war into which India had been drawn by Britain without prior consultation. The year 1943 brought a famine, the effects of which were intensified by the sequestering of river boats by which rice might otherwise have been delivered from Bengal's paddy fields. Several million people lost their lives and many more converged upon Calcutta in quest of food or the means to earn their livelihood. Sister Marie Thérèse recalled the increased number of "war babies" left on the doorsteps of Loreto, and the bedlam which prevailed when she found herself presented with twenty-four babies to bottle-feed. For most of the war, however, while the Japanese forces were in nearby Burma, the three hundred orphans and other children at Loreto Entally were evacuated to convents outside the city. The Entally compound was taken over as a British military hospital, and its dormitories were reserved for the wounded. Mother Teresa, however, remained in Calcutta. The Bengali school was moved to Convent Road, and when she had taken her final vows as a Loreto Sister she succeeded a Mauritian Loreto nun, Mother Cenacle, as its headmistress and Superior in charge of three or four Loreto nuns and a bigger community of Daughters of St Anne. The "Bengali Teresa" was determined that the teaching work would not be interrupted.

The fact that she stayed when others chose to leave did not fail to make an impact on her pupils. She was happy in her work and well-liked by those whom she taught. Her mere absence from the refectory at meal times was enough of a punishment when the girls misbehaved. Not long after her appointment as headmistress she had written to her mother:

This is a new life. Our centre here is very fine. I am a teacher, and I love the work. I am also Head of the whole school, and everybody wishes me well.

By then Drana was living in Tirana, Albania. Her elder daughter, Aga, had remained with her in Skopje until 1932 but had then moved to Tirana to live with Lazar, where she worked first as a translator from Serbo-Croat into Albanian and subsequently on Albanian radio. Together the children had contrived to persuade their mother to join them, and in 1934 she had moved to the Albanian capital.

Dear child, came her mother's somewhat stern reminder from there. *Do not forget that you went to India for the sake of the poor.*

She added another insight which sowed an umistakable seed for her daughter's future:

Do you remember our File? She was covered in sores, but what caused her far more suffering was the knowledge that she was all alone in the world. We did what we could for her but the worst thing was not the sores but the fact that her family had forgotten her.

The story of how she rescued a woman who had been left to die on the streets of Calcutta was one which Mother Teresa would afterwards tell to audiences throughout the world. What caused that woman to weep, she informed them, was not the fact that she was half-consumed by maggots and on the point of death, but that the person who had deserted her was her son, that she was alone and unwanted even by her own family.

Conventional wisdom has it that in the face of the poverty, hunger, ignorance and despair she had seen, albeit so far only in a limited way, Mother Teresa began progressively to feel that something more was being asked of her. Yet those who shared her life as Loreto nuns knew nothing of any dissatisfaction, and neither, when he met her for the first time in 1944, did the priest who was to become one of the closest companions of her spiritual journey for more than forty-five years.

Father Celeste Van Exem was a Belgian Jesuit, an expert in Arabic and the Muslim faith, who had lived for some time with the Bedouin Arabs, imbibing their spirit, their language and their culture. He had also studied Urdu and come to Calcutta in 1944 for the specific purpose of working with the city's Muslims. He and two other professors felt themselves called to an intellectual apostolate and were looking for a place in Calcutta in which to house their books, and from which to carry out their work. Eventually his Jesuit Superior gave them a house in Baithakana, close to the night-marishly congested Sealdah station and also not far from Mother Teresa's community on Convent Road. In 1991 he remembered with characteristic humour his initial response to the suggestion that in view of this proximity he might be prepared to say daily Mass for Mother Teresa: "No, Father. My Provincial called me to India for the Muslims and not for Sisters." "I was a young priest who wanted to work with intellectuals", he confessed. "I did not want to be busy with nuns." Nevertheless, despite himself, he was persuaded. On 11 July 1944 he began his work at Baithakana, and on the following day at Mass he met Mother Teresa for the first time. His impression in those early days was of a very simple nun, very devout, with an interest in the poor but not particularly remarkable in any respect. Yet she undoubtedly responded to something in him, for not long afterwards she asked him to become her spiritual director and father. Once again reluctant to become diverted from what he considered to be his real vocation, he told her she must put her request in writing to Archbishop Ferdinand Périer: "It was the last thing I wanted to do, to become the spiritual father of a nun." The request was formally made none the less, and in obedience he found himself assuming a role he would not have sought but one through which he would come to know her as someone with "an intense spiritual life".

At the end of the war Mother Teresa's community moved back to the old convent at Entally, and Mother Teresa was replaced as Superior by her predecessor, Mother Cenacle. Opinions among the local ecclesiastical hierarchy had been divided about Mother Teresa's competence as a Superior. Mother Cenacle was very elderly, however, and it was Mother Teresa who continued in practice to do most of the work. The year 1946 brought the escalating conflict between Hindus and Muslims which preceded partition and the independence of India. For a period there were no teachers available to teach classes four to ten. Mother Teresa took them all, keeping those children whose families were too far away for them to rejoin them, exceptionally busy in an attempt to take their minds off the bloodshed of the streets. On one occasion when there was no food left, one of her former pupils recalled, "Mother told us, 'I am going out. Children, you stay in the chapel and pray.' By 4 p.m. the store room was full of different kinds of vegetables and food."

On 16 August 1946, a date declared "Direct Action Day" by the Muslim League, Calcutta erupted into Muslim/Hindu violence. All food deliveries were brought to a standstill. With three hundred hungry girls at Entally's boarding school, Mother Teresa went out into the streets alone. She was stopped by troops, who drove her back to the school with a lorry-load of bags of rice, but not before she had witnessed something of the horror of the bloodbath in which over five thousand Calcuttans were killed and another fifteen thousand were wounded.

During that year Mother Teresa herself was weak and ill. In the recollection of Sister Marie Thérèse she was always rather frail: "We were careful of her. I don't know whether she realized it, but we were. . . . When it came to the work and the running around, our Superiors took extra care with her." Mother Teresa had a weak chest and the Loreto Provincial was afraid that she would be stricken with tuberculosis. She was directed to rest on her bed for three hours every afternoon. In all Father Van Exem's years of association with her that was the only time he saw Mother Teresa cry: "I have seen her upset at the death of a Sister, things like that, but I have never seen her cry. But then there were tears in her eyes. It was very hard for her to be in bed and not to do the work." The period of enforced rest culminated in the directive to go on retreat to the hill station of Darjeeling. The intention was that in the interests of her health she should undergo a period of spiritual renewal and a physical break from the work. Instead, as it transpired, she was to be called to another form of work and service within the religious life she had already chosen.

On 10 September 1946, a date now celebrated annually by Missionaries of Charity and Co-Workers throughout the world as "Inspiration Day", on the rattling, dusty train journey to Darjeeling, came what Mother Teresa would subsequently describe as "the call within a call". It was an experience about which she would say little. "The call of God to be a Missionary of Charity", she once confided, "is the hidden treasure for me, for which I have sold all to purchase it. You remember in the gospel, what the man did when he found the hidden treasure – he hid it. This is what I want to do for God." The message, in whatever form it was communicated, was nevertheless both singular and unambiguous: "I was to leave the convent and help the poor while living among them. It was an order. To fail it would have been to break the faith."

CHAPTER TWO

The Will of God

In the recollection of Father Van Exem, "Inspiration Day" might in fact be more accurately described as "Inspiration Days", for Mother Teresa continued to receive divine inspiration relating to the work she was to undertake and how she was to implement it, throughout the retreat that followed. After the experience of the train came a period of silence, solitude and prayer. Father Pierre Fallon, who directed the retreat, noticed how Mother Teresa remained even more deeply engrossed in prayer than usual, and how at intervals she was seen to be busy writing on small slips of paper.

It was to Father Van Exem that Mother Teresa entrusted these slips of paper on her return to Entally in October, with a request for his opinion and direction. He took them with him back to Baithakana and placed them for a while beneath a picture of the Immaculate Heart of Mary, which Mother Teresa had given him as a Christmas gift. When, two hours later, he finally looked at them in the privacy of his room, he found in them all the essential ingredients of what was to follow: "She was to leave Loreto but she was to keep her vows. She was to start a new congregation. That congregation would work for the poorest of the poor in the slums in a spirit of poverty and cheerfulness. There would be a special vow of charity for the poor. There would be no institutions, hospitals or big dispensaries. The work was to be among the abandoned, those with nobody, the very poorest."

The experience on the train to Darjeeling and during the subsequent days had, in some way which Mother Teresa felt appropriate to keep in her heart, sown the seeds for all that was to follow. When she returned to the Loreto School in October she led a retreat on the subject of the cry of the crucified Christ from the

cross, "I thirst", and of the request in St John's Gospel to the
Samaritan woman (4:9): "Give me to drink." From the intensity
with which she spoke then, and from the very specific spirituality
which would eventually be enshrined in the constitutions of the
Congregation she was to found, something of the insight she
received may be inferred. The society would be consecrated to the
Immaculate Heart of Mary because, state the constitutions, "it was
born at her pleading, and through her continual intercession it grew
up and continues to grow". The Congregation's expressed aim, was
to "quench the infinite thirst of Jesus Christ on the Cross for
love of souls". The importance given to this general aim would be
underlined by the fact that in time each one of the Society's chapels
throughout the world would be inscribed with the two simple
words: "I thirst". Those who were called to respond to that thirst
by taking in addition to the usual religious vows of poverty, chastity
and obedience, a fourth unique vow of "wholehearted free service
to the poorest of the poor" would be called "Missionaries of
Charity" – carriers of God's love. Beyond this lay Mother Teresa's
conviction that when Jesus Christ spoke the words "I thirst" on the
cross, he did so as a revelation of God's longing to draw humanity
to himself. She saw that cry as an expression of the same thirst
revealed to the woman at Jacob's Well, a thirst which could not be
quenched by water alone but by love. She also recognized that the
requisite love could itself only come from God. In order to be its
carriers, Missionaries of Charity must themselves therefore
acknowledge their dependence on the directive: "If any one thirst,
let him come to me and drink" (John 7:37), for the words "I thirst"
simultaneously revealed the thirst of man for God. In the hungry,
thirsty, broken bodies of the poor, the Missionaries of Charity
would also see the Christ who in St Matthew's Gospel (25:35) had
so specifically identified himself with those in need: "For I was
hungry and you gave me food; I was thirsty and you gave me to
drink; I was a stranger and you made me welcome; naked and you
clothed me, sick and you visited me, in prison and you came to see
me."

The "call within a call" did not invite a radical change of direction as far as Mother Teresa's spirituality was concerned. The
devotion to Mary and to the Immaculate Heart was deeply rooted

in the Roman Catholic faith of her Albanian childhood and in the spiritual life of Loreto. The memory of a former pupil bears witness to Mother Teresa's strong emphasis, even during her years as a teacher, on the significance of what took place at Jacob's Well between Jesus and the Samaritan woman. Time alone would show how exceptional things were brought about, as if necessarily and with perfect logic, as a result of this intensely private experience of a devout but otherwise apparently unexceptional woman, in such a way that people would speak of charisms and divine grace. Time would reveal her to have a gift for radiating love. She herself would often suggest that the capacity to radiate God's love was dependent first on a personal interior contact with the fire of God's love. Perhaps the "call within a call" involved such a contact. Certainly, those who knew her in the early years of the new congregation she was to found, spoke often of the "fire" that seemed to burn in her. What is clear is that this second call entailed for her an experience of what she saw as God's thirsting love in reality which urged her to respond with a specific apostolate, and having received that enjoinder it was not in accordance either with her own personality or with her religious convictions to delay unduly. The example of the Visitation of the Virgin Mary was undoubtedly constantly before her, for she had frequently told her young pupils, "Our Lady went in haste because charity cannot wait."

Yet the man whom she had chosen as her spiritual father required her to wait. He was beginning to discern in her "a union with God" which exceeded his initial impression of a woman who was "very good, very simple, very humble and very obedient", but it was not for him to decide what was or was not the will of God for her. Conscious that as a young priest he could not carry the responsibility for what was to follow alone, Father Van Exem resolved that before pursuing the matter any further they should pray about it until January. Then, if it seemed to be an expression of the will of God, they would raise the issue with Archbishop Périer. When January 1947 came, he instructed Mother Teresa to write to the Archbishop and went himself to see him. The Archbishop's response to the young man's suggestion that Mother Teresa's request was the will of God was much as he had expected: "You have only just arrived here and already you are telling the nuns to leave their convents. . . . You say this is the will of God, just like that. I am a bishop and I don't profess to know what is the will of God." Such scoldings were very much the tenor of Archbishop Périer's relationship with the younger man when it came to the question of Mother Teresa, but Father Van Exem was able to discern in them a certain wisdom and a valid testing of his own belief in the rightness of Mother Teresa's second calling.

There were a number of other Orders in Calcutta already working with the poor. The Archbishop was doubtful as to whether the founding of yet another could really be justified. The emphasis of Mother Teresa's proposal was very much on the idea of *going out to* the poor. The work of the Sisters of Charity or the Daughters of St Anne, for example, commendable though it was, was undertaken very largely within the confines of their convents, hospitals or dispensaries. Even given this distinction, however, and the fact that there might be a case for an Order committed in this particular way to wholehearted, free service to the poorest of the poor, the Archbishop was conscious of the possible irresponsibility of allowing a woman to live and work alone in the slums of India, a woman who wanted to trust entirely in Divine Providence for the provision of her own needs and the needs of those who might or might not come to join her. It was a time of strong Indian nationalist feeling. Mother Teresa was a European. New Congregations were more usually begun when a group was already established. To what public criticisms might the Roman Catholic Church render itself liable by authorizing a foreign woman to step out alone to undertake what in human terms must appear an act of folly? The Archbishop reminded Father Van Exem of another nun who had felt it was her vocation to leave her convent to work in a not dissimilar fashion. He had prevented her from doing so, and recently she had come back and thanked him on her knees. Mother Teresa would have to wait. The Archbishop would not authorize her application to Rome for a year.

Determined that she must leave at once, Mother Teresa urged Father Van Exem repeatedly to return to the Archbishop, but whenever he did so he received the same ostensibly irate reaction. His spiritual charge was therefore directed to be patient and, above all, not to talk to anyone else about her request, not even to her Loreto superiors. She told nobody, not even a group of Yugoslavian Fathers in Calcutta with whom she was very friendly. Nor did she tell Father Julien Henry, pastor of St Teresa's Church near the Entally compound, who attended the convent every day. Nevertheless the frequent conversations with her spiritual director did not altogether escape her superiors' notice. With hindsight Father Van Exem surmised that they had realized that "something was going on – they did not know quite what", and that it was this realization which contributed to her being transferred shortly afterwards to the Loreto convent at Asansol, some three hours' train journey from Calcutta.

At the time Father Van Exem professed to be delighted at what he assumed to be the end of a responsibility he had only reluctantly assumed, but when he passed on to Archbishop Périer the news of Mother Teresa's removal, the Archbishop insisted that he continue his role as her spiritual director by letter. At that time any correspondence written by a nun would have to be left unsealed, possibly read by her superior and only then sealed prior to dispatch. Father Van Exem protested that this obligatory procedure would put an end to all secrecy and render Mother Teresa's life within Loreto impossible, but his objections were instantly quashed. Mother Teresa was entitled to write to her bishop and he to her in a sealed envelope. Father Van Exem and his spiritual charge would therefore correspond in this way via the Archbishop. Archbishop Périer himself would act as intermediary and postboy. By this means Mother Teresa wrote numerous letters to Father Van Exem, which he found "beautiful" and "poetical". They were letters not only about matters of conscience but also about her life in Asansol, where once again she taught geography and where she prepared a group of children for their first communion. She was also put in charge of the convent garden, and she wrote with sensitivity of the beauty of the flowers she tended, in letters almost all of which would subsequently be destroyed. "At Asansol", Father van Exem reflected in 1991, "Mother Teresa was very happy. There she had time."

Some five or six months later, she was once more in his confessional. She had been brought back to Calcutta at the special request of Archbishop Périer, who had informed her superiors that he had "serious reasons" for wanting her to be there. To Father

Van Exem this was a clear indication that Dr Périer was taking the question of Mother Teresa's second vocation very seriously. All the same, the Archbishop remained adamant that she must wait a full year before any further steps were taken towards her leaving. Shortly afterwards the old man fell gravely ill. From Entally, Mother Teresa sent him a message saying that she would pray for him, and asking that if he recovered he take it as a sign that she was to begin the work. The Archbishop did recover but Father Van Exem's appeals to him, at Mother Teresa's continued insistence that "The Lord wants it now", fell on apparently deaf ears, and the frequency of his visits to the Archbishop's office became a source of irritation to his Jesuit superiors, who suspected him of going over their heads on matters of the apostolate. In confidence, however, without revealing the identity of the person concerned, Archbishop Périer consulted Father Henry as to the feasibility of a "Mother" working for the poor in Calcutta. Father Henry responded positively to the idea and started a novena for this unknown "Mother of the Poor". The Archbishop also consulted the General of the Society of Jesuits and a specialist on Canon Law in Rome, as a consequence of which, when in January 1948 Mother Teresa once again wrote to the Archbishop, he finally gave her his permission to apply to leave the Loreto Order, advising her not to write directly to Rome but to apply first to her own Mother General in Rathfarnam, Eire.

It was Father Van Exem's view that Mother Teresa should apply for an indult of exclaustration, which in allowing her to leave the convent would nevertheless enable her to continue as a religious still bound by her vows and answerable directly to the Archbishop. The alternative, an indult of secularization, would mean that she reverted to being a lay person, a fact which would render her even more vulnerable and liable to lose the respect and confidence generally afforded to religious by the Indian people. Father Van Exem was particularly concerned that she might lose the faith of the Bengali girls for whom she had hitherto set a shining example. The Archbishop was not of the same opinion. His strict instructions were that Mother Teresa must demonstrate her total trust in God by applying for an indult of secularization. She must leave Loreto with no hope of ever returning. When Father Exem explained the distinction between the two indults, Mother Teresa chose first the option which would enable her to keep her vows, but the Archbishop went through her handwritten letter and firmly crossed out the word "exclaustration". "Trust your Mother General," her spiritual director advised her, "she will know what to do." In obedience Mother Teresa altered her request to one for secularization, and the Archbishop himself typed out the final version of her application to Mother Gertrude M. Kennedy, Mother General of the Loreto Order.

During the second week of February 1948, Father Van Exem was summoned from Baithakana to Archbishop's House. Mother Gertrude's handwritten answer dated 2 February was, he claimed, one of the most beautiful he had read in his life. Many years later its essential contents remained engraved upon his memory:

Since this is manifestly the will of God, I give you permission to write to the Congregation in Rome and to apply for the indult. Do not speak to the Provincial. Do not speak to your superiors. Speak to nobody. I did not speak to my own counsellors. My consent is sufficient. However, do not ask for the indult of secularization, ask for the indult of exclaustration.

Still Archbishop Périer insisted that if the application to Rome was to be made through him, Mother Teresa must do as he wished and apply for an indult of secularization. Archbishop Périer was well known and highly regarded among the Indian bishops. The response to any application through him would be made much more expeditiously than to a request from a relatively unknown young priest. Father Van Exem therefore took the news of Mother Gertrude Kennedy's answer to his spiritual charge, together with the Archbishop's directive that she could now write to the Congregation for the Propagation of the Faith for an indult of exclaustration. "How do I write to a Cardinal?" was Mother Teresa's reaction. "She was so simple she did not know. She did not know how to set about it at all. I told her not to worry about 'Eminence' and all that, but just to put 'Dear Father' and explain very simply her call to the poorest of the poor."

Once again Mother Teresa applied, as her Mother General had instructed her, for an indult of exclaustration, but again the

Archbishop corrected it to secularization, and the final formula included the expression of total trust which Archbishop Périer had been seeking from the start: "Since I trust God fully I ask for the indult of secularization." In mid-February 1948 Dr Périer sent Mother Teresa's letter, together with a covering letter of his own providing details of the applicant's life and work in Calcutta, to the apostolic nuncio in Delhi for forwarding to Rome, but it was not until the end of July that Father Van Exem was once more required urgently to cycle to see the Archbishop in response to a telephone call from Archbishop's House. The decree dated 12 April 1948 had been delayed at the nunciature in Delhi. By the time Father Van Exem reached the Archbishop's office, however, Dr Périer had already translated the Latin text into English and made three copies of it. "She has it", he announced, and went on to explain that Mother Teresa had been granted permission to leave Loreto for one year not, providentially, with the indult of secularization for which she had asked in obedience, but with the indult of exclaustr-ation she had really wanted. At the end of that year her right to continue the work on that basis would be dependent on the "good pleasure of the Archbishop".

The decree had arrived on a weekday. The Archbishop was resol-ute that the Loreto nuns' working week should not be interrupted by the announcement of its contents. Mother Teresa, despite her anxious appeals to Father Van Exem to know whether news had come, was not to be told until the following Sunday after Mass. Accordingly on Sunday, after Mass but before his breakfast, Father Van Exem called her to the large convent building at Entally. The unusual earliness of this invitation combined with the sight of the large envelope he was holding was enough to suggest to her that the decree had at last arrived. She asked first to go to the chapel before hearing its contents. In the room known as the bishop's parlour Father Van Exem waited while she went to pray, and then announced to her the good news: "Mother, you have the decree of exclaustration. I have three copies for you to sign: one copy for you, one copy for Rome, one for the bishop. You have the decree of exclaustration for one year. You can do the work. Your Superior is now the Archbishop of Calcutta. You are no longer a Loreto nun."

"Father," came the immediate response, "can I go to the slums now?" Her departure was, however, not to be quite so straightforward. Archbishop Périer had anticipated a shocked reaction from some of the Loreto Sisters and his fears were to prove not unfounded. When on 8 August the decree was made public, Mother Ita, the Superior, took to her bed for a week. Mother Cenacle wept inconsolably at the loss of her invaluable helper and the prospect of carrying the burden of the Bengali school alone in her advancing years. "Either it is not the will of God," Father Van Exem attempted to stem the flow of tears, "in which case do not cry, she will be back, or if it is the will of God, she will never come back." A notice was put up on the blackboard for all the Loreto nuns to see: "Do not criticize. Do not praise. Pray." For most it was at very least a surprise, for Mother Teresa had kept faithfully to her instructions to remain silent. In the recollection of Sister Marie Thérèse, many were saddened because they had all been "very friendly". They were also mystified. "We young ones essentially couldn't fathom her leaving." The Loreto Order was with justification highly regarded in Calcutta. Could the abandonment of such an Order really be the will of God?

In readiness for her departure Mother Teresa purchased three saris from a local bazaar: white saris edged with three blue stripes, which would in time become the distinctive habit of her new Congregation. The fabric was the cheapest she could find at the time, and the blue stripes appealed to her because blue was the colour of the Virgin Mary. In the sacristy of St Mary's chapel at Entally Father Van Exem blessed them, together with the white habits to be worn underneath the saris, in the presence of Mother Cenacle and of Father Henry, who had by this time discovered the identity of the nun who felt herself called to live and work amongst the poor as one of them. Mother Cenacle was still tearful but Mother Teresa knelt silently in prayer, apparently unmoved.

On the evening of 16 August she exchanged the religious habit she had worn for nearly twenty years as a Loreto nun for the new habit of her future congregation, and left the Loreto convent, quietly, by taxi. Her former pupils had been curious to see what she would look like in a sari, but their curiosity was to remain unsatisfied. Father Van Exem had suggested that it would be sensible for Mother Teresa first to acquire some medical know-ledge and experience with the Medical Mission Sisters at the Holy Family Hospital in Patna. Archbishop Périer had given the idea his support, and Mother Teresa's letter to Sister Stephanie, their Superior, had met with a warm welcome and the promise of every possible assistance. So it was that with a view to catching the night train to Patna, she slipped through the convent gates under cover of darkness. She took with her only her ticket for Patna and five rupees. The Loreto nuns would readily have provided her with more but Mother Teresa was resolved to put her trust in Divine Providence from the outset, even as she embarked on what she acknowledged was the most painful step of her life. She had been eager to start the work, the waiting had been a supreme test of her obedience, but it was also true, as she would point out on many subsequent occasions, that Loreto had provided her with the foun-dations for what was to come. It had given her a regular, disciplined religious life which she had loved and a community to which she had been firmly attached. "To leave Loreto", she afterwards acknowledged, "was my greatest sacrifice, the most difficult thing I have ever done. It was much more difficult than to leave my family and country to enter religious life. Loreto, my spiritual training, my work there, meant everything to me."

She was nevertheless happy for a while in Patna. At the beginning of her medical training, she wrote to her spiritual father of how she was nervous of picking up the tiny newborn babies in case she crushed the fragile life out of them, but it was not long before she felt that she had learned all that she needed to know. After only a matter of weeks she requested permission to return to Calcutta and begin work in the slums. Father Van Exem, who had envisaged her training for at least six months, possibly even a year, was incredu-lous. Both he and the Archbishop were emphatic that there could be no question of her starting work without adequate medical know-ledge, but Mother Teresa's letters insisting that in Patna she was learning now about illnesses which she would not encounter in the slums, kept on coming. She would learn far more about cholera, sores and the sicknesses of the slums, the missives insisted, by actu-ally going into them. Finally, Father Van Exem agreed to combine his forthcoming retreat in Patna with a meeting with Sister

Stephanie, the Superior of the Medical Mission Sisters, and one of the Sister-doctors with whom Mother Teresa was training. Having never seen Mother Teresa in a sari before, he failed to recognize her among a group of other nurses in the hospital, until when he finally asked for her, she protested, "But Father, I am here." To his further discomfort, both Sister Stephanie and the Sister-doctor whom he consulted were in agreement that Mother Teresa was ready to begin life in the slums. Father Van Exem was concerned at the possibility of a scandal, and a resulting end to the work, in the event of Mother Teresa making a mistake. Mother Teresa would not make a mistake, Sister Stephanie predicted. Besides, there would be others who would offer their services, doctors and nurses who would come forward and share the responsibility.

In the very short time in which she had been with them, Mother Teresa had learned much from the medical Sisters, including something of the rule of balance prescribed by Mother Dengel, their foundress, who had herself fought to obtain permission from the Holy See for her nuns to practise surgery and midwifery in their hospitals. Mother Teresa was intent upon starting a congregation, members of which would lead the lives of India's poor. She intended that she and the girls whom she expected to join her would live, dress and eat like the poorest of the poor, whom they would tend, feed and clothe as the suffering Christ. The nuns' food would accordingly consist solely of rice and salt, the humblest of Bengali diets. Experience had demonstrated to the Medical Mission Sisters, however, that without proper nutrition it was impossible to work efficiently over a long period of time. On the kind of diet Mother Teresa proposed, her Sisters would become prey to the same diseases that afflicted the poor. In humility Mother Teresa took the advice given to her. When, on the strength of the Medical Mission Sisters' opinion, she was permitted to return to Calcutta to start work in the slums, she did so resolved that those who came to join her in her formidable task should receive the sustenance they required. In obedience they would eat no more, but also no less, than necessary.

First, however, the problem of finding suitable accommodation for Mother Teresa herself must be resolved. There were numerous large properties available at that time, belonging to Muslims who had left Calcutta to make their homes in Pakistan, but they were not necessarily suitable for a woman living on her own. Archbishop Périer rejected Father Van Exem's initial suggestion that she should be lodged in one of the Carmelite houses, on the grounds that their contemplative life must not be disturbed. Father Van Exem appealed therefore to the Good Mother of the Little Sisters of the Poor, who ran a home in which some two hundred elderly poor found shelter and care. The Good Mother received the proposal with caution. If Mother Teresa was no longer a religious she would have to be over sixty in order to qualify as an inmate. On being assured, however, that Mother Teresa had received a decree of exclaustration and that she was under obedience to Archbishop Périer, the superior agreed to make her welcome. Within the confines of their institution the Little Sisters of the Poor were committed to poverty and dependence on Divine Providence in a not dissimilar fashion to that envisioned by Mother Teresa. From a small room on the first floor near to the gate of St Joseph's home she would be able to go out after Mass and breakfast each morning to the slums in which she wanted to work.

By 1991 the memories of Father Van Exem and Mother Teresa were at variance as to the date on which she first ventured into Motijhil, the slum she had been able to see from the windows of the Loreto convent, Entally. Certain documents dating from that period, together with the abundance of letters which Mother Teresa received almost from the very beginning of her new Order, were kept by Father Van Exem. There came a time, however, when Mother Teresa, adamant that the work was God's work and not her work, wanted all such documentation destroyed. The response of her spiritual director was that the documents were not her property but belonged rather to the Congregation. Without the authority of the Bishop he could not destroy them. She must appeal to Archbishop Perier. When she did so, Archbishop Périer's instruction was that he would only direct Father Van Exem to destroy the correspondence on condition that she wrote the history of the Congregation. This she never managed to do. When in 1960 Archbishop Périer retired Mother Teresa appealed to his successor Archbishop Vivian Dyer to give authority for the destruction of the documents but, much to her frustration, Archbishop Dyer asked her what his predecessor's opinion had been and opted to endorse it. Mother Teresa tried again with his successor, again to no avail. By the time Cardinal Lawrence Picachy succeeded Archbishop Albert D'Souza, she knew what the answer to any such appeal would be. Some years later, however, worn down by Mother Teresa's repeated pleading, Father Van Exem sent her the two boxes he had so carefully retained, on condition that she keep anything that rightfully belonged to the Congregation. The issue of the disposal of this documentation was the only one over which they had ever quarrelled. In the end, Mother had had her way: "She will have kept a few things I suppose but not very much."

Mother Teresa lived very much in the immediate moment. She was far too occupied with the present to be unduly concerned about the past. Yet a few records do remain. Extracts from a notebook she kept at the time she initiated the work in the slums recorded the date she first went to Motijhil as 21 December, but her spiritual director, knowing with what little importance she imbued such considerations, remembered it as being on the 8/9 December. What is certain is that she spent eight days in retreat, during which he went daily to give her spiritual instruction, before she finally caught a bus to Mauli Ali, an area which in time would become so much a centre of the work that the local people nicknamed it Missionary of Charity Marg (Road). From there she made her way to Motijhil and the children who would swiftly become her first pupils. On the morning of the very next day the children were waiting for her on the steps of a railway bridge leading down into the slum. By 28 December Mother Teresa had permission to open a slum school in Motijhil. The "school" was an open space among the huts, the children squatted in the dirt, and Mother Teresa scratched the letters of the Bengali alphabet in the mud with a stick. Nevertheless, the twenty-one pupils who arrived on the first day virtually doubled on the second and increased steadily until the noise of the alphabet being repeated was a familiar sound in the muddy alleyways that divided up the row upon row of improvised hovels.

Those who were not clean I gave a good wash at the tank [Mother Teresa noted at the time]. *We had catechism after the first lesson in hygiene*

and their reading. We used the ground as a blackboard. After needlework
class we went to visit the sick.

She also noted how she laughed a good deal on that occasion as it
was the first time that she had attempted to teach such very small
children. There were times when she was confronted with needs
that taxed her abilities to the limit. The story is told that when she
was attending to the poor single-handed she found herself confronted by a man with a gangrenous thumb. Obviously it had to be
removed, so she took a pair of scissors with, undoubtedly, a prayer,
and cut. Her patient fainted one way and Mother Teresa the other.
Gradually, however, as people heard what she was doing, they gave
her money and they came to help. The bus driver on the route
from St Joseph's home insisted on her occupying the seat next to
him. A former fellow teacher from St Mary's came to help her
teach. Mother Teresa rented two huts in Motijhil for five rupees
each. One served as a school, in which pupils were given milk at
midday and awarded bars of soap as prizes. Somehow the love with
which the work was carried out belied the nonsense of teaching the
alphabet to waifs who would probably never read, and hygiene to
those who would never be able to buy soap. The other room was
to serve as the first home for sick and dying destitutes. In her diary
she wrote of how the experience of the rejection of one dying
woman opened her eyes to a pressing need, of how the work began
as the suffering people called for it:

I saw a woman dying on the street outside Campbell Hospital. I picked
her up and took her to the hospital but she was refused admission because
she was poor. She died on the street. I knew then that I must make a
home for the dying, a resting place for people going to heaven.

An old Muslim woman came to her in Motijhil. "I want you to
promise me something", she appealed. "When you hear that I am
sick and dying, please come, I want to die with God."

It would not be long before Mother Teresa started teaching,
visiting the sick and elderly, instructing Christian children in the
catechism, bringing comfort to Muslim and Hindu families alike in
their poverty, in the slums of Tiljala and Howrah. She started a

dispensary at St Teresa's Church. The work, while she was engaged in it, was absorbing, the thirst for souls grew stronger: "When I am in the work, looking at the hundreds of suffering, I think of nothing but them and I am really very happy." Yet it would be untrue to suggest that she was simply carried away on a wave of enthusiasm and God-given grace, and that everything came easily to her. Beyond the rapid growth of the work lay a daily reality of painful effort to keep going. The first months were marked by frequent loneliness, doubt and the temptation to return to the security of Loreto. Again her diary recorded her struggle:

Our Lord wants me to be a free nun covered with the poverty of the Cross. Today I learned a good lesson. The poverty of the poor must be so hard for them. While looking for a home I walked and walked till my arms and legs ached. I thought how much they must ache in body and soul, looking for a home, food and health. Then the comfort of Loreto came to tempt me. "You have only to say the word and all that will be yours again", the Tempter kept on saying. . . . Of free choice, my God, and out of love for you, I desire to remain and do whatever be your Holy will in my regard. I did not let a single tear come.

This, she recognized, was "the dark night of the birth of the Society". "Everyone sees my weakness", she acknowledged, and there were times when the tears did well in her eyes. Not all those whom she approached for support, even the occupants of presbyteries, were ready to understand. One priest whom she approached for financial aid treated her as if she was doing something very wrong. Telling her that he did not understand, he parted from her without even saying goodbye. For the moment she was compelled to acknowledge that she was no good at begging – "But never mind, that too will come."

The search for a house in which others might join her went on. Mother Teresa herself had little time to devote to it, but together Father Julien Henry and Father Van Exem scoured East Calcutta. Eventually, when they were almost at a loss, Father Van Exem had the idea of asking Alfred Gomes, one of four brothers who had a sizeable property at 14 Creek Lane adjoining a compound shared by two Christian families. Two of the brothers had chosen to move to East Pakistan at the time of the partition in 1947. Alfred Gomes| agreed at once that Mother Teresa should be given the use of a room on the second floor. First he must write to his brothers in Pakistan and some repairs must be completed on the top floor, but thereafter Mother Teresa could occupy it free of rent. It was in many ways the ideal location. In those days Mother Teresa stopped work in the slums at 5 or 6 p.m. Her evenings were devoted to prayer and writing. The fact that access to her accommodation would be via the family of Michael Gomes, Alfred Gomes' brother who lived downstairs, would deter any unwelcome intrusions when the work of the day was over. It was also a place which Mother Teresa would describe as "rich in its poverty". When the Good Mother of the Little Sisters of the Poor went to inspect the accommodation for herself she was struck by its extreme spartanness: "Well, you are sure to have Jesus with you", was her comment. "They cannot say that you left Loreto to become rich."

To begin with Mother Teresa had nothing but a bench, which served as a library, a box for a table, a chair provided by the Good Mother, and a green almirah which was used as an altar. The Loreto nuns subsequently sent her a bed. To this was added the picture of the Immaculate Heart of Mary which Mother Teresa had given to Father Van Exem while she was still at Loreto and which he now returned to her. Father Julien Henry had also given her a statue of Our Lady of Fatima for the altar. "I am looking forward to giving the Immaculate Heart her first oratory in Calcutta", she wrote. "Ambition to have her loved, to have her served fills my heart." On the third floor of the building was a large upper room that ran the length of the house. In time this would be made available for her use when the first of those whom Mother Teresa believed would come began to arrive. On 28 February 1949 she moved into her new convent in Creek Lane. There were times when she went hungry and had to resort to writing Michael Gomes notes asking him for a little food: "Mr Gomes, I have nothing to eat. Please give me something to eat." There were times also when she felt very much alone – "Today, my God, what tortures of loneliness." Placing her trust in Divine Providence and in the Immaculate Heart of Mary, she prayed repeatedly: "I have no children as once you told your beloved Son, 'They have no wine'."

On 19 March 1949 Subhasini Das, a Bengali girl who had been one of Mother Teresa's pupils at the Loreto convent school in Entally, joined her in the sparsely furnished room in Creek Lane. Her mother had previously wanted to remove her from school and compel her to marry, but the matter had been brought before a court. Mother Teresa had given evidence, and the girl's devotion to her teacher had been so apparent that the judge had committed her to her teacher's protection. It was she who became the first aspirant and the future Sister Agnes. If Mother Teresa had kept silent about her specific intentions to leave Loreto, she had not failed to sow the seed of a lasting commitment to the poor in some of her young pupils. She had walked with them through the slums of Motijhil, and pointed out to them that someone should care for these people who had so little. Some time before Mother Teresa's leaving was made public, a small group of her pupils had resolved that they wanted to do something for the poor. They gave half their time to serving the occupants of the slums. They made a special novena. Mother Teresa had even gone so far as to ask them hypo- thetically whether, if God asked it of them, they would be prepared to leave school for the service of the poor before they finished their final exams. Magdalen Polton Gomez was among those who said "yes". She was an ardent supporter of the movement for Indian independence and deeply hostile to the British, but Mother Teresa persuaded her to channel her youthful energies into love of the poor, eventually not only those of India but of all nationalities. "It was like a spell", she would afterwards explain. "I was caught up in this spell." Her father was totally against the idea of her joining Mother Teresa. Nevertheless on 26 April Magdalen Gomes, the future Sister Gertrude, became Mother Teresa's second young companion. May brought the prospective Sister Margaret Mary. She was only sixteen at the time, and as yet there was no formal novitiate for the Congregation, but Mother Teresa took her also, simply as a "boarder".

Mother Teresa and the first girls to join her went regularly to Baithakana Church. In the sacristy there they received their instruc- tion relating to the religious life, the spirituality of St Ignatius Loyola, the spirit of the congregation, charity for the poor and the motivation for it: the presence of Christ in them. Gradually the numbers increased, and as they did so Father Van Exem took to going to the convent to give his instruction. The first ten girls who arrived were all former pupils. One by one they began the work of serving the poorest of the poor, going begging from door to door, taking the proceeds to those who were starving in the streets, comforting the sick and the dying, and teaching children the dignity of human life. All this was undertaken, sometimes in the face of rejection and abuse but always in the conviction that they were responding to the message of St Matthew's Gospel: "As you did it to one of the least of these my brethren, you did it to me."

Yet the group that assembled around Mother Teresa was not as yet a formal congregation. It was simply a collection of what Archbishop Périer described as "pious women living together" who were not entitled to have the sacrament reserved in their "convent" in the upper room at Creek Lane. Instead they had to make their way daily to St Teresa's Church for Mass. At the end of the first year Mother Teresa's continuation of the work was still subject to the decision of the Archbishop, as was the application to Rome for the formal erection of the congregation. Archbishop Périer gave it sympathetic consideration, in the course of which Father Van Exem was once more summoned to the Archbishop's presence. This time he found himself questioned as to whether he knew of any criticism of what Mother Teresa was doing. Reluctantly, the young priest was made to acknowledge that the priest of St Thomas's Church had described Mother Teresa's work as "wiles of the devil". Mother Teresa had been doing valuable work at St Mary's school for Bengali girls. No one had been able to match her since. She had left a certain good for something which was desperately uncertain, and such a move, it was argued, could only be the work of the devil. Incensed, the Archbishop dispatched Father Van Exem to the priest in charge of St Thomas's to persuade him either to retract his statement or to cease forthwith to be priest of that parish. Such an inducement was scarcely one easily resisted. The priest of St Thomas's retracted his earlier remarks. Still Archbishop Périer was worried. He made further enquiries but eventually wrote the necessary letter to Rome.

At extremely short notice Father Van Exem was required to produce a polished version of the constitutions for the proposed congregation by April 1950. Mother Teresa herself had written the first "Rules" in 1948 and 1949 in a little yellow notebook, but she had no knowledge of Canon Law or the manner in which they should be formally presented, and when the first version was shown to Father Sanders, a Jesuit priest, he pronounced that the English was poor. The spirit of the constitutions would remain very much the spirit of Mother Teresa but much had to be added by Father Van Exem under her inspiration. They were developed largely on the basis of the Loreto Rule, which had in turn been based on the Jesuit Rule, especially in relation to the rule of obedience and to the devotion to the Sacred Heart of Jesus as the seat of love. As far as the rule of poverty was concerned, Mother Teresa wanted it to be rigorously implemented. She had wanted to stipulate that the Missionaries of Charity would not own the buildings from which they served the poor. She wanted them to belong to the Church and so preserve the poverty of her Congregation, but the situation of the Roman Catholic Church in India had made this idea impracticable. There was nevertheless much of the Franciscan ideal in the Missionary of Charity rule of poverty. Similarly, the relationship between work and prayer had much in common with the Benedictine concept of *ora et labora*. A member of Father Van Exem's congregation was employed at the High Court in Calcutta where he knew a proficient typist. Thus six copies of the Constitutions of the Missionary Sisters of Charity were typed in the High Court of Calcutta in time for Archbishop Périer to take them with him to Rome in April 1950.

Questions were raised in connection with such practical considerations as the Sisters' dress, an issue which was left very much to Mother Teresa's discretion. One of the aspiring Missionaries of Charity had to be dressed up as a postulant in a plain white sari and short-sleeved habit, another as a novice in a white sari and a habit, the sleeves of which covered the whole arm. Mother Teresa herself posed as a professed Sister with the distinctive blue border to the white sari. Photographs were then taken and submitted to Rome for approval. Thereafter Pope Pius XII's endorsement of the erection of the new congregation came swiftly.

On 7 October 1950, Archbishop Périer said Mass for the first time at the altar in the tiny chapel on the top floor of Alfred Gomes' house in Creek Lane. A large congregation assembled to hear Father Van Exem read the decree of erection, which described how "a little group of women under the guidance of Sister M. Teresa" had devoted themselves "with generous heart and with great profit for the souls, to helping the poor – the children, grown-ups, the aged and also the sick, in this our Metropolitan City". It went on to speak of the "earnest examination" of the group following the request to be erected into a religious congregation, and the conclusion that "no other Congregation already in existence answers the purpose which this new Institute is intending". Finally it spoke of how "those who join this Institute are resolved to spend themselves unremittingly in seeking out, in towns and villages, even amid squalid surroundings, the poorer, the abandoned, the sick, the infirm, the dying; in taking care of them assiduously and instructing them in the Christian Doctrine, in endeavouring to the utmost to bring about their conversion and sanctification. . . . And in performing any other similar apostolic works and services, however lowly and mean they may appear." It was given under Archbishop Perier's signature and seal on the day of the Feast of the Most Holy Rosary, 7 October 1950, and on that same day the eleven who had by that time joined Mother Teresa began their postulancy as Missionaries of Charity.

At that time the postulancy, which now lasts one year, took only six months. Father Van Exem was accordingly assigned to compile a ceremony of reception in time for 11 April 1951. Drawing his inspiration from the reception of the Carmelites and other congregations in Calcutta, he compiled a vestition ceremony in which the novices to be came to the cathedral dressed as Bengali brides. During the service they withdrew to a room close to the sanctuary to have their hair cut by Mother Teresa, and then reappeared dressed in their religious habits as novices. It was a beautiful and memorable order of service, with which Mother Teresa, who had herself to be received as a novice Missionary of Charity, was very satisfied. For a Bengali girl the cutting of her hair represented a particular sacrifice. Its inclusion in the liturgy was significant and justified the time involved – at least in the view of some. With characteristic amusement, years later Father Van Exem recalled the reaction of the local people to so many Bengali brides arriving by bus, and the comment of one priest on the duration of the ceremony occasioned by the cutting of the hair: "The ordination of a priest takes two hours, the consecration of a bishop three hours, the reception of a Missionary of Charity four hours!"

In their convent the new novices maintained the spirit of the society which had been defined not only as one of "loving trust" and "total surrender" but also of "cheerfulness". The duties of prayer and work were faithfully observed. In her journal Mother Teresa wrote of how beautifully silence was kept, of how the fervour of the young novices compelled her to follow them, and of how the poverty "which seems so clear in the plans" was actually taking shape. The novices washed themselves and their clothes in communal buckets. They cleaned their teeth with ashes. Their "garment things" were contained in a small *potla* or bundle, which was also used to raise the pillow of anyone who coughed at night. Despite the improvised nature of its furnishings, the top floor of Creek Lane was spotless and tidy and remained so, even as the single large room and tiny chapel could barely provide adequate dormitory and living space for the growing numbers. It became obvious that the Missionary Sisters of Charity must seek larger living quarters. As the need became pressing the small Congregation began to pray fervently for somewhere to form a more permanent mother house. "I had promised Our Lady 85,000 Memorares", Mother Teresa later confided, but the Congregation was still so small that, ever practical, she taught all the children and people in their care the Memorare and enlisted their help in meeting the requisite number. "And soon we got the house."

A certain Doctor Islam, a retired magistrate who had been educated by the Jesuits in Calcutta, was among the many Muslims seeking to move to Pakistan, and therefore desiring to sell a property he had built for himself on one of Calcutta's main arterial roads. In an encounter with Mother Teresa and Sister Gertrude he was taken aback one day to find the subject of the sale of his property broached. He had, he insisted, told no one of his intention to sell, it was only a plan that he had formulated in his mind. When Father Julien Henry began negotiations on Mother Teresa's behalf, Dr Islam found himself agreeing to sell his house for less than the price of the land on which it stood. Father Van Exem retained the memory of the venerable old man's last farewell to his property. The priest had waited in the parlour alone while the Muslim went to the nearby mosque to pray. On his return, the old man stood outside the property and wept. "I received that house from God", he said. "I give it back to him." Father Van Exem would hear no more from this generous benefactor, but the concession he had made over the sale of the property was to prove of momentous importance. The Archbishop of Calcutta swiftly approved the purchase and advanced the necessary money, and the Missionaries of Charity moved into what remains their mother house to this day, a property really made up of two houses surrounding a central courtyard at what was then known as 54A Lower Circular Road and is now Acharya J. Chandra Bose Road, in the very heart of Calcutta. The move took place in either February or March of 1953. That even those who were directly involved in it cannot agree on a precise date is an indication of just how all-consuming the work with the poor had already become.

Looking out onto a humming vortex of noisy pedestrians, trams and traffic, where the sound of the city's congestion, of passing Hindu processions, rickshaw bells and political parades would interrupt and sometimes even completely drown the Sisters' prayers, the building provided its initial occupants with a degree of space to which they were unaccustomed. It had a larger chapel and a refectory, and for the first time, Mother Teresa would have a small room of her own. Nevertheless the Congregation would continue a life shaped by the extreme poverty which Mother Teresa saw as so vital. "Our rigorous poverty is our safeguard", she would insist when, later, people wanted to give the Missionaries of Charity things which they themselves saw as basic necessities of life but which for the Sisters were unnecessary luxuries. "We do not want to do what other religious orders have done throughout history, and begin by serving the poor only to end up unconsciously serving the rich. In order to understand and help those who have nothing, we must live like them. . . . The only difference is that these people are poor by birth, and we are poor by choice." In the earliest days, however, maintaining the poverty of their life was not a problem.

Officially the young Missionaries of Charity possessed only their cotton saris and habits, coarse underwear, a pair of sandals, the crucifix they wore pinned to their left shoulder, a rosary, an umbrella to protect them against the monsoon rains, a metal bucket for washing and a very thin palliasse to serve as a bed. Totally dependent as they were on the generosity of others, unofficially even these basic items were often in short supply. Mother Teresa herself had become more accomplished in the art of begging and those around her learned from her: "Mother gave us a love for begging from door to door. We used to take a large oil can and brought left-over food from Canal Street families which Mother then carried to the dispensary for poor children in the afternoon." Canal Street was an area not far from Lower Circular Road, the occupants of which were themselves quite poor but what they had, they were willing to share. The Sisters' priority, however, was begging for the poor for whom they cared and not for their own needs. The memories of the first Sisters are thus punctuated with tales of improvization accepted with boundless humour, of how, for example, on one occasion Mother Teresa allocated the same pair of sandals to three different Sisters, all of whom needed to use them at once. The problem was resolved by allowing the youngest to wear them.

On another occasion the only pair of shoes available for one Sister to wear to church was a pair of red stiletto heels. Her hobbling appearance in such unsuitable footwear occasioned much amusement. Habits had at times to be made up out of old sacking that had originally contained bulgar wheat. The labelling on it could not always be completely washed out and was sometimes visible through the thin cloth of the sari. Beneath the neat pleats across one Sister's behind the words "Not for resale" were still discernible to those who looked closely. American Army khaki was used to make bags for the Sisters in which they carried a bottle of drinking water when they went out to work in the heat. Mother Teresa was concerned that they should not have to take water from the poor, who would have gone without in order that their visitors might drink. One Christmas there were not enough shawls in the house for the Sisters to wear for midnight Mass, yet somehow they all had to look the same for their walk to the Sacred Heart Church in Dharamtala. Those without shawls were consequently obliged to wear their bed-covers.

Poverty of life was something which the young aspiring Sisters had expected, even craved. In fact the discipline of eating more than their appetites would naturally have dictated was often more of a trial to them than going hungry. Days were long and hard. During the week they rose at 4.40 a.m. to the call of *Benedicamus Domino* and the response of *Deo Gratias*. On Sundays the rising time was 4.15 a.m. They dressed at their bedsides with a sheet over their heads. They went downstairs to wash their faces with water scooped out of a tank in the courtyard with empty powdered milk tins, and collected ash from the stove in the kitchen with which to clean their teeth. They washed themselves with a tablet of soap which had been divided into six and was used for washing both their clothes and their bodies. Morning prayers, meditation and Mass consumed the time between 5.15 and 6.45 a.m. Then for breakfast they had to drink a glass of water before they ate. There was no tea in those early days. Cold milk made out of American milk powder accompanied an obligatory five chapattis spread with ghee. They were made to eat quickly and to take a vitamin pill, and by 7.45 a.m. they were out into the streets of Calcutta to work amongst the poorest of the poor, having somehow managed, with the limited facilities available, to have their obligatory daily bath and wash all the previous day's clothes in a bucket. Shortly after noon they returned to the mother house for prayers, a meal of five ladles of bulgar wheat and three bits of meat if meat was available. After lunch there was housework to be done, and then Mother Teresa was very insistent that they should have a rest for half an hour. Afterwards they had prayers and afternoon tea, which consisted of two dry chapattis followed by half an hour of spiritual reading and instruction from Mother Teresa. Then it was back to their duties in the city. At six they returned to the mother house for prayers and adoration of the sacrament, followed by a meal of rice, dhal and vegetables, during which they had ten minutes of spiritual reading. Then came time for mending – using a razor blade, needle and darning thread contained in a cigarette tin – and recreation before evening prayers and bed by ten o'clock. Recreation was one of the few times at which conversation was permitted other than for communication essential to the work. The signal for them to be free to talk was the invitation *Laudetur Jesus Christus* to which the response "Amen" was sometimes almost shouted with relief at the opportunity to share some of the experiences of the day.

It was not only the poor whom the Missionaries of Charity sought to serve who sometimes rejected them. The girls' own families were frequently ashamed of coming across them in the streets or markets dressed in the white sari of Indian widowhood and in the company of outcastes, and they made their objections felt. Years later one Sister's father would undergo a change of heart, but in the early days he reproached his daughter for accompanying Mother Teresa into the slums. "My son died," he wrote to her, "my only son. And you walk around with Mother Teresa in the slums. I cannot bear it." In a way which would subsequently cause her to wonder at her own toughness, the Sister in question wrote back to the father she loved so deeply, "My brother died and I am dead to you also".

The physical conditions of the work were rigorous in the extreme. On Sundays on their way to collect children for Sunday school, the young novices sometimes had to cross railway lines, jump ditches and wade through pools of water. On one occasion two of them were caught in a heavy downpour of rain. The roads through the slums flooded to above waist height. Mother Teresa had instructed them to say their rosaries wherever they went, as "a beautiful way of continuing prayer", and the practice was so much a part of their lives that distances were measured in terms of rosaries, but in the stench and filth and rotting carcasses of the flood water even the rosary was not enough to distract their minds. Instead they sang the entire High Mass in Latin.

There were times when there was no fuel to cook meals but in a spirit of cheerful sacrifice the Sisters undertook to eat raw wheat, occasionally soaked over night. When the curry was bitter and they had nothing to improve it or substitute for it, at Mother Teresa's suggestion, they ate it for the conversion of the Mau Mau in Africa. Only on Thursdays were the girls granted some respite. Because Sundays were taken up with catechetical work, Thursday was kept as a recollection day, free of work outside the house and set aside for prayer and meditation. Often in the beginning, at Archbishop Périer's insistence, on Thursdays Mother Teresa would take her charges to a Calcutta doctor's garden for a picnic.

As her talent for begging developed, Mother Teresa was to

become something of a thorn in the flesh of some who were on the receiving end of her persuasive powers, but in her Sisters' eyes she was from the very beginning a marvel. Privately, they conducted a competition to beat Mother Teresa into the chapel in the mornings. Rarely if ever did anyone succeed, despite the fact that she invariably worked late into the night, even struggling at times to write the history of the Congregation which would free her from the possibility of future personal disclosures which she considered irrelevant. Throughout the day she laboured with tireless zeal and always with evident joy. Nothing appeared to frighten or daunt her. Spurred on by the conviction that with the strength of God she could accomplish anything, nothing was too menial, nothing too great an obstacle in her path. "In Mother we saw really the living Constitutions", one early Sister would later record. "The joy of being poor, of working hard." As a newcomer she had found the toilet dirty one day and hidden herself away in disgust. Mother Teresa happened to pass by without seeing the Sister. She immediately rolled up her sleeves and took a broom and cleaned the toilet herself. It was a lesson that Sister would never forget.

Acts of obedience were constantly required of them. Quite apart from the requirement to eat five chapattis whether they were hungry or not (if they could not then, Mother Teresa informed them, they were not made of Missionary of Charity material) they must speak English with each other at all times. The young pupils from Loreto who had left without finishing their exams were required to make up their studies on top of their work as future Missionaries of Charity. In fact some were afterwards able to continue their studies with the Loreto Sisters. Realizing that the Congregation would need people with medical skills, Mother Teresa asked some of the first to join her to study to become doctors, despite the fact that for a Bengali girl the study of medicine which brought men and women together in conditions of unacceptable intimacy was considered taboo. The students' exercise books were made out of wrappers taken off tins of milk and chocolate powder. The former Loreto girls, bright and from caste-conscious families as they were, were subject to all kinds of humiliation, but Mother Teresa required them to shine and they did so. When one of her former pupils, after considerable struggle, won a gold medal for her studies, Mother Teresa directed her to surrender it to the student who had come second. The Missionaries of Charity would not have need of such things.

The visionary fervour that burned in her was not the kind that invited compromise, but she asked nothing of those around her that she was not prepared to do herself. She coached them, worked late into the night long after they had gone to bed, and was constantly protective of them, keeping to herself, for example, the knowledge that the small tin box in which she stored the money for their daily needs was once again empty. Of those early days of the society, Mother Teresa herself would insist that they had not been all that difficult: "After all, I had been in India a long time and I knew the people. It was not so difficult to get started. Divine Providence is much greater than our little minds and will never let us down." Certainly Divine Providence appeared to be at work in many and obvious ways. When once in Calcutta the small community was left with absolutely nothing to eat, suddenly there was a knock at the door. A woman, completely unknown to the occupants of 54A Lower Circular Road, was standing at its unpretentious entrance with some bags of rice. She told them simply that some inexplicable impulse had brought her there. In the bags was exactly enough rice for the evening meal.

This was just one of innumerable similar examples which would feed and confirm the conviction that God would meet the needs of those who trusted totally in him. One day Father Julien Henry appealed to Mother Teresa for money to print St Joseph leaflets. Mother Teresa searched the house and found only two rupees. At Father Henry's request, she parted with those very last rupees. Just as he was leaving, however, Father Henry remembered a letter he had been asked to deliver to her. Later that evening Mother Teresa opened the letter to find that it contained a gift of 100 rupees. Her generosity had been abundantly repaid. On another occasion the Sisters started making a mattress in readiness for a new arrival, but ran short of cotton. Mother Teresa immediately volunteered her pillow, but her Sisters were reluctant to accept her sacrifice, feeling that she needed to rest properly at the end of a rigorous day's work. Mother Teresa insisted, but even as she did so an Englishman appeared at the door with a mattress under his arm. He was leaving for England next morning and the thought had come to him that the Missionaries of Charity might have some use for his mattress. Commenting on the incident, Mother Teresa would later remark: "It might have happened the next day or the previous day but no – God in his Providence had sent the stranger at the precise moment when the mattress was needed."

"We had to start the work, we couldn't wait for money because life and poverty were everywhere", Mother Teresa explained. Yet somehow where there was a need, the means of meeting it was provided, and there was joy and peace to be derived from the experience, and a fresh appreciation of small things. In the early 'fifties Monsignor Barber, then Vicar General of Calcutta, said of Mother Teresa that she had a fire in her which had to be communicated to her Sisters. It was done by daily instruction. Even when she returned tired from the work, from begging or from meeting people, she would make time in which to teach her young companions. It was done also by lived example. One of the early Sisters recalled her first Christmas as a Missionary of Charity as an illustration of the tender concern Mother Teresa had for each of her Sisters, and the joy that was derived from small things within the context of a life of poverty:

The refectory was beautifully decorated with streamers, balloons etc, and at each one's place at table was a white paper bag on which was written "Happy Christmas to dear Sister . . . from Mother". Mother had stayed up doing all this for us. Inside was our mail and Mother's presents to us. We all got the same except for the pencils. I got a cake of Sunlight soap, a clothes peg, a red and blue pencil, a St Christopher and the Miraculous Medal identity card, a leaflet with beautiful words, sweets and a balloon. . . . We were thrilled with our gifts, the Sister wrote in January 1956, *as there is nothing else we could possibly want. The Sunlight was a real god-send.*

By then the work of the Missionaries of Charity was proceeding at such a rate that they had become known as the "running congregation". On 12 April 1953 the first group of Missionary Sisters of Charity took their first vows in Calcutta's Roman Catholic cathedral, and during the same ceremony Mother Teresa made her final vows as a Missionary of Charity. Only then did the Sister renowned for her inability to light the candles for Benediction succeed Archbishop Périer as Superior of the Order she had founded. Despite his ostensibly ungenerous testing of her vocation, the Archbishop had given the Congregation his warmest personal support and interest throughout its earliest years, to the point of even involving himself in decisions concerning the Sisters' footwear. Contrary to usual Indian practice he insisted that for their own protection they must wear shoes inside the house. The Missionaries of Charity apparently passed the test of this close attention. Such was the exceptional growth and singular spirit of the work begun by a woman with no particular outstanding skills that by the late nineteen-fifties Archbishop Périer would finally be heard to announce: "Manifestly the finger of God is here".

CHAPTER THREE

Contemplatives in the World

"What a wonderful thing is M.C.", wrote Mother Teresa while the Missionaries of Charity were still at Creek Lane. "The highest and the lowest are brought together." She had been to the house of Lady Hazra, one of Calcutta's influential figures, to talk to members of the All India Women's Conference about work amongst the poorest of the poor, and to enlist their support. "Ladies Sinha, Bose and Hazra" had proved to be "extremely interested". They would find helpers for her among their number.

Gradually the first of Mother Teresa's Missionaries of Charity were joined by other helpers. Doctors, nurses and other lay people worked with them on a voluntary basis, and an increasing number of dispensaries were set up to cope with the sickness arising from malnutrition and overcrowding, a problem in the face of which the Calcutta Corporation, the governing body of the city, had already acknowledged itself to be virtually powerless. Calcutta after Partition was a city beset with human misery. Even the three thousand official slums could no longer contain the two million or so destitute who sought to scratch their daily bread from the streets of the metropolis. The starving destitutes who made their pathetic homes on the platforms of the railway stations, or simply slept and struggled for a pitiful existence on the pavements, could not all be arrested or taken into care. The prisons were already overflowing, and the hospitals filled to a dangerous bursting point. The Indian government, backed by international relief organizations, set up dispensaries and soup kitchens, and managed to send some medicine and clothing into the slums, but the flow of destitute refugees from East Pakistan was seemingly interminable, the relief efforts were hopelessly inadequate, and the starving and the disease-ridden lay dying where they fell.

One wet day in 1952, a naked beggar boy of thirteen or fourteen stretched out his emaciated limbs to die by a roadside in a residential area. The occupant of a nearby house telephoned for an ambulance and the boy was taken to hospital, but being naked, he obviously did not have the necessary funds for treatment. The hospital, already overcrowded, rejected him, and his poor matchstick body was deposited back where it had been found. The young beggar boy died alone and untended in the gutter. The incident was, however, reported in the press. Public attention was drawn to the plight of this boy and the thousands of others like him, who could not even die with dignity.

This heightened public awareness gave an additional impetus to the application Mother Teresa made to the municipal authorities. Indeed, part of her success at that time was undoubtedly due to the fact that the work to which she felt herself so uncompromisingly called also fitted in with the needs and schemes of government and town officials constantly embarrassed by the number of poverty-stricken people on their pavements. The municipality was seeking a solution to the problem of destitutes dying in the streets and there, quite unexpectedly, was a woman of considerable energy and determination offering to take care of them. Her first care for the dying had begun in a hut in the slums but almost immediately she had found herself short of space. She had neither funds nor credit but she applied to the municipality for a "house". It was, she acknowledged, understandable that the hospitals should prefer to grant their limited number of free beds to patients who had some hope of recovery, rather than to those who were obviously and inevitably destined to die very soon of malnutrition or old age. What she was offering to do was take care of the starving, the unprovided for, those for whom there was little if any likelihood of recovery. Some of the officials had already noted the work of the Missionaries of Charity and their helpers in the slums. They realized also that in exchange for the gift of a "house", Mother Teresa was offering to salve the consciences of Calcutta's more socially minded citizens. There would be no more criticism in the newspapers of a city which allowed some of its inhabitants to die without so much as a roof over their heads. They granted her, provisionally, a monthly sum of money and the use of the pilgrims' dormitories attached to the Kali Temple, an imposing building which rises high above congested streets, pilgrims' rest houses and "ghats" where the dead are cremated.

The Kalighat district is a popular place of pilgrimage for Hindus. It lies on the banks of the Hooghly River, into which flow the sacred waters of the Ganges, and its temple is dedicated to the powerful Kali, goddess of death and fertility. Hindu legend records how Kali's father made a sacrifice in order to guarantee the birth of his son but failed to include Shiva, Kali's husband, in the ceremony. Kali, insulted by this omission, committed suicide, and the grief-stricken Shiva roamed the world, bearing his wife in his arms and threatening destruction wherever he went. The world was saved by Vishnu, who hurled a discus at Kali's corpse, whereupon the scattered pieces of Kali fell to the ground sanctifying the places where they landed. Most sacred of all was the spot where the toes of Kali's right foot came to rest, the Kalighat. The temple of Kali, surrounded by its street stalls laden with brightly coloured pictures of the deity, with garlands and multi-coloured powders steeped in symbolism, is thus a vital centre of worship and devotion for Hindus, and it is the wish of every devout Hindu in the city to be cremated in the Kalighat.

The corporation health officer, who happened to be a Muslim, showed Mother Teresa two great rooms at right angles to each other and linked by an adjoining passage. Once used as a resting place for pilgrims who had completed their devotions to Kali, Mother Teresa found them particularly acceptable: "This is a very famous Hindu temple and people used to come there to worship and rest so I thought that this would be the best place for our people to be able to rest before they went to heaven; so I accepted there and then." Mother Teresa and her Sisters rolled up their sleeves and set to work. Within twenty-four hours she had transformed the filthy, disused building into her Nirmal Hriday, a "Place of the Immaculate Heart" at the very centre of Hinduism and only a short distance from the walls of a temple regularly daubed with the blood of sacrificial sheep and goats. Low cots or mattresses were placed on the ledges which ran along either side of the two great rooms, and the almost fleshless frames of people consumed by disease and maggots were given a place to rest in the cool half-light which fell from small windows high up in the walls. The professed intention of those who tended them without any sign of repugnance was not, as some suggested, to convert Hindus to Christianity, to offer them food and shelter in exchange for acceptance of the Christian, and more specifically, the Roman Catholic faith, but to allow them to die according to what is written in the book: "Be it written according to the Hindu or Muslim or Buddhist or Catholic or Protestant or any other religious faith." The sick and the destitute, the beggar picked up from the streets, the leper rejected by his family, the dying man refused admittance to a hospital – all were taken in, fed, washed and given a place to rest. In the beginning conditions in the home for the dying were rudimentary in the extreme. There were times when Mother Teresa transported people in dire need in a workman's wheelbarrow. Of those brought in, those who could be treated were given whatever medical attention was possible; those who were beyond treatment were given the opportunity to die with dignity, having received the rituals of their faith: for Hindus, water from the Ganges on their lips; for Muslims, readings from the Koran; for the rare Christian, the last rites. To Mother Teresa and those who worked with her, restoration to health was not the all-important factor. What was equally important was enabling those who died to do so "beautifully". For her there was no incongruity in the adverb. "A beautiful death", she maintained, "is for people who lived like animals to die like angels – loved and wanted." It was for one old man who had never slept in a bed in his life to clutch the metal side of his simple camp bed frame and proclaim with a radiant smile, "Now I can die like a human being".

In the early days of Nirmal Hriday there was nevertheless a considerable amount of hostility towards the foreign woman and her companions, who were considered to be encroaching on Hindu territory with the co-operation of a Muslim health officer. Conversion to Mother Teresa meant the "changing of heart by love". Conversion by force or bribery was something which she regarded as a shameful thing, and the relinquishing of religion for a plate of rice a terrible humiliation. There were those, however, to whom this was not immediately apparent. Stones were thrown at the Missionaries of Charity as they tried to carry the sick into the dimly lit refuge. On several occasions Mother Teresa and her Sisters were met by Hindus protesting against their presence. One man even threatened to kill Mother Teresa. Then, as on other occasions when she found herself confronted with possible death, her response was simply that this would only expedite the process of "going home" to God: "If you kill us, we would only hope to reach God sooner."

Another leader of a group of young people, who feared the intentions of the Christian women tending the non-Christian dying, entered Nirmal Hriday resolved to turn Mother Teresa out. Having witnessed, however, the care with which the suffering, emaciated bodies of the poor were tended, he returned to his fellow protesters outside with the directive that he would evict the Sisters but only on one condition: namely that they persuade their mothers and sisters to undertake the same service. Gradually Mother Teresa's insistence on the pre-eminence of charity above all things commanded recognition. Those who came to criticize watched as the Sisters applied potassium permanganate to the maggot-ridden wounds of the dying. They learned how Mother Teresa had lifted a young Hindu priest from a pool of his own vomit and filth and brought him to be nursed and eventually die in peace. "We worship a Kali made of stone," announced another priest from the adjacent temple, "but this is the real Ma-Kali, a Kali of flesh and blood."

The resentment and the menaces subsided, although opposition to the proximity of corpses, which to the orthodox Hindu carry strong associations of impurity, did not die altogether. At one point a city councillor actually introduced a motion demanding the removal of the home for the dying from the environs of the Kali temple to some other location. The City Fathers, after considerable deliberation, resolved that "as soon as a suitable place was found, the Nirmal Hriday Hospital be removed from its actual premises". Apparently no suitable alternative site was found, for with this resolution the matter was laid to rest. Hindu pilgrims paused en route to the temple to bring contributions to the work. Every month a marwari businessman sent a delivery boy with a supply of *bidis*, Indian cigarettes, for the occupants of the home for the dying. Each time Mother Teresa parted from them with her habitual valediction, "God bless you". Finally the marwari came himself to deliver his bidis. He wanted to receive her blessing himself, he explained, rather than have her bless his servants. On Sundays, wealthy businessmen and high-caste Hindu ladies would come to Nirmal Hriday to help wash and shave the destitutes.

The word spread and in the course of time the small statue of the Virgin Mary which stood in the corner of one of the two great rooms, was adorned with a crown made from the golden nose rings of the Indian women who had died there. Mother Teresa saw the nose rings as a beautiful gift: "Those who had nothing have given a crown to the Mother of God." Nirmal Hriday was, she claimed, really the treasure house of Calcutta, for the people who died there went straight to God, "and when they go, they tell him about us". It was also, she discovered, a place with a capacity to transform. There were few who went to the Home for the Dying to cleanse the wounds or wash the excreta from the men and women who lay upon the rows of low cots, to cut their hair or coax small morsels of food into their mouths, or even just to scrub down the floors and ledges with a mixture of water, ashes and strong smelling disinfectant, who did not come away in some way changed. There were people there who had starved for too long even to consume the lightest of foods, people whose bodies were half-consumed by maggots, and yet it was not the place of horror that it might have been. The simple act of cutting hair could engender the most luminous of smiles. Just holding the hand of a person whose suffering and previous isolation defied imagination could induce the relief of sleep. Such experiences, Mother Teresa saw, brought greater understanding. In order to understand poverty, she would insist with growing frequency, you had to touch it, not necessarily in the broken bodies of the dying but wherever you encountered it. "Don't just look around like a spectator," she directed those who came to work with her, "really look with your ears and your eyes, and you will be shown what you can do to help."

The work with children which had begun so humbly in an expanse of mud among the huts of Motijhil was also growing. It grew in an attempt to achieve the impossible – in an effort to provide love and care for the apparently unlimited number of unwanted children who must otherwise fend for themselves or die on the streets of Calcutta, orphans, sick, crippled or mentally handicapped children whose parents found themselves unable to support them, children whose mothers had died in Nirmal Hriday, babies born to unmarried mothers who would never be accepted back into their families – in all these Mother Teresa and the Missionaries of Charity saw the infant Christ for whom a Nazareth must be provided. Other charities were already at work in this field but the need was still overwhelmingly great. Once again, Mother Teresa's identification of this need coincided with official embarrassment, and the work of the Missionaries of Charity began to find recognition in the highest quarters.

Dr B. C. Roy, an eminent statesman and for many years the Chief Minister of West Bengal, was also a medical doctor who kept in touch with medical practice by giving daily free consultations at his residence. Mother Teresa would join the queue there at 6 a.m., not necessarily for medical advice but with some practical request relating to the provision of water or electricity for a slum area. After he had written memos on several occasions to the person directly responsible for the matter in question, Dr Roy began to take notice of the persistent little woman who was apparently concerned for the poor of his "problem state". He told her to come to his office. The doors of Government House were opened to her and the Chief Minister trusted her fully. She could call on him freely without previous appointment. So it was that when, on 23 September 1955, Shishu Bhavan, the first of a whole series of children's homes, was opened in a very ordinary two-storeyed building with a large courtyard, only a few hundred yards from the mother house in Lower Circular Road, Dr Roy tried to spur her on to larger things: "Bigger, Mother, we need a much bigger home here. Enlarge this one. Try to buy the adjoining property. I shall help you."

In fact, like all Missionary of Charity undertakings, it began in an unassuming way with a group of tiny sick children in a few cots on the downstairs verandah. Soon, however, the relief distribution initiated at St Teresa's church was moved to Shishu Bhavan and it rapidly became an expanding refuge for crippled and unwanted babies and children. Some of them were found in dustbins and drains. Others were simply abandoned on the city railway platforms. Nearly all were suffering from acute malnutrition and tuberculosis; all were crying out for love. Each day children were discovered and brought to the home by the Missionaries of Charity and, perhaps even more tragically, by parents who were forced to accept their own inability to feed and support their families. Gradually the word spread – children were sent to Shishu Bhavan by the police, by social workers, by doctors and eventually by hospitals. Some of the babies were so tiny that the prospect of their survival was minimal; some of the older children with emaciated limbs, distended stomachs and eyes that seemed prematurely old, were permanently scarred by their experiences. No child was ever refused a home, however, even if it meant that the babies slept three or more to a cot or were coaxed into life in a box heated by a light bulb.

Mother Teresa's approach to caring for these unwanted waifs was always an essentially practical one. One of the first things she did when she opened Shishu Bhavan, Calcutta was to acquire three old typewriters on which she taught some of the older girls how to type and thus improved their chances of getting a job. Whenever possible the sick must be restored to health and those capable of learning must be given some form of education or training to equip them for the future. In a normal child a tremendous transformation took place in the first year alone. First there was a physical change, an increase in weight. The shy ones lost their shyness. As the children grew stronger the aim was to send those capable of pursuing regular studies to proper schools. Those who were unfortunate enough to have no parents should at least be given either a skill, such as carpentry for the boys and needlework for the girls, or a good education. The slum schools which the Sisters ran were not recognized by the government and no recognized school in Calcutta would accept the children without fees, although some would make certain financial concessions, but a generous Hindu lady in Calcutta sponsored the first ten children for the first ten years, and other benefactors would in time adopt a similar system of sponsorship. The future of individual children was thus guaranteed for some years. A baby sponsored by an Indian "parent" or, in the years that followed, by "parents" throughout the world, would be provided with a regular sum of money which would be placed in a bank account until the child reached school age and then used to finance his or her schooling. Later, in 1975, this system of individual sponsorship would be replaced by a general World Child Welfare Fund which would share any financial assistance fairly between all the thousands of children who were by that time in the care of the

Missionaries of Charity. Writing to the "Dear Parents of our Spon-sored Children", Mother Teresa, still very much in control of such administration, would explain that the legislative requirements of individual sponsorship for five thousand children were becoming impossible to meet:

It is becoming nearly impossible to fulfil all the wishes about reports etc, as we did in the beginning when we only had a few children. Second reason is that the number of our children is much higher than five thousand since we have opened houses in sixty-one cities. Therefore we have decided to have a General Child Welfare Fund from which we can help all the children that we know need your help.

Whatever the means of providing for the children, in India Mother Teresa, whose identification with the Indian people was deep-rooted and who herself became an Indian citizen in 1948, was acutely conscious of the need to equip these children for the requirements of Indian society. Some of the youngsters who came to Shishu Bhavan were returned to their parents once their strength and health had been restored. Others were adopted: Hindu children by Hindu parents, Christian children by Christian parents, and so on. Some went to families in other parts of the world, to wherever a secure and stable background could be guaranteed, although legal restrictions could make this a difficult and protracted process. For those who remained in her charge, however, Mother Teresa endeavoured to arrange marriages in accordance with Indian cus-tom. The social backgrounds of the majority of girls in her care would not make the traditional role of marriage broker easy, but it was ensured at least that each girl had a dowry of a new sari, a few trinkets and a wedding ring.

The joy of brides and bridegrooms welcomed back in traditional fashion to Shishu Bhavan, of children successfully raised to lead worthwhile and dignified lives, of smiling young faces inviting attention and love pervaded the atmosphere of Shishu Bhavan. There were those for whom the care offered by the Missionaries of Charity came too late. For all those babies who survived the shock of premature birth, attempted abortion or simply of being unwanted, there were always those who died within an hour of arrival. Mother Teresa's attitude made the transition from the practical to that of unqualified love without apparent question: "I don't care what people say about the death rate. Even if they die an hour later we must let them come. These babies must not die uncared for and unloved, because even a tiny baby can feel." If they were to die then they must do so "beautifully". They must not do so without experiencing, if only for the most fleeting of instants, all the love it was within her power to give.

To Mother Teresa the suggestion that the solution to the problem of India's rapidly increasing population lay in sterilization or abortion was utterly abhorrent and incomprehensible. To her every child was the infant Christ; its destruction by abortion must be seen inescapably as a crucifixion. She did not approve of government sterilization programmes in India. When, during Indira Gandhi's first term of office as Prime Minister, the government sponsored a policy of sterilization of both men and women, inducements were offered in the form of material benefits and the issue became a source of controversy. Indira Gandhi had already shown her solidarity with Mother Teresa in a multitude of ways. Often, as Prime Minister, she would telephone the Missionaries of Charity in Delhi to offer them food left over from State dinners. She was always available to Mother Teresa when she came to the capital, but her support for sterilization brought about one of Mother Teresa's rare attempts at intervention on an issue which could be considered political but which she saw as essentially moral. She delivered a letter from the Catholic Bishops Conference stating their opposition to the programme. She also informed the Prime Minister that she would not be blessed for what she was doing. Shortly afterwards Mrs Gandhi was defeated at the polls.

Even for leprosy victims, Mother Teresa could not accept the idea of sterilization, despite the fact that they frequently infected their children: "A child is their only joy in life. The rich have so many other things. If you remove a child from the home of the poor, or from those with leprosy, who is going to smile at them and help them to get better?" It was a logic consistent with her insistence on the principle of "loving until it hurts" the Christ she saw in every man, the same logic that induced her to go where others feared to tread, to tend the nauseating wounds of the leper or work at great personal risk in places of violence and pain. To her the "beautiful" was to be found in the most unexpected places: "Very often we see a leper woman who is scarcely able even to walk, walking for miles, just to come to Sister to make sure that her child is all right. She has spotted the sign of leprosy in the child so she comes walking . . . all the way walking. We had the wonderful case of a woman who scarcely had any feet to walk on and she had walked more than six miles. She came with this baby in her arms and said, 'Sister, see, my child also has leprosy'. She had seen a spot. The Sister examined the child and took the smear but it was not leprosy, and the woman felt so happy that her child did not have leprosy that she took the child and walked all the way back again. She didn't even stop for a rest. That's a very beautiful thing." It was not then for humankind to determine that the potentially beautiful was merely one more dispensable commodity. When, in 1968, Pope Paul VI in his encyclical *Humanae Vitae* condemned abortion and all forms of birth control except the "rhythm method", Mother Teresa instructed her Sisters to encourage the people they served to accept joyfully the papal instruction, and not to engage in any discussions or arguments to the contrary.

Mother Teresa set about combating abortion with adoption. She sent word to all the clinics, hospitals and police stations: "Please do not destroy the child. We will take the child." She set her young Missionaries of Charity to work on making posters that would convey the same message. At Shishu Bhavan unmarried mothers appeared at all hours of the night and day, looking for a home for the babies they could not keep. The demand Mother Teresa discovered among childless couples for these "unwanted" children became yet another "blessing of God for us". The Missionaries of Charity also began to give instruction in what Mother Teresa described as "Holy Family Planning". When a young woman from Mauritius joined the Missionaries of Charity, who had experience of instructing young married couples in the use of the rhythm method in her own country, she became actively involved in the setting up of an information programme in India. By 1967 a carefully structured natural family planning programme had been established. Despite Mother Teresa's insistence on the beauty of "abstaining out of love for each other" and the simplicity of the rhythm method, teaching such practices to leprosy patients, slum dwellers and street people was not without its limitations. The story is told, for example, of how one woman who had already given birth to a number of children, wished to avoid becoming pregnant again. She was given instruction in "Holy Family Planning" and a string of beads of various colours to help keep a record of the safe period. Some time later she returned to one of the Missionaries of Charity natural family planning centres confused as to why she was once again expecting a child. "I hung the beads round the neck of Kali," she protested, "and still I am pregnant." Nevertheless, by 1979, Mother Teresa would be able to refer in her Nobel Prize speech to the fact that in Calcutta alone, in the space of six years, there had been 61,273 fewer children born to families who would otherwise have had them, because of their use of the rhythm method.

When asked what she intended to do with her wages, the first girl to get a job on the strength of the typing training Mother Teresa had given her at Shishu Bhavan replied that she would move her father, mother and two brothers out of Motijhil slum. Shishu Bhavan in Calcutta was to become the catalyst for many other similar success stories. It became one of the largest work centres of the Missionaries of Charity, a hive of constant activity, always teeming with children and always the focal point of a queue of people waiting for food or medicine. In time, in addition to the care provided for children, free treatment and medication would be given to hundreds of sick adults each week. Cooked food or "kitcherie" was also distributed daily to the hungry, and from here an ambulance donated by Pope Paul VI would set out each morning to distribute rations and carry helpers to no fewer than eight leprosy centres each week, giving free treatment to thousands of victims of the disease.

The need to alleviate the plight of leprosy sufferers had long been a concern of Mother Teresa's. As a disease which ran rife in areas of great poverty, cramped living conditions and malnutrition, leprosy constituted a particularly pressing problem in and around Calcutta where poor nutrition, overcrowding and inadequate medical attention determined the tragic struggle for survival of so many. In India, a substantial proportion of leprosy cases were non-infective, but ignorance of the real nature of the illness and of available treatment was widespread. More difficult than the treatment of the actual symptoms of the disease, Mother Teresa recognized, was the combating of the irrational fears and myths associated with it. A sufferer, fearing the ostracism, unemployment and rejection which frequently accompanied the revelation that he was a leper, would conceal the illness until it had reached its more advanced stages, and even then might well be reluctant to undergo treatment in the alien world of an impersonal hospital far removed from his home and his family, which might ultimately reject him anyway. The Missionaries of Charity ran a leper asylum at Gobra, a district on the outskirts of Calcutta. It so happened, however, that plans for the city's development included the site occupied by the one hundred and fifty or so lepers who would otherwise have been driven to scavenge for a wretched existence on the city's rubbish tips. Their houses and large compound were to be expropriated and incorporated into the new development. Calcutta's healthier citizens would never accept accommodation in close proximity to people carrying a disease they abhorred. Mother Teresa's persuasive powers succeeded only in inducing the authorities to delay evacuation of the colony until alternative accommodation had been found for them. She was offered a place in Bankura district, but with some indignation she pointed out that the area proposed lacked even the most fundamental necessity for the well-being of leprosy patients: an adequate water supply.

The predicament of the lepers who were still, it seemed, the "unclean" of biblical times or of medieval Europe, was brought home to her with increasing intensity, and with the help of a growing number of interested lay people among the British community in Calcutta, she became an active campaigner on their behalf. Someone once somewhat rashly remarked to Mother Teresa that he would not help or touch a leper for a thousand pounds. "Neither would I," was the instant reply, "but I would willingly tend him for the love of God." A Leprosy Fund and a Leprosy Day were started. On the collection boxes were inscribed the words: "Touch a leper with your compassion." In the vision of Mother Teresa the invitation was not merely to give at a distance from a surfeit of wealth, but rather to reach out in love to the Christ whose maimed hands and feet could feel no pain and were therefore susceptible to every conceivable form of injury. There were those in Calcutta who responded with great generosity, and there were others whose fear and suspicion were less easily overcome.

Ann Blaikie, an Englishwoman and the wife of a British solicitor working for a large company in Calcutta during the nineteen-fifties, who would in time become the international link for the Co-Workers, recalled Mother Teresa enlisting her and her husband to take her to view a plot of land between two railway lines as a possible site for a new leper clinic. The local councillor who was present at the time clearly disapproved of their proposition, and asked the crowd of villagers who had inevitably gathered to witness their arrival whether they wanted a leper clinic. The response was unmistakably hostile. The villagers picked up stones and started to throw them, forcing the well-intentioned intruders to run for the car. Mother Teresa, always quick to perceive the hand of Providence at work, saw in their disapproval an indication that God might not want a a leper clinic in that particular location and resolved to pray for two months and see what God did want. In the course of the next two months, 10,000 rupees were given to Mother Teresa by Philips Electric Light Company. Dr Sen, a Hindu specialist in leprosy treatment at the Carmichael Hospital for Tropical Diseases, retired from his official post and offered the rest of his working life to Mother Teresa, and an ambulance was sent to her from the United States. The foundations for the first of Mother Teresa's mobile leprosy clinics were laid.

Mobile leprosy clinics could reach out to a far greater proportion of India's leprosy sufferers. The discovery of the sulphone drug, dapsone or DDS, meant that patients could be treated in their own homes. Ambulances carrying this and other medicaments to those areas where they were most needed could arrest the disease and in some cases cure it and, what was of vital importance to Mother Teresa, they could do so without removing the patient from his family, his essential source of love, or from his employment, the mainspring of his dignity. In September 1957, Mother Teresa's first mobile leprosy clinic was actually opened by Archbishop Périer at Shishu Bhavan on Lower Circular Road. Work started on 1 November of that year, and by the following January six hundred lepers were attending regularly. Dr Sen, whom Mother Teresa would describe on his death in August 1972 as "such a wonderful holy man", also proved to be invaluable in providing the Sisters with the skills they needed for the leprosy clinics. The work spread and more centres, which the ambulance visited once a week, were opened. By 1958 the work of the mobile clinic had been recognized by one witness at least as verging on the miraculous:

Here in Howrah, I saw an experiment in mercy – a miracle it would have been called in a less cynical age. Into the clearing drove an ambulance and in minutes people crowded about its open doors. And no ordinary people these. Beyond the lines of abysmal poverty and undernourishment etched upon their faces, below the tell-tale marks of frustration and harsh treatment, were the scars of a deeper distress – leprosy.

Wherever there were large concentrations of lepers, it was Mother Teresa's hope to establish "static all-weather dispensaries". The first of these began as a mobile clinic under a tree on a piece of land between a railway line and the Titagarh Municipal Sewage pumping station, providing treatment for an already existing community of people with leprosy. Experience showed her, however, that the process of walking to and from a clinic frequently prevented ulcerous feet from healing. Indoor facilities were needed to accommodate such patients. The dispensary developed into a permanent centre which was formally opened in March 1959. Mother Teresa was naturally shy of public speaking. Time would gradually impress upon her the need to speak out in the interests of the poor of the world, but in 1959 she was still reluctant to do so. She also had an intuitive talent for discerning other people's gifts and abilities and using them to the full. At the opening ceremony, therefore, it was Ann Blaikie who, on her behalf, thanked the Volkart Foundation Trust for financing the building of a Leprosy Dispensary at Titagarh, the Titagarh Municipal Council for making the necessary land available, and the Speaker of the West Bengal Assembly for opening it. The speech was given in the presence of what one reporter described succinctly as the "social élite". Also listening if not understanding were 240 Titagarh lepers sitting in rows, awaiting a promised feed and a handout of blankets. After the speech, buns, biscuits, oranges and blankets were distributed amongst them:

"A crippled woman peeled an orange to feed her child. A man fumbled with fingerless hands to offer cake to a pariah puppy cradled in his lap" – and all this took place against the backcloth of the new clinic, blessed by the Archbishop of Calcutta, its paint new smelling and its promise a bright beacon on the very edge of bustee land.

No sooner had the Titagarh clinic opened than the municipal chairman, fearing that it would otherwise be besieged by lepers flocking there from miles around, urged Mother Teresa to start another nearby. At the time there were 30,000 known lepers in Calcutta, and Mother Teresa was already treating 1,136 of them. "So wonderful is the way of God," she commented, "we will eventually get them all."

Treating the lepers involved not only the dispensing of sulphone drugs, the tending of subsidiary ailments, and the distribution of free milk and rice; it involved, above all, the restoration of the dignity and confidence of the patients whose sense of identity had frequently been undermined by fear. For this reason patients who attended the clinics were encouraged wherever possible to provide for their own needs. Those who were able to use their hands were shown how to make shoes from foam rubber cuttings and old rubber tyres. They wove their own bandage cloth, made their own clothes and even managed some carpentry. In the knowledge that so much could be achieved, particularly if the disease was caught in its early stages, Mother Teresa encouraged her Sisters to go out spotting it. In some cases lepers could be completely cured after a year or two, and even those who were severely disfigured could be given a sense of their own value. "In India," Mother Teresa explained some years after the opening of Titagarh, "the idea is, once a leper – a leper for life. Very often it happens that there are broken homes, broken lives. Among our disfigured beggars there are people who have been somebody in life. Last Christmas we had a party for all our lepers. Every leper was given a parcel of food and clothes. At every centre we have made them choose their own leader and they have their own council so that we can deal with them when we have so many thousands in a group." She recalled one of these leaders getting up to thank the Sisters for their gift and their work: "Some years back," he had told her, "I was a very big man and I was

working in offices in a large building as a government official. I had
air conditioning and people to answer my every call. I had people
bowing to me when I came out of my office and I had a big family.
But as soon as they discovered I was a leper all that went. There
was no more air-conditioning, no fans, no home, no family – only
these young Sisters who wanted me and who are my people now."

Experiences such as his spurred Mother Teresa on to implement
one of her most cherished wishes: a place where lepers could live
and die with dignity, where they could work gainfully and lead
constructive lives. Thirty-four acres of land donated by the Indian
government and funds raised by German children singing at a
charity concert on the Feast of the Three Kings, made it possible
to initiate the venture. The gift of a white Lincoln Continental car
brought it to fruition. The vehicle in question was one provided
for the use of Pope Paul VI during his visit to India in 1964. On
his departure the Pope elected to give it to Mother Teresa to help
with her work. When the needs of the poor required it, Mother
Teresa was not infrequently seen in cars made available for her use
by British businessmen and others in Calcutta, but she treated no
one to the incongruous vision of a slight figure dressed as one of the
poorest of the poor riding through the city streets in a ceremonial
limousine. Instead, she raffled it, raising very much more by this
means than she would have by an outright sale. To the thirty or so
dwellings already under construction some six motoring hours from
the heart of Calcutta, the Pope's gift added a substantial hospital.
A further contribution from the Papal Propagation of the Faith in
Germany provided a convent and a chapel. Shanti Nagar, "The
Place of Peace" and the fulfilment of a dream, began to form a
green oasis in what had previously been merely an expanse of dust.

A well was constructed, ponds were stocked with fish, and banana
and palm trees were planted several years before the first leper
families moved in. The idea was to make the inhabitants self-
sufficient. The first arrivals learnt how to make bricks and so helped
to build homes for those who were yet to come. Despite, in some
cases, the handicap of severely maimed limbs, the villagers looked
after their own cattle, grew their own rice and tilled their own
paddy fields. They ran their own grocer's shop. They made baskets
to be sold for use in the coal mines and even started a printing

press. Mother Teresa's original plan for Shanti Nagar envisaged the settling of about four hundred families who must all somehow be accommodated in inexpensive, easily maintained but attractive huts and who must all be given the appropriate medical treatment. Her answer to sceptical queries about the availability of resources or of surgical skills was, as always, that God would provide. One doctor at the Leprosy Study Centre in London recalled with some amusement how, in his case, the will of God was brought about. He received a telephone call apparently out of the blue:

"I'm speaking on behalf of Mother Teresa", said the voice on the telephone. "Can you tell me where I can buy a million tablets of dapsone?"

I could and I told her, and I added for good measure that I should like to know that they would be given to the right people at the right dose for the right disease.

Not long afterwards the doctor in question found himself in India with the Missionaries of Charity, helping to "add a modicum of medical knowledge to their Christian compassion, a smattering of diagnosis and treatment to their love and concern".

Humanly speaking it was all still fearfully fragile. The provision of professional knowledge and skills, of vital medicines and equipment was as completely dependent on Divine Providence as were the lives of the Sisters themselves. If an increasing number of occupants of the home for the dying began to recover it was not because Nirmal Hriday could provide efficient medical care which hospitals could not. There were those trained doctors and nurses who came to work there on a voluntary basis who were horrified at the failure to observe the kind of fundamental rules of hygiene which would protect the Sisters from infection and the "patients" from contaminating each other. The Missionaries of Charity were not to wear gloves to touch the maggot-ridden bodies of the dying, any more than they were to hold the lepers at arm's length because they were tending the body of Christ. One anecdote which Mother Teresa loved to tell and retell was of a young novice who was sent for the first time to work in Nirmal Hriday, who returned at the end of the day with shining eyes, protesting her joy that she had been touching Christ throughout the day.

The same kind of reasoning determined that it was not by its efficiency or effectiveness that an action should be judged but by the amount of love that was put into it. It also meant that the vocation of a Missionary of Charity was not to be perceived as a call to work with lepers or to resolve any other particular form of poverty, even if an individual manifestly had a talent in a particular direction. Hard though it sometimes was for some of her Sisters and Brothers to accept, the vocation of a Missionary of Charity was not to give such talents to the poor. It was to "belong to Jesus". Essentially hard working and practical though Mother Teresa was, this primary focus was one on which she was totally uncompromising. The Missionaries of Charity were not social workers. The mere suggestion that they were was enough to cause her pain, for what they must be was "contemplatives in the world".

Impressed by the success of Missionary of Charity ventures, government officers in Delhi once wrote to Mother Teresa, asking her to train some of their social workers. They wanted her to share her secret, which they imagined must take the form of some novel and advanced technique, a new chapter in the manuals of sociology. In fact Mother Teresa was obliged to decline their request. The "success", as she saw it, was entirely dependent on the recognition of Christ in the poor and on spiritual values to which social work, very good and commendable though it might be, gave insufficient credence. Mother Teresa's relationship with God was a very personal one. "I have no imagination," she once acknowledged, "I cannot imagine God the Father. All I can see is Jesus." When she looked at the poor she saw Jesus in his distressing disguise. When she wrote of the poor, she wrote "Poorest of the Poor" in capitals, as she did all references to God or Jesus. It was the rejected Jesus whom her Sisters must see and touch in those they served:

Each time Jesus wanted to prove his love for us, he was rejected by mankind. Before his birth his parents asked for a simple dwelling place and there was none because his parents were poor. The innkeeper looked at the poor dress of Joseph the carpenter, thinking that he will not be able to pay, and he was refused. But Mother Earth opened its cave and took in the Son of God.

Again, before the Redemption and the Resurrection, he was rejected by his people. They did not want him; they wanted Caesar. They did not want him; they wanted Barabas. At the end, as if his own Father did not him also because he was covered with our Sins – in his loneliness he cried, 'My God, my God why hast thou forsaken me?'

The yesterday is always today with God, therefore today in the world Jesus stands covered with our sins, in the distressing disguise of my Sister, my Brother. Do I want him? If we are not careful the riches of the worldly spirit will become an obstacle. We will not be able to see God for Jesus has said "Blessed are the clean of heart for they shall see God."

Without this essential spiritual perspective, without the purity of heart vital to the seeing of God, without the framework and grounding of the religious life, Mother Teresa was firmly convinced that her Sisters would be unable to bring peace to the dying, touch the open wounds of the leper and nurture the tiny spark of life in babies whom others had abandoned. It was not possible to engage in the apostolate without being a soul at prayer.

Prayer, centred on the Eucharist, because in the Eucharist Christ offered himself to sustain, was therefore essential. Quite apart from the shared offices that punctuated the day, the Missionaries of Charity were to pray while dressing. There was a specific prayer to be said as each major article of clothing was put on. Of the habit they prayed that it might be a reminder of their separation from the world and its vanities: "Let the world be nothing to me and I nothing to the world." The girdle they tied round their waists was to remind them that they must try to imitate the angelic purity of Mary, "surrounded and protected by that absolute poverty which crowned all you did for Jesus". As they put on their saris they were to pray the words: "Oh Most Blessed Virgin Mary, cover me with the mantle of your modesty and let this sari make me more and more like you." The crucifix was to remind them that they were the spouses of Christ crucified: "And as such I must in all things live the life of a victim and do his work of a Missionary of Charity." As they put on their sandals they committed themselves to following Jesus "wherever you shall go in search of souls, at any cost to myself and out of pure love of you." As they walked the streets they were to use their rosaries as a "beautiful means to keep on praying".

Mother Teresa directed them to make use of all their senses to help them pray, to pay special attention to how they genuflected, how they joined their hands, how they took the Holy Water. They were to use holy pictures to raise their minds to God. At night they were to pray, holding their crucifixes, as they knelt at their bedsides before sleeping. Throughout the day they were to undertake the work in such a way that prayer and action became one. They were in fact to be "professionals in prayer". Each year every Sister underwent an eight-day retreat based on the spiritual exercises of St Ignatius Loyola. Some years later Mother Teresa would confide to a friend that she could lead a retreat for her Sisters, direct and listen to them, and still be on retreat herself. So constant and so perfectly fused were prayer and activity in her.

The striving for perfection was what she wanted from her Sisters. She was a faithful daughter of the Roman Catholic Church. She had, she would often tell them, promised to give saints to Mother Church and she was rigorous in forming them with that intention. She would not be satisfied with their just being good religious. She wanted to be able to offer God a perfect sacrifice and, as far as she was concerned, only holiness perfected the gift. The Rule or constitutions was the expression of the "Will of God". She and those whom she regarded as her "dearest children" must therefore know it and submit to it everywhere and always, down to the last breath. The meditation on Thursday mornings, the day of their reflection, would invariably be devoted to a point of the constitutions. Mother Teresa had never been a student of theology but she was steeped in the gospels, and her knowledge of the lives of the saints was extensive. She herself would join in the half-hour of spiritual reading which she prescribed for her young Sisters each day. For all their poverty, even in the early days, Mother Teresa had managed to beg a comprehensive library with which to provide them with the spiritual resources she was convinced they needed, and her spiritual instruction of them was rooted in her own not inconsiderable reading of Catholic religious writing. So it was that she could reinforce her own insistence on the significance of the Rules with St Vincent's comparison of the Rules to "Wings on which to fly to God", and with the examples of numerous saints and others called to the religious life.

The directions to her Sisters were those of a firm believer in discipline – Obedience was to be "prompt, simple, blind, cheerful, for Jesus was obedient unto death". Charity was to be manifested in "words, deeds, thoughts, desires and feelings, for Jesus went about doing good." Poverty was to be applied to all "desires and attachments, in likes and dislikes, for Jesus being rich made himself poor for us". Chastity was to be lived "in thoughts and affections, in desires and attachments". In the street they were not to look at worldly pictures or magazines. Nor were they to listen to idle conversation. They were to shun "dangerous occasions" and to avoid touching each other for "Jesus is a jealous lover". Twice a day they were called upon formally to examine their consciences in relation to these and other matters.

With Mother Teresa, however, charity was always paramount. If her requirements were direct in their wording and strict in their expectations it had to be borne in mind that she was attempting the formation of girls, some of whom she had known as pupils and many of whom were fresh from school. Her instructions were given in the context of the deep and tender affection she had for them, and with the clear understanding that kindness was always a priority. She told them she preferred them to make mistakes in kindness than to work miracles in unkindness, and she lived what she preached. Her close attention to the small details of their daily life was necessary before there were any other Superiors amongst them. It was she who admonished them, for example, when complaints were made that the Sisters were so engrossed in saying their rosaries as they walked through the streets of Calcutta that they failed to greet people who knew them. They must, Mother Teresa stressed, always be the first to smile in greeting: "If you take a little trouble to bow to Jesus in the heart of these priests and religious you meet, won't that help you to pray the Rosary with greater love?" Their vocation, to be beautiful, must be full of thought for others. It must also be full of joy. Candidates wishing to join the Missionaries of Charity need not have any particular educational qualifications though they must have common sense and be capable of acquiring knowledge (especially the language of the people they were to serve), but they must be healthy in body and mind, guided by the right intention and of a cheerful disposition. "Smiling Novices,"

Mother Teresa would say, "I can hear the music of your laughter of joy. Learn, my children, to be holy, for true holiness consists in doing God's will with a smile."

Christ present in the hungry one so that "we can satisfy his love for us"; Christ, the bread of life, the Word made flesh, silently present in the Eucharist, "to satisfy our hunger for love" – Mother Teresa had been granted a sacramental vision of God fully present in the world, her own understanding of which would become more comprehensive with time. Somehow she must communicate to her young Sisters something of the depth and richness she already knew. If she was concerned with small practical considerations such as how the Sisters cut their hair, she never lost sight of the deeper vision. Ultimately what she sought to develop in them was "the constant awareness of the Divine Presence everywhere and in everyone, especially in our own hearts and in the hearts of our Sisters with whom we live, and in the poorest of the poor". She wanted them to live in union with God and with one another. Silence was at the root of that union, for God was the "friend of silence":

We need silence to be alone with God, to speak to him, to listen to him, to ponder his words deep in our hearts. We need to be alone with God in silence to be renewed and transformed. Silence gives us a new outlook on life. In it we are filled with the energy of God himself that makes us do all things with joy.

Of necessity theirs must often be an interior silence, surrounded as they were for much of the time by noise and restlessness. To make possible true interior silence she told her Sisters they would practise:

Silence of the eyes by seeking always the beauty and goodness of God everywhere and closing them to the faults of others and to all that is sinful and disturbing to the soul.

Silence of the ears, by listening always to the voice of God and the cry of the poor and the needy, and closing them to all the other voices that come from the evil one or from fallen human nature, e.g. gossip, tale-bearing, uncharitable words.

Silence of the tongue, by praising God and speaking the life-giving Word of God that is Truth that enlightens and inspires, brings peace, hope and joy, and refraining from self-defence and every word that causes darkness, turmoil, pain and death.

Silence of the mind by opening it to the Truth and knowledge of God in prayer and contemplation, like Mary who pondered the marvels of the Lord in her heart, and closing it to all untruths, distractions, destructive thoughts like rash judgement, false suspicion of others, revengeful thoughts and desires.

Silence of the heart, by loving God with our whole heart, soul, mind and strength and one another as God loves, desiring God alone and avoiding all selfishness, hatred, envy, jealousy and greed.

Fidelity in small things became an expression of something much more profound: self-sacrificial love. In preparation for Christmas, the season when "the Word was made flesh and dwelt among us", an empty crib would be placed in the Sisters' chapel. Also in the chapel was a box containing some straw. During advent the Sisters were encouraged to make small personal sacrifices, to allow some- one else readier access to the water tank, for example, by relinquish- ing their own place. Then, discreetly, they would go to the chapel, remove a straw from the box and place it in the crib. Thus when the infant Jesus was laid in the manger at Christmas it would be in a crib warmed by their love and sacrifice.

Mother Teresa taught her Sisters the relevance of their acts of obedience to the Church and the world as a whole: "I hope and pray you are conscious of your responsibility to the Church. You are the sign of God, the proof of his living love for men." At her careful prompting the Missionaries of Charity's prayer life followed the liturgical calendar of the Roman Catholic Church's year. May was specially devoted to the Virgin Mary; June to the Sacred Heart; in August came the special feast of the Society, the Feast of the Immaculate Heart of Mary. Their devotions were related not only to special events within the life of the Society – as new houses were opened, the anniversary of their beginning was marked on the blackboards in all the chapels of the Missionaries of Charity for special remembrance – but also to events in the life of the Church, the mystical body of Christ, which she once said was "everything" to her. When, in November 1964, news of Pope Paul VI's forthcoming visit reached Calcutta, she called upon her Sisters to offer "many acts of silence in preparation for the coming of the Holy Father". After his departure, in the month of December they would undertake "many acts of charity in thanksgiving for the Holy Father's visit".

As the work began to spread it did so, according to Mother Teresa, entirely as the need was identified and the means to meet it were given. "It is the presence of Christ which guides us", she would emphasize. "We do not make plans, we do not prepare an infrastructure. Everything is made according to the necessities of the poor. If they ask us for bread, we try to get it for them. If they do not have anyone to wash their clothes, we wash them. It is Divine Providence who guides us in the execution of the work and in the obtainment of means for it." Such dependence on Divine Providence did not, however, prevent her from recognizing the need to ensure that the growth was that of a "straight, beautiful, fruitful tree". She knew that she would have need of Superiors who would "take the place of God" among their Sisters, that her own presence amongst them would not be as constant, but even as the demands upon her time grew she wrote to them regularly. The Sisters too would begin to travel. As the ships' sirens resounded in Calcutta at midnight on 31 December 1961 to herald the beginning of a new year, she thought of each one of her Sisters and "longed to offer to God a perfect sacrifice made of your hearts". She wrote to them in a way which betrayed an extraordinary capacity to keep in touch with the difficulties and demands of their daily lives, and she told them that she wanted to be with them wherever they were: to love them, to help them and to guide them to become saints.

CHAPTER FOUR

Poor on the Moon

For nearly ten years after the inception of the Congregation of the Missionaries of Charity, its work was confined to the diocese of Calcutta. Canon law forbids the opening of further houses outside the diocese by institutes less than ten years old, and the Archbishop of Calcutta was most emphatic in enforcing this rule. Mother Teresa was able to accept the general wisdom of the restriction. Ten years in which to communicate the fire that burned in her to others, in which to shape some of her young Sisters into superiors imbued with the spirit of the Society and capable of taking charge of new foundations elsewhere, was not an excessive period. By 1959, however, a year before the probationary period proscribed by the Roman Catholic Church was complete, the Sisters were eager to extend the work begun in Calcutta throughout India, and the Archbishop relented a little. Almost immediately they were invited to establish houses in Ranchi, Delhi and Jhansi, for news of the work was spreading, and bishops in need of their services welcomed them readily into their dioceses. In Delhi the Missionaries of Charity opened a children's home. Its inaugural ceremony was attended by the Prime Minister, Jawaharlal Nerhu who, when asked by Mother Teresa if she should tell him about the work of the Congregation, paid tribute to the achievements of the first ten years: "No, Mother," was his reply, "you need not tell me about your work. I know about it. That is why I have come."

The work that had won the recognition of Pandit Nehru spread swiftly to many other towns and cities – even to the glamour city of Bombay, which prided itself on a display of palatial mansions and an abundance of Roman Catholic schools, colleges and charitable institutions. Mother Teresa was convinced not only of the possibility of finding vocations among Bombay's well-educated Catholic community but also of the necessity to meet a real need in the city. She offered her services to Cardinal Gracias, who responded instantly with an invitation to come and work in his archdiocese. As head of the Roman Catholic Church in Bombay, Cardinal Gracias had already identified many areas of need which his limited number of clergy were unable to meet. Mother Teresa was quick to endorse his diagnosis. After a short tour of inspection of his city, she made the unpopular comment that the slums of Bombay were even worse than the slums of Calcutta. The citizens of Bombay were reluctant to admit that the city which boasted an impressive marine drive and opulent villas also embraced heavily overcrowded "chawls", buildings which rose several storeys high, where ventilation was minimal, the only available water had to be carried up narrow stairways, and children had nowhere to play or even breathe fresh air. The uncared for of Bombay, Mother Teresa insisted, were crying out as vociferously for love as the inhabitants of the Calcutta "bustees". Not long after the arrival of the Missionaries of Charity in Bombay, a newspaper headline depicted the fate of a woman who had died alone and untended in one of the city streets. Her body had remained there for several hours before anyone came to remove it. The pattern of need was repeating itself. With the help of Cardinal Gracias, Mother Teresa opened a home for the dying in Bombay.

The gift of Pope Paul VI's Lincoln Ford Continental in 1964 was not the only manifestation of papal support for her work. If Mother Teresa was diligent in her fidelity to the Church and to the Vicar of Christ, even in the early stages of the Missionaries of Charity, the fact did not go unrecognized. There were to be other gifts. On one occasion Paul VI provided her with a substantial donation for Christmas which enabled the Missionaries of Charity to give five thousand children and leprosy patients a good meal and a small present. On another he gave them the means to buy four thousand beds and mattresses for the poor, and a "pontifical" lorry which got stuck one day in a one-way street. When the policeman endeavouring to clear the congestion was told it was a present from the Pope to the needy, the driver was allowed to proceed with the remark: "Oh, the Pope – all right carry on."

On 1 February 1965, only six years after the Missionaries of

Charity had been allowed to extend their activities beyond the boundaries of the Calcutta Archdiocese, the Congregation was granted the Papal Decree of Praise through the Sacred Congregation for the Propagation of the Faith. In November 1960, Mother Teresa had gone to Rome on her return from the United States, where she had been in search of funding for the work in India, to ask the Pope, then John XXIII, for pontifical recognition. It was during the first international journey that would take her away from her Sisters in India. She had left them with an expression of her confidence in them and in Sister Agnes, whom she had made Assistant General, and with the assurance that she would carry each one of them, just as they were, to the feet of Christ's vicar on earth because she was going to beg the Holy Father to take the small Society under his special care.

As it transpired, the stay in Rome also gave her an opportunity to meet again the brother whom she had not seen since 1924. Lazar was by then living as an exile in Italy with his wife Maria and their daughter, Aggi. Drana and Aga Bojaxhiu, however, were still in Tirana, and it was a source of continuing sadness to both Mother Teresa and her brother that they remained cut off with no apparent means of leaving a country which was by then widely regarded as one of Europe's most rigorously socialist states.

The wait in Rome was a nerve-racking one for Mother Teresa, for whom the application for papal recognition of the Missionaries of Charity was a crucial step in her religious life. Yet according to one of the Sisters who was close to her at the time, when it came to actually making the request in person to Pope John XXIII Mother Teresa lost her nerve and asked only for a blessing. It was Cardinal Agagianian who at the Sacred Congregation of the Propagation of the Faith questioned Mother Teresa rigorously about the constitutions and work of the Missionaries of Charity, and her answers apparently met with his approval, for on 2 May 1965 the "little Society" in India was formally appointed a society of pontifical right.

The Papal Internuncio, Archbishop Knox, came from Delhi to Calcutta to read the decree in public in the presence of, among others, Archbishop Perier, Fathers Van Exem and Henry, and the Provincial of the Loreto Sisters. Benches and chairs and fans had to be borrowed for the occasion, while Mother Teresa squatted on the ground to hear the expression of the Holy See's endorsement:

In order that the apostolate among the poorer people might be promoted more efficaciously, the Ordinary of the Archdiocese of Calcutta, India, some years ago, instituted a Pious Union of women which he later raised into the religious Congregation of the Missionary Sisters of Charity.

As with the help of God's grace the above named Congregation has grown much and has sent its Sisters into many other dioceses of India to carry out the works of charity, the Ordinaries of the said dioceses submitted to this Sacred Council for the Propagation of the Faith a petition that the Decree of Praise might be granted to this Congregation.

Our Most Holy Father Paul VI by Divine Providence Pope, gladly received this petition communicated to him by the undersigned Cardinal Prefect of this Sacred Council at the audience of the 1st February AD 1965 and awarded the Decree of Praise to the Congregation of the Missionary Sisters of Charity whose Mother House is in the Archdiocese of Calcutta.

Moreover this Sacred Council approved the Constitutions of the said Congregation for seven years according to the text which is joined to this Decree. Given at Rome from the Palace of the Sacred Congregation for the Propagation of the Faith.

The decree conferred on a hitherto diocesan Congregation the approval of the Holy See. Henceforward no change could be made to the Congregation's constitutions without its consent. In his homily the Internuncio gave the Missionaries of Charity three words to remember: *Dependence* on God every day; *detachment* from the goods of this world; and *dedication*. Through their fourth vow they were, he said, to be a holocaust for God and for the poorest of the poor, holding constantly before them the example of the model of Jesus on the cross, the Son of God who made himself poor for love of mankind.

The "holocaust for God" continued to expand within India. "Our discernment of aid is only ever the necessity", Mother Teresa would claim on more than one occasion. The necessity always perceived as that of the thirsting Christ seemed to call for an expanding range of responses: clinics for those suffering from tuberculosis, ante-natal clinics, general dispensaries, mobile leprosy clinics, night shelters for homeless men, homes for abandoned children, homes for the dying and the destitute, nursery classes and crèches, primary schools, secondary schools, provision for further education, feeding programmes, villages for lepers, commercial schools, training in carpentry, metal work, embroidery, needlework or other skills, child-care and home management, and aid in the event of emergencies and disasters arising from riots, epidemics, famine and flooding.

In late 1977 a cyclone hit the state of Andhra Pradesh and made two million people homeless, and the accompanying floods and devastation took the lives of thousands. A tidal wave, described by one eye-witness as a wall of water eighteen feet high, swept inland for fifteen miles, destroying everything in its path. Mother Teresa immediately gathered together a group of Sisters to help the victims of the disaster. Her verdict when confronted by the scenes of desolation was one of horror: "Nowhere have I experienced such utter destruction, such hopeless suffering, such an appalling stench of death." In the middle of the disaster area she established a house as a base from which ten Missionaries of Charity, together with Christian Aid, the Red Cross and two other charities, could work round the clock, feeding, housing, clothing and inoculating an endless stream of bewildered people, too dazed and shocked to seek out and reconstruct their own homes. The incident proved to be only one of many similar disasters to which Mother Teresa was frequently able to respond with conspicuous speed and efficiency, because she had at her disposal a growing number of Sisters, bound in obedience to move as directed and rendered free to do so by the poverty which meant that they travelled only with such personal luggage as could be contained in a bucket or a cardboard box.

When Pope Paul VI gave Mother Teresa his car, he did so in order that it should be put towards what he described as her "universal mission of love". His words were to prove to be prophetic. The first invitation to start a foundation outside India came in 1965, when Mother Teresa was invited to open a house in Venezuela in order to help meet the needs of the millions of baptized Roman Catholics in Latin America who had lapsed in their faith largely because of the lack of priests and religious to instruct and guide them. During a visit to Rome for the Second Session of the Second Vatican Council, Archbishop Knox, the Internuncio to New Delhi, had met Bishop Benitez of Barquisimeto, a South American bishop, who had impressed upon him the need for help to combat the spiritual poverty prevalent in some of the isolated communities of his diocese and for a congregation of Sisters to work especially among the women, to give them a sense of their own dignity and train them in practical skills. Archbishop Knox was eager that Mother Teresa should accept the invitation to Venezuela, but she was at first reluctant to do so. She did not feel that her Sisters were as yet ready to move so far afield. She was not certain that they were sufficiently steeped in the spirit of the Congregation and it was, above all, the spirit which she insisted was important, for without the spirit the work would die. The Missionaries of Charity did not need the additional requirement to go to Venezuela, she protested, but the Archbishop pointed out that the needs of the Church and not those of the Missionaries of Charity were paramount and the matter was settled. For Mother Teresa the authority and the requirements of the Church were not issues to be challenged. By mid-July 1965 she had left for Venezuela with five Sisters.

Venezuela, with its isolated mud hut communities nestling in lush jungle vegetation, would present new challenges for the Missionaries of Charity. The requirements of work within the framework of the South American culture were very different from anything they had experienced in India. The encounter with unconsecrated marriages in which sometimes only a proportion of the children were actually true brother and sister was entirely new to them. Nevertheless the Sisters set swiftly to work. They set up their headquarters in a small town called Cocorote, in a rectory which had been deserted for many years. They ran sewing and typing classes for the girls of the neighbourhood. They taught English, and they visited the poor and the sick, bearing soap and clean clothes. The local governor Dr Bartolome Romero Aguero became their champion. He supplied them with free petrol for a four-wheel-drive vehicle in which they sped along the Panamanian Highway at 90 km an hour on regular visits to the "campos".

Venezuela also marked a departure for the Missionaries of Charity in that they began to co-operate directly in the work of religious education. In an area where priests were in desperately short supply, they were asked to take over the preparation of children for First Communion and confirmation. Later in 1970, when they opened a foundation in the Caracas area, Cardinal Quintero would grant three Missionaries of Charity, together with Sisters from other Congregations, the right to administer Communion. The Sisters took Holy Communion to the sick, conducted funeral services, washed and cleansed the elderly, fed the hungry and, when in 1972 strong winds swept the coast of Venezuela leaving many homes without a roof, they inevitably became volunteer roof repairers. In return the local people shared the little they had. They came bearing gifts of an egg or a banana for the Sisters, who many years afterwards would remember them for their honesty, simplicity and kindness.

By the second half of the 1960s Mother Teresa was beginning to travel with greater frequency. "I am here, far in land distance, but my heart and the very soul is with each one of you", she would write, having just left her small nucleus of Sisters in Venezuela. "Love one another; help one another; be kind to one another." Her journeying imposed upon her the need to give authority to others. Sister Agnes was left in full charge of the Society while she was away from India. Full legal powers of attorney would be given to the Superior in Venezuela to act on her behalf. Her directions to her Sisters became very specific about obedience and the exercising of authority. If the Sisters were to see God in their Superiors, the Superiors were to serve and not to be served. Mother Teresa's journeyings would also take her with increasing frequency to Rome. On 15 July 1965 Mother Teresa was among forty people to have a private audience with Pope Paul VI. Afterwards she would describe how at the meeting with the Pope of "six little MCs with nothing to their name", Paul VI showed great joy but no words would come to him. Eventually he asked her for prayers. He also told her to write to him and that he would see her again, in heaven if not before. The Sisters themselves were so absorbed in looking at him that they could remember nothing more of their audience.

In 1968 came the invitation to work amongst the poor of Rome. At first it was difficult to believe. Rome already had twenty-two thousand nuns belonging to twelve hundred other Orders. The request, however, stemmed from the Pope himself, and in the light of Mother Teresa's strong ecclesiastical sense the opportunity to serve at what she saw as the very centre of Christianity was not to be declined. In August she and a handful of Sisters arrived at Rome airport, from where they were taken by a welcoming bishop to St Peter's to pray and give thanks. The greatness and beauty of the building left Mother Teresa feeling slightly "like a prisoner", but her thoughts were primarily for the Holy Father, who was due to leave next day for a Eucharistic Congress. Attempts to find a suitable place for the Sisters were initially abortive. "There was no place in the inn," pronounced Mother Teresa, "it was very beautiful." Next day, however, she found a very small house amongst the city's poor. Mother Teresa was delighted that it was probably the poorest house the Missionaries of Charity had yet occupied. As far as she was concerned, Our Lady had worked yet another wonderful act of love. The Sisters moved into the slum area and began their work with refugees from Sicily and Sardinia who could only obtain unskilled work and who were not entitled to such State benefits as medical schemes and social security.

From then on the invitations to open houses began to flow in with extraordinary rapidity (see Appendix A). In September 1968 the Missionaries of Charity opened a house in Tabora, Tanzania. For Mother Teresa, who crossed the ocean to prepare the way for them, it was cause to wonder at the way in which her childhood yearning to go to Africa had been fulfilled in a manner she had not expected. Also in 1968 the call came from Archbishop Knox in Australia for the Missionaries of Charity to come to Melbourne. "Necessity" this time took the form, not of extreme physical poverty, starvation or of destitutes dying in the streets, but rather of drug addicts, alcoholics, prisoners in need of rehabilitation and juvenile delinquents crying out for attention.

In July 1970 Archbishop Pio Laghi, Apostolic Delegate to Jerusalem, and Monsignor John Nolan, President of the Pontifical Mission to Palestine, travelled across cease-fire lines from Jerusalem to Amman to welcome Mother Teresa and five other Missionary of Charity Sisters to Jordan. The population of the Jordanian capital had almost doubled to 650,000 since the 1967 six-day war between Israel and the Arab countries, and large numbers of refugees were living in desperate conditions in camps on the outskirts of the city.

The Sisters made their temporary home in a college run by a local religious Congregation, while they struggled to learn some colloquial Arabic and looked for three rooms to form their permanent residence in the poverty-stricken Jebel el Jausa neighbourhood. They had brought with them from India bedding and cartons of tinned food for the poor of Amman. During the nine-day civil war, one of the Sisters kept a diary. The entries record "bombs falling very near – big cannon balls flying like flies, and bullets too". They include an account of how armed men came at night to the house where the Missionaries of Charity were staying and insisted on entering, and of days and nights spent only in the corridor because the glass in the outer rooms had been shattered by heavy artillery.

That poverty was not simply a question of material deprivation was a reality which was to be brought home to Mother Teresa in an ever more pressing way. In the winter of 1970 she visited England to open a home in London in which to train her Sisters. Typically, she chose a drab suburban terrace house in Southall, and during her stay Mother Teresa spent many hours in the slum and vice areas of the metropolis. She was taken on a tour of the nightspots by the Simon Community, a charity committed to the care of the city's derelicts, alcoholics, drug addicts and "down-and-outs". She saw the strip clubs of Soho. She was shown the people sleeping under the tarpaulins which draped the scaffolding of St Martin-in-the-Fields and the drop-outs huddled under the railway arches at Charing Cross. She met some of the homeless curled up on the gratings where warm air rose from the kitchens of West End hotels. Among the methylated spirit drinkers and the drug pushers a young man, well-fed and well-dressed, took an overdose of barbiturates before her very eyes. Mother Teresa was shocked and upset then as she was shocked and upset again in April 1988 when, having witnessed the plight of the occupants of London's "Cardboard City", she pleaded with Mrs Thatcher to help those whom she had seen sleeping in the bitter cold in "little cardboard coffins".

The physical suffering of a woman frozen stiff beneath the railway arches moved her in 1970 to protest at the tragic irony of the fact that "people here send things to me in India when a woman in London is living like this!" Above all, however, it was the spiritual poverty of materially rich societies which touched her: "Here you have the Welfare State. Nobody need starve. But there is a different poverty. The poverty of the spirit, of loneliness and being unwanted." File, the woman covered in sores to whom Mother Teresa's mother had devoted so much care in Albania, had suffered not so much from her physical wounds as from the fact that she had been forgotten by her family; what made death on the streets of Calcutta so terrible was the fact that it was frequently the consequence of a lack of concern on the part of others; there was in the world today a disease more awful than leprosy or cancer – namely that of being unwanted. The recognition of this crucial fact induced the Missionaries of Charity to found Homes of Compassion for destitute men and women, to feed the "down-and-outs" on the banks of a city canal, to knock on the doors of the lonely and the elderly, and to touch areas of human suffering from which others shied away.

In the East End of London the Sisters made repeated attempts to visit a resident of one of a row of council houses occupied for the most part by patients discharged from mental hospitals, some of whom were still unable to look after themselves. The Sisters had noticed an unpleasant smell issuing from the home of an elderly woman who refused to open the door to anyone. Eventually one Sister put her foot in the door and the woman was obliged to allow her to enter. The toilet was blocked in the house and the contents of both of its two rooms were covered with excrement. The Sisters borrowed shovels and filled five sacks with faeces. They washed and cleaned the furniture and curtains, and while they were doing it the old woman enquired of one of them, "Do you still love me now?" "I love you even more now", was the unflinching response.

This was by no means an isolated incident and nor was this kind of need confined to London. The apparent wealth of other European cities and of the United States of America concealed a similar form of poverty. Yet Mother Teresa's response was not to stand in judgement on rich societies which apparently did not know how to use and appreciate the riches God had granted them. She was capable of pointing out in an unequivocal way that if there were poor in the world it was not because God had made them poor but because "you and I do not share enough". Her reaction to the

succession of advertisements for slimming products she once witnessed during a commercial break in an interview she was giving
on United States television was telling if wistful rather than critical:
"And I spend all my time trying to put an ounce of flesh on bare
bones." Invariably, however, her response was to seek immediate and
practical ways to meet the need as she found it, rather than to
condemn what might be seen as the causes of that need. In doing
so she paid little heed to considerations of personal safety or the
kind of reasoning that pointed out the magnitude of the need in
relation to the capacities of her growing but none the less small
Congregation. In 1971 the Missionaries of Charity set up their
simple convent in the very heart of the South Bronx area of New
York, where even the local police did not dare to venture alone.
Outside their building the Sisters created a small haven of green
where they kept chickens, undeterred by the fact that the outside
walls of their chapel, the interior of which was dominated by the
words, "I thirst", were sometimes daubed in two-foot-high letters
with such slogans as "Sons of Satan". "The Sisters are doing small
things in New York," Mother Teresa would explain, "helping the
children, visiting the lonely, the sick, the unwanted. We know now
that being unwanted is the greatest disease of all. That is the poverty
we find around us here. In one of the houses where the Sisters visit,
a woman living alone was dead many days before she was found
and she was found because her body had begun to decompose. The
people around her did not know her name." Someone had ventured
to suggest to Mother Teresa that the Sisters were not achieving
very much: "I said that even if they helped one person, that was all
right. Jesus would have died for one person, for one sinner."

"I do not think the way you do", she would say when it was
pointed out to her, as it frequently was, that her Missionaries of
Charity's efforts were but small drops in the ocean of need, or that
she and her brave companions were like innocents bearing cups
against tidal waves. Her mathematical calculations, like her geography, were based only on principles of compassion: "I do not add
up. I only subtract from the total number of poor or dying. With
children one dollar saves a life. Could you say one dollar buys a
life? No, but it is used to save it. So we use ourselves to save what
we can." Had she ever stopped to "reason" in terms which gave

priority to numbers, results, efficiency and the magnitude of an action, she would never have picked up the first dying person from the streets of Calcutta, and yet by the early 1970s the number of lives that had been saved as a consequence of that first "irrational" action was already running into the tens of thousands. And so she would continue to pick up the dying from the streets and to focus on the particular needs of individuals. The call to change social structures and deal with the root causes of collective problems was a valid one but it was for others. "Begin in a small way", she directed those who worked with her. "Don't look for numbers. Every small act of love for the unwanted and the poor is important to Jesus." "Every human being", she also insisted, "comes from the hand of God and we all know what is the love of God for us."

Where there was discord and disharmony, there the need to be instruments of the love and forgiveness of God was simply perceived as even greater. In the first few months of its life as a new nation, tragedy struck Bangladesh, formerly East Pakistan. In October 1970 a cyclone drowned more than three hundred thousand people in one of the worst natural disasters of the twentieth century, and in the following year occupation by West Pakistan troops claimed a further three million lives. Two hundred thousand women were reported to have been raped, and nearly ten million men, women and children fled to India to escape the violence. At the request of the Bangladesh Government, Mother Teresa and two teams of Missionaries of Charity rushed to do what they could in the stricken country. The victims of rape were to suffer particularly from rejection by their own families. Muslim tradition dictated that despite the fact that they had been violated against their will, these girls should be abandoned. Some of the Freedom Fighters who had fought for the liberation of East Pakistan made a dramatic break with Muslim tradition by offering to marry these "heroines of the nation", and the Prime Minister, Sheikh Mujibar Rahman, called upon the Bangladeshi to recognize the sacrifices of their women and to honour them rather than punish them, but there were still many who were reduced to committing suicide by tying their saris round their throats.

Mother Teresa set up one home in Dhaka and several more in Bangladesh to care for these women and girls in what she saw as a "beautiful work to be done for the Church". As it transpired, fewer of the violated women came forward than had been anticipated, and so the Sisters explored the needs of the surrounding villages. They opened clinics and gave practical training to women who were not equipped to fend for themselves without their men. In one village in particular, out of twenty-three male heads of families, seventeen had been shot in one day. The village had been put to the torch and most of the homes destroyed. The widows, ill-equipped as they were to earn money for their families, were reduced to begging on the streets of Dacca. The Sisters, recognizing that every Bengali woman knew how to make puffed rice, set up a business in the "widows' village". The women's puffed rice was sold in the Dacca market and their fatherless children did not go hungry.

In 1971 Mother Teresa took four Sisters to Belfast, to a place where hatred was preached even from the church pulpits. A report at the time described the arrival of four Sisters, equipped with two blankets each and a violin. They were to take up residence in the Catholic "ghetto" of Ballymurphy, in a council house previously occupied by a curate of the parish who had been shot dead by "the forces of law and order" as he had just finished administering Extreme Unction to a wounded man. The house was completely empty, bereft of all furniture. It had also been ransacked by vandals while it was standing tenantless. Mother Teresa's plan was for her own Sisters to work in conjunction with a small group of Anglican nuns as a sign of unity in a strife-ridden city. The Missionaries of Charity set about quietly helping the local people and their children. At one point, during a prolonged shooting match between Springhill (Catholics) and Springwater (an adjoining Protestant area), the Sisters themselves were reduced to sitting on the stairs for four hours as the only relatively safe place in their home, but the door of their house remained constantly open to others as a refuge from violence and desolation.

In Gaza in 1973 the Missionaries of Charity turned their attention to the deprived Arabic-speaking people living in Israeli-occupied territory. During the uncertainty of a cease-fire, among the 380,000 Arab refugees who had been squeezed into Gaza by the tide of armies fighting in 1948, 1956 and 1967, they searched for the poorest of the poor. In Gaza Old Town they took over a house once occupied by a priest who, cut off by the barriers of war and politics, had undertaken a lonely struggle to keep the faith. The priest had been killed shortly prior to their arrival, in a murder which reflected the violence and tension of the area. The Missionaries of Charity cleaned up the house and the neighbouring church and struggled to banish the fear and the sorrow of many whose lives appeared devoid of hope.

In Peru the Sisters established a home for abandoned children, paralysed young adults and old men and women, in a large dirty pink convent at the heart of the "thieves' market", in one of the poorest districts of Lima. During the disturbances between the police and their adversaries witnessed by many an overseas television screen in February 1975, the home shook with the rumblings of passing tanks, and bullet holes in the dispensary and chapel windows bore witness to how exposed the occupants had been to the hazards of life in Lima.

Homesickness, "culture-shock" and linguistic difficulties were among the lesser sacrifices the young Sisters were required to live through whilst still communicating joy to those around them. A letter from Tabora, Tanzania, provides an insight into some of the other problems encountered by a Sister there in the course of one of the worst days of her life:

Early in the morning, one of the old men in our home came and called me, saying that another of the old men had died. I thought it was the usual heart failure, but when I went in I had the greatest shock of my life – the wall in one of our rooms had fallen in on him and he was stone dead. We had been having heavy rain, but we did not realize there was dampness in the foundations. As a matter of fact one cannot see the dampness at all. The police were very good and helpful.

Then one of our ladies, while yawning, dislocated her jaw, so I had to drive her to hospital in the pouring rain. Our car, which is a huge affair and as old as can be, is not suited for this country at all as the clearance is very low, so each time I go down a road the bottom of the car hits the corrugations on the roads which are made of red sand only. The car, being very heavy often gets stuck, as the only type of car that can run here is one with a four-wheel drive. When I came home we started re-arranging the house in order to fit in everyone, and it was nearly night before

*everything was settled. When one of our ladies cried out for help I thought
another wall had fallen, but when I rushed to the scene, I saw a poisonous
snake gliding round the room. Thank God, one of our workers saw it and
rushed in with a stick and killed it. So ended the day.*

From the Bronx, New York, another Sister described the exhaustion
of working from early morning to late in the evening with children
between the ages of six and sixteen milling about their house and
courtyard during a leisure programme for the inner city kids:
"climbing walls, hanging from trees, scattering playthings, making
everything dirty, eating half their sandwiches and throwing the
other half in the bin, drinking their orange juice and firing the
unopened cellophane packets into the pools." New York and other
American cities spent an enormous amount of money for thousands
of ghetto children. They provided mobile swimming pools, films,
puppet shows, free tickets to the zoo and museums as well as daily
lunch. "This is the difficulty," commented the Sister, "everything
for the body but nothing very much for the mind and soul." Each
summer saw an increase in criminal activity which was not just a
consequence of the heat.

Despite difficulties, dangers and personal hardships, however,
they were still able to recognize in every act of human love – be it
the self-denial of a small child who went without sugar in order
that another might eat, or the gift of ICI's Laboratory Building in
its own compound of five acres – the proof of an eternal love.
Mother Teresa was able to see even the fighting and the flooding
in Bangladesh as a "blessing in disguise" because it had brought
out the best in the Indian people. Many had gone without in order
to assist the refugees. Even the children had brought an onion or
a spoonful of rice, and the four thousand who were being fed daily
at Shishu Bhavan and who ate only when the Sisters could provide
for them, offered to go without food for a day in order that the
refugees might eat.

In the beginning the Sisters had been carefully formed and
shaped by Mother Teresa's direct personal example, by the manner
in which she bathed sores, scrubbed floors and pressed babies to her
heart with apparently unlimited energy, tenderness and joy. Now she
visited the different houses as often as she could and endeavoured still

to write to them, although increasingly often with an apology for not having done so sooner. There were times on her travels when she slept in the luggage racks of third-class train compartments, and times when with a polite but unyielding smile she would wedge herself onto a seat already occupied by the wife of an Indian farmer and her livestock. On trains and planes, however, where sometimes she had three seats to herself, she would savour the rare opportunity for silence and reflection. In her large rounded handwriting she compiled small letters and notes which became an inspiration and guide to those who could no longer learn so much by direct association with her. She wrote to the Sisters' parents thanking them for the gift of their daughters, and she wrote to the Sisters themselves urging them to smile in the face of adversity and if someone did not smile to "make them". Nuns who looked sad were, she pointed out, the greatest stumbling block to vocations because young people, like God, loved a cheerful giver. She shared with them the news of other foundations, of her meetings with the Pope, and incidents that tickled her sense of humour: the time when she was given a bed to sleep in large enough to accommodate three Missionaries of Charity, which she deduced must have been meant for a bishop; the time when she arrived back in India unexpectedly early to be challenged at the door of the mother house which she always referred to as "home". "Who's there?" "Mother." "Whose Mother?" "Your Mother" "Our Mother?" "Your Mother" – she afterwards relayed the experience with much amusement.

Even as she travelled she remained closely concerned with details of discipline within the various foundations. The Sisters must be careful not to expend unnecessary money on postage. Extreme care must be taken not to use donations carelessly, because the sacrifices of others had made them possible. Medicine and food must be distributed promptly, before they were spoiled. The preservation of the spirit of poverty, which was not only a means of identifying with those whom they served but which was also an expression of faith in Divine Providence, was something she saw as vital. Even of those priests who were directly concerned with the spiritual welfare of the Sisters she asked that they refrain from intervening in the internal affairs of the houses when it came to the question of poverty. In India some tried to suggest that the Missionaries of

Charity should, for example, hang curtains in the communal rooms, but the poor whom the Sisters sought to serve there had no curtains and Mother Teresa was quick to point out that the majority of her Sisters still came from relatively poor backgrounds themselves. It was unthinkable that they should raise their standard of living by joining the Congregation. The blue bulgar wheat "bedspreads" had a way of finding their way into foundations far removed from Calcutta. In the West creature comforts such as fitted carpets and labour-saving devices such as washing machines, albeit given with the best of intentions, met with a similar response. The Sisters were not allowed to accept anything but a glass of water by way of hospitality, for often that was all that the poor could offer and they must not be made to feel outdone by others who had more luxurious provisions at their disposal.

Increasingly Mother Teresa stressed that fund-raising for her work was contrary to her wishes, and she declined the offers of regular income that were beginning to arise: "I don't want the work to become a business but to remain a work of love. I want you to have that complete confidence that God won't let us down. Take him at his word and seek first the kingdom of heaven, and all else will be added on. Joy, peace and unity are more important than money." Firmly convinced that if God wanted her to do something, he would provide the necessary funds, she once rejected – in a manner which in anyone else might have been construed as ungracious – an offer made by New York's Cardinal Cooke of five hundred dollars a month for each Sister working in Harlem: "Do you think, Your Eminence, that God is going to become bankrupt in New York?"

In a scientific age she believed there was still room for the miraculous:

In Calcutta there were floods and we worked day and night cooking for five thousand people. The army gave us food. One day something told me to turn off the road towards an unknown area and we found a little village where people were being swept away. We got boats for them. We found out later that if we had come only two hours later they would have been drowned. Then I said to the bishop that I was going to ask our novices to pray for the rain, which had been pouring down for many days, to stop.

I told him, "The novices are very earnest. They pray with great energy. It will be a strong expression." So we put them – 178 of them – in the church of our mission. Outside it was raining; inside they began to pray, and I brought out the Blessed Sacrament. After a while I went to the door of the church and looked out. The rain had stopped and there was a patch of clear sky above us – yes, I believe in miracles.

The list of such miracles was growing. There was the time in Calcutta when there appeared to be no food with which to feed the seven thousand expectant people for the next two days. For some unanticipated reason the Government closed down the schools for those days, and all the bread that would have been provided for the schoolchildren was sent to the Missionaries of Charity for their seven thousand dependants. On another occasion a Sister telephoned from Agra to say that a children's home which would cost 50,000 rupees was desperately needed there. Mother Teresa was compelled to tell her that because of lack of funds it was impossible. The telephone rang again shortly afterwards, however, to inform her that she had been awarded the Magsaysay Award from the Philippines. The award money amounted to some 50,000 rupees. "So I called the Sister back to tell her God must want a children's home in Agra."

When Mother Teresa visited Britain in 1971, hoping to start a novitiate outside India, the choice of possible locations had been narrowed down to Dublin or London. One of her first visits in England was to a priest in Southall who wished to consult her about problems among the immigrant community. In the course of her visit it was suggested that Mother Teresa should bring her novitiate to Southall, and it was agreed that if within two weeks she had heard nothing from the Bishop of Dublin, she would do so. A fortnight passed by and nothing was heard so Mother Teresa sought amongst the properties of Southall for a suitable house. The ideal place was found but the asking price was £9,000. Mother Teresa insisted that she could not pay more than £6,000, but as always when she found what she felt was a suitable house for her Sisters, she tossed a miraculous medal into the garden of the property. By the time Mother Teresa had returned to the priest in Southall, the estate agent had telephoned to say that the owner was prepared to sell for £6,000 because she wanted the house to be filled with love. Mother Teresa still did not have the necessary funds in England and money could not be taken out of India. As planned, however, she set off on a tour around England during which she mentioned the possibility of opening a novitiate in Southall. She made no appeal for money but by the end of her tour the old knitting bag which she carried with her had been stuffed full of donations. The total, when the money was counted, amounted to £5,995. It seemed that the house in Southall was meant to be.

Experiences of this kind were by no means confined to Mother Teresa herself. Those who shared in the work were frequently witnesses to the manner in which the needs of the poor were mysteriously met, despite their own limitations and the apparent lack of means. Inevitably this served to increase the mystique and the mythology surrounding the small woman who was already being credited not simply with the belief in miracles but with the capacity actually to work them. As early as 1962 the press had reported as one of Mother Teresa's "miracles" an account of how a maddened bull had charged down a slum lane, injuring its terrified occupants. As it approached Mother Teresa, who was busy treating a group of lepers, she was said to have raised her hand, whereupon the beast came to a halt in front of her and allowed itself to be led quietly away. Mother Teresa did have a Franciscan way with animals. At one time she kept a dog in Calcutta which was so savage that it was the bane of some of her Sisters' lives, but which was invariably docile and well-behaved in her presence. The Sisters who did not share their Superior General's affection for Kala Shaitan (Black Devil) finally prayed to be delivered from its menaces, and shortly afterwards thieves came in the night and poisoned it. Mother Teresa's strange attachment to it was not enough to save its life.

She herself consistently countered all attempts to credit her with exceptional skills by protesting her own ordinariness all the more vehemently, and pointing constantly to the God at work through his imperfect instruments. Undoubtedly also, however, the manner in which her prayers and those of the people about her were frequently answered in a very concrete way, served to endorse Mother Teresa's faith in Divine Providence and to confirm her in her audacity.

On a personal level there were times when she was compelled to accept that not all things were possible through love and prayer. On 4 January 1970 her sister, Aga, wrote to her from Tirana to tell her that her mother's health was growing steadily worse, that she now weighed only 39 kilos, and that life for them both was very difficult. For the woman who could move mountains on behalf of the poor of the world it was not easy to accept that she could do nothing to help her own mother and sister.

The year 1970 was one which took her very close to her roots. On Wednesday 8 June she landed at Belgrade airport, having been invited to Yugoslavia by the Red Cross. It was only a short visit because she was due to leave for Jordan to open a house for Palestinian refugees in Amman, but she managed to make the journey to Prizren where her family had its origins, and from there she went on to Skopje, the city of her birth, which had suffered a dreadful earthquake in 1963. She had a meeting with the local bishop, visited a Red Cross centre for Macedonia, and then went on to Letnice where she knelt before the statue of the Madonna which had featured so significantly in her adolescent years. In Skopje she let it be known that it was one of her greatest wishes to see a Missionary of Charity house opened in the city. The emotional ties were still there. In 1962 a priest from Ohrid in the extreme south of Yugoslavia had written to Mother Teresa with news of the place she had left some thirty-three years previously, and she had written back to thank him in Serbo-Croat:

I thought that the people of Skopje had completely forgotten Agnes, as you are the first to write to me in such a long time. Pray for me. I will also pray for our people in Skopje, that they might pray for me. My mother and sister are still in Tirana. Only God knows why they have to suffer so much. I know that their sacrifices and prayers help me in my work. It is all to the greater glory of God.

Mother Teresa and Lazar had tried to keep in touch with their mother and sister by letter – it was by this means that Mother Teresa kept up her knowledge of the Albanian language – although even this form of communication had broken down for a while under the post-Second World War Marxist regime. The letters written by her sister bringing news of her mother's welfare touched her deeply, and when Drana wrote to her son that her only wish was to see his family and "Agnes" again before she died, Mother Teresa did her utmost to bring about a reunion. Exile that he was, there was a limit to what Lazar could do. During a visit to Rome, however, in the company of Eileen Egan, Mother Teresa, in her capacity as one who had "come from Albania" and brought great honour to the country, appealed to the Albanian Embassy to allow her mother and sister to leave Albania. Eileen Egan, in her book *Such a Vision of the Street*, would later describe how Mother Teresa moved an embassy official to tears when she told him in Serbo-Croatian that she "came as a child seeking for its mother". Catholic Relief Services, the organization which Eileen Egan represented, was prepared to assist Lazar Bojaxhiu in the resettlement of Drana and her daughter in Italy in the event of the Albanian authorities allowing them out of the country, but this and other attempts to obtain exit visas proved abortive.

For Mother Teresa it would have been easier to accept her own suffering than that of an elderly mother who wanted only to see her children once more before she died. Her love for her own family betrayed itself in her appreciation of the sacrifice other families had made in giving their daughters to the congregation, in her eagerness to meet such families and pass on news of their daughters, in her concern to know if any Sister had suffered a bereavement in order that the whole Society might hold that person in prayer, and in her constant assertion that love began in the home. She explored the possibility of going to Albania herself before her mother died, but was given to understand that whilst permission would be granted for her to go to Albania no guarantee could be given that she would be allowed to leave again afterwards. At the price of great personal anguish Mother Teresa opted not to go to her mother, "for the sake of the poor of the world". On 12 July 1972 a telegram arrived in Calcutta announcing that Drana Bojaxhiu had died in Arans, Albania. Her daughter, Aga, would also die in Albania, on 25 August 1973 in Tirana, without ever seeing her sister or brother again.

There were setbacks in the history of the Missionaries of Charity also. After a relatively short period of time in Belfast, the Indian Sisters were made to feel they were not wanted, and so abandoned the challenge which had appeared to present itself to them. To Mother Teresa, however, even this retreat proved to be only one more example of a wisdom which passed understanding. Triumphant even in "failure", in November 1973 she wrote a letter of reassurance to her Co-Workers in Ireland:

Leaving Belfast was a very big sacrifice – but very fruitful – for our Sisters are now going to Ethiopia to feed the hungry Christ. The same Sisters who so lovingly served him in Belfast will now be giving his love and compassion to the suffering people of Ethiopia – pray for them and share with them the joy of loving and serving.

Shortly after the Sisters left Belfast, Mother Teresa had broken her journey from Rome to Hodeidah in Addis Ababa to investigate the possibility of reaching out to the victims of a dreadful drought in Northern Ethiopia. The general opinion of others involved in relief work there was that it would be impossible for a Christian religious Congregation to obtain permission to enter the country. Undeterred, Mother Teresa managed to arrange a meeting with the Emperor's daughter. The Princess showed considerable interest in the work of the Missionaries of Charity, and Mother Teresa was able to ask her to tell her father, Emperor Haile Selassie, that on the occasion of the forty-third anniversary of his coronation, which was to be celebrated that week, she would like to offer him her Sisters to help his suffering people. Next day Mother Teresa received the news that despite a day of heavy engagements with Archbishop Makarios, the Emperor would see her that afternoon. A series of questions from the Minister of the Imperial Court preceded the interview:

What do you want from the Government?
Nothing. I have only come to offer my Sisters to work among the poor suffering people.
What will your Sisters do?
We give whole-hearted free service to the poorest of the poor.
What qualifications do they have?
We try to bring tender love and compassion to the unwanted and the unloved.

I see you have quite a different approach. Do you preach to the people, trying to convert them?
Our works of love reveal to the suffering poor the love of God for them.

Mother Teresa was then ushered into the presence of the eighty-year-old Emperor. The encounter was short, the outcome completely contrary to all anticipation, and yet somehow inevitable: "I have heard about the good work you do. I am very happy you have come. Yes, let your Sisters come to Ethiopia."

*

The Sister left behind in Ethiopia to seek out accommodation went out each morning, clinging tightly to her rosary, meeting Jesus at every corner in the innumerable poor, and trusting firmly that she would be guided to the right place. The managing director of a local firm adjacent to a small house which seemed suitable was persuaded to let the Missionaries of Charity use the property free of charge. The basic plumbing and whitewashing was sorted out under the Sister's supervision. An appeal from the parish priest produced three good tables, a cupboard, a gas cooker and a bench, and four beds were purchased from Addis Ababa market so that when three more Sisters arrived at the end of the week they were able to set up home in relative comfort. From the disappointment of Belfast, Mother Teresa was quick to point out, something vital and constructive had sprung.

In March 1980 ten of the twenty residents and one young volunteer helper died when fire broke out in the early hours of the morning in the home for destitute women run by the Missionaries of Charity in Kilburn, London. A trial for murder subsequently took place at the Old Bailey, during which witnesses recalled the horror of that night when Sister Anawim, then the London Superior, was woken by screams and threw open the door of the small room in which the residents slept to face the horror of a wall of flame already out of control. The jury eventually returned a verdict of Not Guilty. Later at the Coroner's inquest the official verdict was "Unlawful killing by arsonist unnamed".

There were other heartbreaks and disappointments. A handful of

professed Sisters left the Congregation, two of whom belonged to
the original twelve. In view of the rigours of the life the number
was surprisingly small, but for Mother Teresa their going was the
cause of personal pain. It was also in some way a falling short in
her promise to bring saints to Mother Church. A vocation to her
was like a tiny flower. It must be nurtured in order to bloom. Some
who left did so for reasons of ill health. Some fell in love, despite
the fact that Mother Teresa was stringent in her warnings about the
temptations of being alone with the young men they encountered in
the course of their work. Others found that they wanted to serve
God in a different way. Whatever the reason for their going,
Mother Teresa did not hold it against them but was grateful rather
for the time and the service that they had given. Her instructions
to the remaining Missionaries of Charity echoed the directive circulated in the Loreto Congregation when she herself had been due to
leave Entally: "Pray for all those who have been in the society –
that God may protect them and keep them in his love. Do not pass
judgement – do not gossip – but show your love and kindness for
them as you would like others to do to you – if this happened to
you."

Yet others, in the words of Mother Teresa, "went home to God".
On 7 May 1966 a Sister who was herself a homeopathic doctor
died under particularly tragic circumstances. She had failed to pay
adequate medical attention when she was bitten by a young puppy
in the course of her work at Raipur. Only some weeks later, when
she began to foam at the mouth and experienced a fear of water,
did Sister Leonie realize that the dog had been rabid. It was too
late for her life to be saved. The young Sister took the news very
badly but found peace while Mother Teresa sat at her bedside
holding her hand for the final forty-eight hours of her life. "Our
loss in the world is our gain in heaven", Mother Teresa would
always maintain. Years later, in August 1986, Sister Stanislaus, the
Superior in Dehra Dun, and her assistant, Sister Carrol were
drowned. It was a time of torrential rain and the Sisters need not
have gone out but they chose to do so because they did not want
people in desperate need to wait for them in vain at the dispensary.
On their return journey an old wooden bridge suddenly collapsed
and their ambulance plunged into the river. In reporting afterwards

what had happened Mother Teresa did not shrink from the harsh realities of the incident. Sister Carrol had died immediately, her head cracked open by a huge boulder. Sister Stanislaus, though she could swim, was impeded by her sari, and had been carried away by a strong current. Her body was found two hours later. Her sari was tangled round her legs and her lungs were full of water. Mother Teresa was able to present the occurrence to her Sisters as "the story of our two dearest Sisters who went to serve the poor and the sick, and their reward was that Jesus was very pleased with their effort so he took them to himself. . . . When a gardener comes to pluck the flowers, he takes the best. The same with this Jesus of ours." Mother Teresa's acceptance did not, however, mean that such events did not loom large in her consciousness.

The Congregation grew none the less. On 6 May 1978, a few months before he died, Pope Paul VI once more granted Mother Teresa a private audience, together with the Sisters in Rome and a group of Italian Co-Workers. Mother Teresa, her face shining with joy at the privilege, spoke of their coming as a tribute of loyalty to him as the Vicar of Christ on earth. One of the Sisters presented him with a garland of roses, which he in turn placed upon Mother Teresa with the words, "Mother Teresa, I feel an unworthy servant of yours." By the year 1979 there were 158 foundations scattered throughout the world, 1,187 professed Sisters, 411 novices and 120 postulants. The flow of Sisters emerging from the novitiates in Manila or Rome, or returning from Calcutta's cathedral to the mother house on Lower Circular Road after making their vows, was a steady one. While the number of vocations for other religious orders was tending to diminish, apparently the total surrender, the wholehearted commitment and the poverty of life required of a Missionary of Charity continued to appeal. In the courtyard at Lower Circular Road the returning Sisters were welcomed by a group of others dancing after the Bengali fashion, with small candles in their hands. Mother Teresa herself would greet each one, touching their heads with both hands in a gesture of blessing and then, when the celebrations were over, she would read from a list the destinations for which the newly professed were bound: "Sister M. . . Jesus needs you in Essen, West Germany", or in Kigali, Rwanda, or in any one of a multitude of other possible locations.

The streets of Calcutta, it seemed, led to Everyman's door. Within a matter of days the young Sisters would then be dispatched, with the curious assortment of parcels and cardboard boxes which had by then become the distinctive luggage of the Missionaries of Charity, to wherever the poorest of the poor seemed most urgently to require their presence. "If there are poor on the moon," Mother Teresa was once heard to remark, "we shall go there too."

CHAPTER FIVE

Sharing the Vision

"You can do what I can't do. I can do what you can't do. Together
we can do something beautiful for God." It was undoubtedly this
principle, one which Mother Teresa applied to many things, that
underlay the founding of the Missionary Brothers of Charity. By
the beginning of the 1960s, with the kind of thinking which would
raise the hackles of those inclined to a less traditional view of male
and female roles but which took into account such practical realities
as the limitations of her Sisters' physical strength, Mother Teresa
had decided that there were certain aspects of the work which were
more suited to men than to women. Initially one or two priests
tried working with the Sisters in the slums, but Mother Teresa's
plans were for something much more extensive. At the time Father
Van Exem was a parish priest in Asansol, but Mother Teresa made
the journey to see him there to tell him of her ideas for a new
foundation: a Congregation of Brothers very similar to that of the
Sisters, trained in the same spirit and working in conjunction with
them. Father Van Exem in his turn, and not without a certain
apprehension, relayed the request to start such a foundation to
Archbishop Vivian Dyer, who had succeeded Archbishop|Périer
as Archbishop of Calcutta. The response, to his amazement, was
unequivocally positive: "Father, in the whole of India you will not
find a bishop more in favour of Brothers than myself. In India
people have understood the vocation of a priest. They have understood the vocation of a Sister. They have not understood the
vocation of a Brother. Tell her to begin."

By 1963 three candidates had come forward, and on 25 March,
with the help of Father Julien Henry and the blessing of Archbishop
Albert D'Souza, Mother Teresa formed them into a Society. In the
chapel at 54A Lower Circular Road she pinned crosses on the chests

of three young men sprucely dressed in white shirts and trousers. For a while they and the others who came to join them would remain under the direction of the Sisters. The men occupied a floor of Shishu Bhavan and were given part of their training by a Sister in her tertianship. Father Henry gave them spiritual instruction and, at Mother Teresa's specific request, taught them carpentry. For recreation, she allowed them to play volley ball to let off steam. Rome, however, was not so swift to approve her creation of a Congregation of Brothers as the Indian bishops had been. Recognition by Rome depended on substantial numbers and hence a certain guaranteed stability, but priests were reluctant to send candidates to join the Brothers until they had become a recognized institute. A less readily articulated reason for caution on the part of the authorities in Rome lay in the fact that a number of other Congregations of Brothers had been initiated by bishops in India and had foundered. The earliest years of the Order were stunted by this impasse, and the fact that the Roman Catholic Church does not permit a woman to be head of a religious Congregation of men presented further difficulty.

Mother Teresa considered two priests she knew as possible leaders of the Missionary Brothers. One was Father Ante Gabric, a member of the Society of Jesus who had been born in 1915 in Metkovic in Croatia. He belonged to a band of Jesuit missionaries of Croatian and Slovenian origin who planned to evangelize the region south of Calcutta between the Hooghly, Matala and Gosaba rivers. He was a priest very much after Mother Teresa's heart – dedicated to the poor, spiritual, dynamic, austere and habitually seen going about his work with his rosary in his hand. Mother Teresa always conversed with him in their common language, Serbo-Croat, and she was full of admiration for him and others like him who gave their lives to the hidden poor in a not dissimilar fashion to the way in which she was giving hers. The other priest who particularly impressed her was Father Robert Antoine, a Belgian of ascetic appearance who was deeply immersed in the Bengali culture and who had given his services as a chaplain in Nirmal Hriday. One day after saying Mass at the mother house in Calcutta he had remarked to Mother Teresa over breakfast that when he thought of the poor the food he ate stuck in his throat. It was the kind of remark which did not fail to have its impact on Mother Teresa. The General of the Jesuits was not prepared to grant her any more of his local priests, however. The Missionary Sisters of Charity were already absorbing much of the attention of Father Henry and Father Van Exem. A Monsignor from Kerala actually came and spent over six months with the young Brothers before feeling that he must leave. It was only in 1965, however, that the solution to the problem presented itself in the form of Father Ian Travers-Ball, an Australian Jesuit who was spending his tertianship at Sitagarha and whom Mother Teresa with her impish humour would afterwards claim to have "kidnapped" from the Jesuits.

In 1962, a year before he was ordained a priest, he had heard Mother Teresa speak in Poona to a group of seminarians. She was little known then and the actual words she spoke did not remain with him, but the indelible impression she left was of a person "very close to God". Not so very long afterwards, during his tertianship he was given permission to work for a month amongst the poor. He had recently heard of the Pious Union established by Mother Teresa on the very same day that he was ordained a priest (a fact which Mother Teresa would later regard as something more than a beautiful coincidence), and he went to spend a month with them in the hope not of joining them but of gaining experience and knowledge of working with the poor which he could afterwards apply in working as a Jesuit in Hazaribagh.

The need for a priest to form and lead the twelve very young men he met in December 1965 was one which made itself quickly apparent to Ian Travers-Ball. For her part, Mother Teresa discerned in his arrival an answer to prayer. Having watched the Australian priest at work with the young Brothers, she almost immediately arranged for a meeting with him. It was not an occasion of much discussion. Mother Teresa simply presented him openly with her problem and so implied a request for help. Her Jesuit visitor sought an interval in which to reflect upon his response. He spent three days with Father Van Exem gaining a little more insight into the background to the Brothers, and within no more than ten days he had decided that here was the very opportunity he had been seeking. With permission he left the Jesuit

Order for a provisional period initially, and on 19 February 1966 joined the small group of men in Shishu Bhavan, Calcutta. The occasion was marked with the simplest of ceremonies, during which Mother Teresa gave him the small crucifix which, worn over the heart, remains to this day the only distinguishing mark of the Missionary Brothers. The Brothers were entrusted to his care because, as Mother Teresa put it, "He is a very holy person, really very holy." Holiness was above all the quality which she looked for in a priest. She had no illusions about the human nature to which even priests were susceptible – Jesus, she once pointed out, hand-picked twelve disciples, one of whom proved to be a crook and the others ran away – but she continued to crave their holiness. Often in later years when her voice was given a more public platform she would be heard urging priests to be holy, and in Father Ian Travers-Ball she had discerned the holiness she sought.

The man who was to become Brother Andrew had been born in Melbourne on 27 August 1928. There were certain very striking points of similarity between him and Mother Teresa which extended far beyond the fact that their birthdays fell within a day of each other. They shared the vision of their second callings to serve the poor as an integral part of their initial vocation. They shared the sense of their own poverty as humble instruments of a higher purpose, for Brother Andrew would subsequently refer to his own life as the "hard-to-believe story of an unfaithful man used by God". Above all, they shared the common conviction that the wholehearted love they were committed to giving to the suffering and the poor, they gave for and to Christ. In fact, in what Brother Andrew described as the "essentials" they differed little. In *Something Beautiful for God*, the book which first brought the attention of so many to the work which Mother Teresa was doing in the slums of India, Malcolm Muggeridge wrote: "I cannot pay Brother Andrew a better tribute than to say that he is a perfect associate for Mother Teresa." It is a tribute which many would endorse. Brother Andrew's entry into the small Congregation of Missionary Brothers marked the beginning of a relationship of mutual regard and trust with their foundress. They did not share their spiritual journey in great depth but they did "encourage each other spiritually at a personal level". Beyond this mutual respect and the coincidences and parallels discernible in their lives, they remained, however, very different personalities, a fact which they both recognized and openly acknowledged. "We are so different," Mother Teresa commented, "but both of us have the same mind." As for Brother Andrew, looking back on their relationship over the years, he would stress their differences in the light of Mother Teresa's sanctity: "Actually we are very different characters. Apart from the obvious factor, she is the one with the very extraordinary 'charisma'. She is called a 'living saint', and she is a very wonderful spiritual person. I am aware I arrive nowhere near to her and I think it has been a grace from the very beginning that I did not feel that I had to be like her."

The Roman Catholic Church finally approved the Brothers' institution as a diocesan Congregation on 26 March 1967. With that approval it became possible for the new Congregation, which already consisted of thirty-three aspiring Brothers, to establish its first novitiate in June of the same year. Still a Jesuit as he was, Father Ian Travers-Ball found himself simultaneously co-founder, novice-master and novice. By 1967 the Sisters numbered nearly 250, had some twenty houses in India and had opened their first centre in Venezuela. The Brothers, meanwhile, were in urgent need of more room. At the beginning of July 1966 they had moved out of Shishu Bhavan into rented accommodation, but soon they had outgrown that also. Then, under what Brother Andrew described as "truly extraordinary circumstances", the Brothers came by a house in Mansatala Row, Kidderpur, Calcutta which was to become their mother house. The next year, 1967, also brought with it the opening of a second foundation in the slum area of Dum Dum, Calcutta's major airport.

At first the Brothers' role seemed to be very much one of supplementing that of the Sisters: of lifting and carrying and providing a masculine presence and physical strength as required. They were young, raw and guided by the Sisters. They were also open to the guidance of Divine Providence, and as the male Congregation underwent an initial period of rapid growth, it began to seem increasingly appropriate to operate with a certain independence as a community which could manage its own affairs. In his own words, Brother Andrew set about "liberating them". The Brothers laboured alongside the Sisters in the work with lepers. In the Home for the Dying they would look after the men while the Sisters cared for the women, and the two Congregations would continue to collaborate very closely. If the Brothers found women in need, or girls or babies, they would send them to the Sisters. If the Sisters found men and boys requiring care, then they would send them to the Brothers. At the same time, the Brothers' work also developed independently. Only a year after the purchase of the Dum Dum house it was occupied by a substantial number of boys, nearly twenty of whom the Brothers were able to send to boarding schools. Those who were too old for boarding school education were sent as day scholars to various local schools. The handicapped and crippled ones studied at home. Only the mentally deficient children were not as yet really provided for from an educational point of view, but the way in which they contributed to the joy of the house was something which the Brothers valued highly and which the other boys seemed readily to accept. In another part of the grounds surrounding the house near Dum Dum airport, shelter was pro- vided for some thirty men who were sick, disabled or destitute. A number of men with families were also given a welcome. Often they were very weak after suffering from some illness or other, and a month or two of nourishing food, medicine and rest could work wonders. A number of them were subsequently able to return home and go back to work to support their families.

In June 1968 the first group of novices completed their novitiate and prepared to make their profession as full Brothers. Father Ian Travers-Ball formally and definitively left the Society of Jesus and became a Missionary Brother of Charity, and at his profession on 2 June changed his name to Brother Andrew. One of Brother Andrew's initial acts of service as General Servant of the small but expanding Congregation was that of revising and updating the constitutions which shaped their life and work. When Mother Teresa had first initiated the Missionary Brothers of Charity she had presented the new Society with the same constitutions as those used by the Sisters. By the time Father Ian Travers-Ball joined the Order, however, the language of constitutions drawn up in response to the call on the train to Darjeeling some twenty years previously seemed somewhat formal and legalistic and – in the light of the call from the Second Vatican Council for the "adequate renewal of religious life" – in need of some revision. In the years 1970–73 the Missionary Sisters also would revise their constitutions to embody the spirit of Vatican II. It was the wish of the Church, and by October 1973 they were required to submit the new constitutions to the Holy See for final approval.

Brother Andrew's revisions of the Brothers' constitutions reflected the deep respect he had for Mother Teresa. He was careful to preserve the original key rules established by her but added to them a number of directives cited verbatim from the decrees of the Second Vatican Council, and also incorporated some further explanation in an attempt more clearly to convey the spirit of the Missionary Brothers of Charity. The opening words of the revised constitutions were indicative of the desired orientation of Brother Andrew's own life:

The general aim of the society comes from the lips of Christ our Lord himself: "I give you a new commandment: Love one another. As I have loved you so you are to love one another. If there is love among you then all will know that you are my disciples. . . ."

The special aim of the Brothers as set down in Article 2 of their constitutions is:

To live this life of love by dedicating oneself to the service of the poorest of the poor in slums, on the streets and wherever they are found. Leprosy patients, destitute beggars, the abandoned, homeless boys, young men in the slums, the unemployed and those uprooted by war and disaster will always be the special object of the Brothers' concern.

"From the beginning Brother Andrew went his own way", one close observer would comment. "To some extent it was the spirit of Mother but they were not the constitutions of Mother." Mother Teresa had no difficulty in accepting the decisions of the Second Vatican Council itself, welcoming, for example, the approved New Mass and the use of the living language instead of Latin, but she was not happy with some of the ensuing developments in the Roman Catholic Church. That the Church wanted renewal she recognized, but renewal did not mean the changing of a habit and a few prayers. She did not approve of individual innovations, with laxity or the lack of discipline which she found in certain quarters. She could not accept, for instance, priests who did not wear vestments at Mass, the movement of tabernacles containing the Blessed Sacrament into obscure corners, the neglect of attention to the Virgin Mary or the rosary. Nor would she tolerate the lack of respect in prayer or a person's demeanour in chapel, any more than she would condone diminished respect for the Pope, for the teaching of the Catholic Church on marriage or sexual morality, or nuns or priests who did not wear religious dress. One newly ordained priest who was sent to give instruction to the Missionaries of Charity experienced precisely how uncompromising she could be in relation to such matters. The priest was somewhat disdainful of the traditional beliefs held by the Sisters. Among other things, he claimed that there was no need for them to genuflect before the Blessed Sacrament outside the Mass because the presence of Christ was limited to its duration. After he had finished speaking Mother Teresa led the priest to the door, thanked him for coming and informed him that he need not come again. She then spent an hour with the Sisters refuting all that the priest had said and explaining to them the decrees of the Second Vatican Council which reiterated the Roman Catholic Church's traditional doctrine on the Eucharist.

Mother Teresa in shaping her Missionaries of Charity, whilst seeking to live amongst the poor as one of them, had none the less also preserved what some would regard as the traditional and necessary separation between the Sisters and those whom they served. At the end of the day, the Missionary Sisters of Charity returned to their convent to sleep. Guests, even longstanding friends of the Congregation, did not eat with the Sisters but in a room apart. Theologically and temperamentally Mother Teresa was a firm believer in the strict adherence to regulations, in details of discipline, tidiness in housekeeping, in religious dress, uniformity of forms of prayer and devotions. She liked details to be fixed and adhered to.

Brother Andrew, on the other hand, whilst sharing her respect for many of these elements, was somewhat more flexible. The freedom he had acquired as a Jesuit pressed him to loosen up certain

aspects of the Brothers' way. He was uncertain about the necessity
for the extreme rigidity of religious training to which the Sisters
were subjected. Mother Teresa had opted to make the language of
her Order English, for the very sound reasons that even while the
origins of her novices were confined to India a common working
language had to be found and that Christian religious literature was
available in English. Brother Andrew could see the wisdom of this
option but regretted the energy that had to be expended by relatively uneducated young men on learning the language. He had
been impressed by his own reading about Dorothy Day's Houses
of Hospitality in America, and stressed the importance of offering
hospitality not just to those whom the Brothers set out specifically
to serve but to any visitor. The Brothers slept in the houses in
which they offered a home to the poor. Visitors prepared to accept
the simplicity of their food and accommodation were welcome to
eat at their table or sleep on their floor. When the Brothers in their
turn were invited as guests they accepted whatever hospitality might
be provided. As to the Brothers' dress, like the Sisters' sari it was
an attempt to identify with the poor, but for men in India there
was no standard dress. The Brothers adopted trousers and shirts
such as poor people throughout the world might wear. The crucifix
was there to show their commitment to Christ but there was no
uniformity or special dress to set them apart from those about them.

For many of the young Brothers Mother Teresa would remain
very much "Mother" but they also valued Brother Andrew's role
in establishing the Missionary Brothers with their separate identity
as "male" religious living in community. He provided them with
the space in which to grow as men, while at the same time sharing
the same charism as the Sisters. The freedom he introduced did
not mean, however, that there was any laxity on the four essentials
without which, Brother Andrew maintained, a Missionary of
Charity was not a Missionary of Charity: seriousness in prayer, love
for the poor, simplicity of life and the need for a community life.
If anything, one Missionary Sister of Charity would point out, not
without some amusement, the Brothers' training and life were more
arduous: "They think because they are men they can take it." Then
more seriously she added, "They are very, very poor and very holy."

The manner in which Mother Teresa dealt with the fact that the man to whom she had entrusted the Brothers differed from her and possibly, according to Brother Andrew, sometimes disappointed her, was revealing. Mother Teresa was a woman whose love and interest in others went much deeper than disagreement with their ideas or ways. Even if disagreement did at times come to the fore, given a little time and space, she would invariably recover her relationship with the "straying one", especially in a quiet, one-to-one encounter. As far as Brother Andrew was concerned, she was the closest he had ever been to a great saint. The richness, beauty and meaning she gave to his life were beyond his ability to acknowledge, but that did not necessitate denying her her humanity. In the close working relationship he had been privileged to share with her in co-founding the Congregation of Brothers he had, he volunteered many years later, been quite lacking in due respect and taken much for granted. Part of it had surely been his male pride asserting itself. At very least he had brought to the task his ego and conceit, which had coincided with traces of the same in her, daughter of Eve that she was. Their differences over certain points had resulted in very real human disagreement: "I must say that she gave me total freedom, even when she disagreed with me. But it has to be said that she could be annoyed and piqued – and show it. On such points, I could have given way, and she would have been very happy to have her way. Where I held my ground she accepted – always graciously in the end, I must add. She was wonderful in not taking offence."

The history of the Brothers was, like that of the Sisters, to be shaped largely by the recognition of a need and the dependence on Divine Providence to meet it. In the village of Noynan, the Brothers set up a centre for village work. From there they cared for five hundred poverty-stricken families, ran a primary school where the children could attend classes and receive a daily meal, and treated patients suffering from tuberculosis in a home opened specifically for that purpose. At a centre in Pipe Road, Calcutta, five Brothers shared the upbringing of no less than thirty-five boys who were without one or both parents and who, because they spoke and wrote different languages, had to be dispatched to a number of different schools. On the overcrowded platforms of India's railway stations the Missionary Brothers tried to show children who had had to make their homes under a piece of discarded matting that someone actually cared for them. They took a bar of soap with them on these visits and made sure the boys washed themselves under the water towers used for filling up the engines of the steam trains.

In the early 1970s, while Mother Teresa was establishing the Sisters' foundations in Jordan, England, the United States, Bangladesh, Mauritius, Israel, the Yemen, Peru and elsewhere, a group of Brothers went to live in one of the desperately overcrowded alleyways of underworld Saigon. The first floor of their house provided sleeping accommodation for thirty or so shelterless people. The second floor served a similar purpose but was also used for classes during the day. The third floor, which consisted of two small rooms invaded by rats driven in by heavy rain, provided an area in which the Brothers themselves ate, slept, read and prayed. Each brother had a sleeping pallet such as the local people used, which had to be rolled up during the day. There was no privacy and always much noise, for during the day they fed hundreds of people there. Other houses were planned for the crippled, disabled and retarded of Saigon who had no one to care for them. It was the assistance and dedication of a former prostitute which enabled the work in Saigon to develop. One of many bar-girls and prostitutes whom Brother Andrew encountered while the country was still alive with foreign troops, the girl had been reduced to earning her living in this way after her husband had been killed by a stolen jeep driven by a drunken Australian civilian. She had taken to the streets in an attempt to support her three small children, and by the time the foreign soldiers began to withdraw she was more than ready to abandon the kind of life she had been leading. With her help the Missionary Brothers were able to create a haven of stability at the heart of economic, emotional and political insecurity. With the pull out of the Americans, jobs and money were scarce, and many widows were left to struggle for their own and their children's survival against an all-enveloping tide of inflation. The aim was to provide a home for those poor who did not fit into the categories catered for by other organizations.

In 1975, however, the Communists took over the houses the Brothers had opened in Saigon and so forced them to abandon their mission. With no possibility of work, no hope of beginning anew and no place in which to live, Brother Andrew caught a plane for

Bangkok and India. In his Christmas letter for that year he wrote in a far more personal way than Mother Teresa would have been prepared to do of the pain of leaving:

This year has been heartbreaking. We lost five houses in Vietnam and Cambodia. The buildings don't matter. But to be separated so finally from all the people one came to know and love is unbelievably painful. I shall never be the same again after this, and I know that I shall have an ache in my heart for them until the day I die.

The full story of the fall of Saigon and the change-over will never be told. The journalists who stayed on lived mostly in the downtown hotels. They did not penetrate the alleys and lanes of the overcrowded parts of the city. They did not really have the chance to share the feelings of the people I knew in Saigon in the reports of the media or in the general idea that people outside Vietnam have of what has been happening there.

The story remains untold, and it will remain untold perhaps until the voice of some Vietnamese Solzhenitsyn is heard. But if that ever happens, it will be after many years. As for myself, I don't have the heart to even attempt the telling.

And so Vietnam and Cambodia is a closed book for me and the Brothers. And what unfolds there in the lives of the voiceless many in the coming years will not be known.

There was encouragement to be derived from what was happening in India. In 1974 Mother Teresa had handed over to the Brothers the Gandhiji Prem Nivas Leprosy centre at Titlagarh. Faced at first with a problem of increasing violence among the lepers, in an attempt to resolve the psychological suffering that gave rise to it and channel destructive energies more creatively, they had set up a modest handloom section on a small plot of railway land. The step was a great success. The violence diminished in the wake of the lepers' renewed sense of their own dignity and value. By September 1978, a much larger plot of railway land would be given to the Brothers officially. Onto this the Brothers would transfer the old handloom section together with a further thirty looms, and open a cobblery and carpentry section. The rest of the space was used for wards, a vegetable garden and piggery and poultry yards constructed by the patients themselves. In time the leprosy centre would be granted even more land, not without opposition and even stone-throwing from local hooligans, but peace would eventually prevail and the rehabilitation unit would grow to include a dairy and a tailoring unit. Ponds would be dug and stocked with fish to meet the fish requirements of the centre. In its operating theatre volunteer doctors performed amputations and other operations free of charge. Artificial limbs were also provided. Some five hundred people were served daily with cooked rice. The indoor section could provide 148 beds and on average five hundred patients would be released from treatment every year.

In a way which was quite unexpected and unplanned the painful departure from Saigon was turned into something fruitful. In mid-summer of 1975, five Brothers – one Dutchman and four Americans who had been working in Vietnam and Cambodia until conditions had compelled them to leave – arrived in Los Angeles. In the Skid Row area of the city's downtown they found a tiny place to serve as living quarters from which to reach out to those people who had somehow fallen outside the scope of the giant welfare system, and above all to those men, women and children who, surrounded by materialism, remained unloved and estranged. From these encounters the Brothers were led into lonely hotel rooms, where in desperate isolation, the dignity of human life had been slowly neglected. They cleaned rooms filled with empty bottles or human excrement, they read to the blind, they accompanied the helpless to the large, sprawling complex of Los Angeles County Hospital, and they gently returned an old man living under cardboard in an alley to a nursing home from which he had escaped because he "found no love there".

Gradually young men began to join the Brothers in Los Angeles as "Come and Sees" – a term used by the Missionaries of Charity to describe those considering the life and work of the Order as a possible vocation. Brother Andrew, having left Vietnam, came to Los Angeles and in the midst of the city's suffering and apparent lack of love, he resolved to found a second novitiate. The spiritual formation of young men wishing to become Brothers from the Americas, Europe, Australia and New Zealand need not necessarily be undertaken in Calcutta. They could be formed in the work and spirit of the Congregation in downtown Los Angeles. Another house was rented. As part of their formation, the novices were sent to work in the Skid Row area, visiting the old, the sick, the alcoholics and the neglected, trying to inject love into a place where violence and alienation had become frighteningly ordinary. In Los Angeles as in Calcutta, there were people dying, unwanted and neglected. Los Angeles might not have actual lepers but it had social lepers; and there were the children, living under terrible conditions of physical, spiritual and emotional want. The work grew, the number of Brothers increased, albeit not as rapidly as that of the Sisters, and homes of hospitality were opened for the homeless and those in need of emergency shelter, a shower, clean clothes, or simply a chat.

Los Angeles proved to be the starting point for new openings in Latin America. In the Far East more houses were established and work would soon begin in Japan, Hong Kong and eventually in Europe – in France, Sweden and England.

In the course of his travels Brother Andrew wrote about what he described as "our funny little Missionary of Charity thing that grows, expands, is full of life – as it exists with such weakness, fragility and folly." He wrote of the expansion of the work as the result of an impulse which did not come from him: "I have felt very clearly that there is the guidance of God's spirit in these new openings and I am aware that I have not made them." He gave expression to his conviction that ostensibly prosperous societies had their own distinctive pressures, their own form of blindness and their own brand of poverty:

Sometimes people wonder why we go to more prosperous places like Los Angeles, Tokyo, Hong Kong, when there is such desperate poverty in India and on such a large scale. I believe that there is much more terrible poverty than that found in India. Hong Kong illustrates this for me. When I was in Calcutta recently during the floods which devastated so much it struck me one day that the people of Calcutta are somehow much more humanly rich than people in Hong Kong. It is a strange paradox that may be saying something to us. It is true of much of the more affluent world. In Hong Kong we have a small home for severely mentally disabled men. We get public funds – and much interference. The men in the home are severely retarded. They have been in various institutions where they did not respond much to training or treatment. They lived with their families in the impossibly small rooms of Hong Kong housing conditions. Since joining us, all have responded well – and the big thing, it seems to me, is that they are happy. But that is not enough, we are told. They must be doing something, they must be programmed. There can be few places as rushed in the world as production-centred Hong Kong. The stress and pressures here are great. It seems we are not allowed to be satisfied that these disabled men are happy. They have to be got into the rush, into the rat-race that is driving everybody else mad. There are basic questions involved in this about where the dignity and value of a man lies, whether it is in his being or in his performance. And so India, with its greater material poverty, has a quality of life that is often lost when the gods are materialistic and must be got down in a report. It is a question of the human and spiritual enjoyment of life. I feel, in places like Hong Kong, we are meant to be a little witness to this as "Animal Farm" bears down on all sides.

His letters spoke of the hidden value of small things and small people, of the miracle of love that was sometimes glimpsed in life in its most bruised and broken forms, a miracle which brought joy and encouragement to those who were sometimes overwhelmed by the smallness of their efforts in relationship to the magnitude of the need:

We are blessed to see the seemingly broken who are healed, the seeming sinner who is a saint, the seeming poor man who is rich in ways we could never imagine. Yes, God has blessed us. He brought us here today to witness the miracle of his presence born anew in the hearts of the poor. He is here among us, disguised in rags and dirt. It is he – hungry; it is he – thirsty; it is he – homeless and lonely. It is he, in Los Angeles, who walks the streets so disguised as even to be shocking to us.

Brother Andrew's emotions were more easily discernible than Mother Teresa's. His letters reflected a readiness to share more widely his own thoughts and reactions to events, although such disclosures were still made out of a desire to convey a spiritual message without appearing to preach. They were written in a very different language and style from Mother Teresa's but they reflected very much the same fundamental message. To that message he also brought, however, the fruits of his own experience as a Missionary of Charity and a vision born of his early life as a compulsive gambler and his training as a Jesuit.

The bond which existed between the Missionary Brothers and Sisters was a strong one and extended far beyond the fact that they shared the same foundress. As the years went by, because of their respective commitments in so many countries, Mother Teresa and Brother Andrew met with decreasing frequency – perhaps once or twice a year, when both happened to be in India at the same time. She was not Brother Andrew's superior, nor was she the superior of the Missionary Brothers of Charity. Brother Andrew was not in obedience to her, but her influence on the Brothers, he was quick to assert, remained great. Her advice and ideas were greatly respected. The Brothers' novice masters were always glad to have her come and talk to the novices, but it was fully recognized that her great influence did not derive from the frequency of her visits, but from her spirit and the living example of her life which was a continual inspiration.

Mother Teresa looked upon the congregation as a part of the same family as her Sisters, and one with which she was well pleased. Yet there remained certain aspects of the Brothers' life which did not quite conform to her original idea. Without great singleness of purpose and vision and considerable strength of character she could never have achieved all that she did. Such people do not easily deviate from what they see as essential to their path, and it would be unreal to expect Mother Teresa to be an exception. She remained eager to have a male branch of the Missionaries of Charity which would emphasize some of the aspects of life that Brother Andrew had altered, which would be closer to the Sisters in details of prayer life, discipline and general tidiness. This factor, it has been suggested, was not without some bearing on the founding of two further male branches of the Missionaries of Charity, the Contemplative Brothers and the Missionary of Charity Fathers.

In 1970 en route to Mauritius, Mother Teresa had hurt her shoulder. Her method of convalescing consisted of spending a time in quiet contemplation in a Carmelite convent in Rome. It was there that it had come to her that when the Sisters became sick or elderly there might be a role for them to spend more time in prayer: "When our Sisters will no longer physically be able to go in search of souls, we still have the better part of our life to spend for Jesus – in silence and adoration – therefore we will spend it in perpetual adoration." Out of this initial inspiration germinated the seed for a contemplative branch of the Missionaries of Charity which would include not only the sick or the elderly. The idea of a life which incorporated greater time for prayer was one to which a number of Sisters responded. On the feast of the Sacred Heart of Jesus, in June 1976 in New York, Cardinal Cooke, in the presence of Mother Teresa, blessed a new contemplative branch of the Missionaries of Charity. Under the leadership of Sister Nirmala, a pioneer of the first foundation outside India in Venezuela, it would at first be known as the Sisters of the Word but later in 1977 be renamed simply Missionaries of Charity, Contemplative.

The particular mission of these Sisters would be to "live the Word of God in Eucharistic Adoration and Contemplation and to proclaim the Word to the people of God by their presence and spiritual works of mercy in order that the Word made flesh will remain in the hearts of men." The Missionaries of Charity were already to be "contemplatives in the world". The new branch, however, was to provide a role for those whose vocation was to a life in which the greater part of the day was dedicated to contemplative prayer. At the same time the rule of life differed from that of traditional contemplative communities, in that it made provision for several hours in the afternoons for active apostolic work amongst the poorest of the poor. The Sisters would also leave the convent for Mass in the adjoining parish, and welcome lay people into their own chapel if they wished to spend time in prayer and meditation. The house in New York was a convent rededicated by Cardinal Cooke for the new foundation, at the very heart of the Bronx. There were those who were frightened to venture into an area where violence and vandalism were rife and some of the surrounding houses had been burnt out, but the Sisters were glad to be among the most needy, with people whose spirit had been broken. The contemplatives' chapel provided an oasis of peace. A drunkard would come in and ask for a rosary and return with a small bouquet of flowers for the tabernacle. Children rang at the doorbell. "We want to see Jesus", they said. "I want to pray with God."

Sensing accurately that Brother Andrew was not keen on the idea of a similar contemplative branch of the Brothers, Mother Teresa simply confronted him with what amounted to a *fait accompli*. Soon after the Contemplative Sisters were founded, in 1978 she established a branch for men in a slum area of Rome. When Brother Andrew refused to endorse the move the contemplative branch was kept clearly separate from the Missionary Brothers. The Brothers of the Word were placed under the direct supervision of a Roman prelate. Only in 1985 would the Contemplative Brothers become, like the contemplative branch of the Sisters, an integral part of the Missionaries of Charity and no longer known as "Brothers of the Word".

Similarly a branch of the Missionaries of Charity for priests wanting to exercise their ministry in the spirit of Mother Teresa, and to bind themselves to the Missionary of Charity ideal of life by the four vows of poverty, chastity, obedience and wholehearted free service to the poorest of the poor, would develop independently of the Brothers. From the time Mother Teresa had first begun to formulate the idea of a Congregation of Brothers she had also expressed a desire for one or two sympathetic priests to work with the Sisters, to visit the slums and "do much spiritual good". The initiative for a branch of the Missionaries of Charity for priests came substantially, however, from an American priest, Father Joseph Langford who, having read *Something Beautiful for God*, felt profoundly called to use his priesthood in some way in the service of Mother Teresa and her work. There were times during his seminary training when he wanted to abandon everything and join the Brothers, but in some sense he had felt that inconsistent with his call to be a priest. In the Missionary Brothers there was nothing to distinguish between the service undertaken for the poor by ordained priests and that done by the other Brothers. The spiritual ministry entailed in their priesthood was used strictly for and within their own community. Father Joseph Langford felt called to something not overlapping with, but complementing the existing role of the Brothers, which would give more direct expression to his spiritual ministry. In 1978 when, at the time of his ordination, Mother

Teresa happened to be in Rome, his idea of what form his relationship to the Missionaries of Charity might take was as yet a dim one. He asked only that he might adopt one of Mother Teresa's communities and hold it up in prayer. Mother Teresa gave him the home for the dying in Calcutta, and he found this spiritual adoption so valuable during the first year of his priestly ministry that he felt it was something that should be shared with other priests and ministers, no matter what their denomination.

What would subsequently develop out of this initial spiritual adoption would remain distinct from the Congregation of Brothers and its priest members. Brother Andrew, whilst acknowledging that Mother Teresa had been fully entitled to found the two additional male branches, was (to use his own expression) "peeved" at the furtiveness with which she had acted. What he saw as his male pride had been stung. The passage of the years, he said in 1991, made his reaction look petty: "The failings of great souls call for a tolerant eye in view of their magnificent achievements, especially from much lesser mortals." Nevertheless a little more openness might have been expected.

Mother Teresa could be quite blind to many considerations when she felt that something important was in question. She was strong in her sense of the direction and purpose she felt came from God, and nothing and no one could be higher than that. There were occasions on which this could be interpreted as a weakness, but at the same time her directness in pursuing her goals avoided the potential quagmires of diplomacy and politeness, quagmires which might well not have produced anything worthwhile and would possibly have hindered the development of the whole. "I was by-passed," Brother Andrew would insist in 1992, "rightly and happily so."

CHAPTER SIX

For the Brotherhood of Man under the Fatherhood of God

For Mother Teresa one of the great joys associated with "giving the poor for love what the rich could get for money" was derived from the fact that from the very beginning it had become a point of union for people of different creeds, social backgrounds and faiths. In Calcutta a high-caste Hindu lady, resplendent in her silk sari, used to go regularly to the home for the dying to wash and tend to the needs of people whom her ancestors had for generations regarded as untouchables. Mrs Chater, a Chinese lady who lived in Entally, used to lend the Sisters an open truck for the picnic/pilgrimages which were their Christmas treat. A Jewish doctor operated free of charge on children with hare lips and cleft palates who came into the Sisters' or Brothers' care. Students from the university started going on Saturdays to shave the dying men. English women went to the mother house on Lower Circular Road to teach the Sisters English, and at festivals volunteers were inveigled into filling bags with gifts for children.

It was in 1954 that Ann Blaikie first became involved in such activities. The fact that she was pregnant had compelled her to give up the kind of voluntary work undertaken by many of Calcutta's European memsahibs: working in a charity shop selling high quality handicrafts in aid of mission work. At the time she knew nothing of Mother Teresa except what she had gleaned from newspaper articles, mentioning that on one occasion she had retrieved a baby from a dustbin, and on another held a children's party at a nearby school. Yet with time on her hands and the encouragement of another "memsahib" from Britain who had a vague knowledge of Mother Teresa's work, she felt impelled to seek her out.

On 26 July she went with Margaret Mackenzie, the friend in

question, to Mother Teresa's first clinic. Mother Teresa took them with her to the Kalighat and in the car en route they suggested that they collect some of the unwanted toys belonging to the children of Calcutta's sizeable British community and repair them for a Christmas party. Mother Teresa's priority, however, was dresses, shirts and pants for her Christian children whose mothers wanted to give them new clothes for Christmas. A dozen European women promptly set about making angels out of tin foil and beads, and sold them to raise the necessary funds. At Christmas the Christian children were duly provided with the clothes they needed. They were also given carefully repaired toys. After Christmas the women gathered together with something of an air of understandable self-congratulation and waited for Mother Teresa to come and thank them. This she did but added that now she needed clothes and presents for the Muslim children's annual festival of Ramadan. Inevitably a party for the Hindu children followed in October for Diwali, the Hindu festival of light.

The group of early well-wishers who provided for this series of children's parties became known as the Marian Society because their work had begun in Marian year. Their efforts were not initially directed exclusively towards helping Mother Teresa but included the support of other missions. Gradually the society expanded to include Indians and Anglo-Indians, Americans and people of other nationalities. It incorporated some who were not Roman Catholics, and, in a way that was quite unplanned, the work done to assist Mother Teresa increased in scope. Groups of women formed working parties to roll bandages out of old sheets and to make paper bags out of newspaper, in which the leper pills could more easily be distributed. As the leprosy work developed, Margaret Mackenzie designed the stickers appealing to those in a position to touch a leper with their compassion, and not without some difficulty contrived to produce a letter heading which at Mother Teresa's express request made India the centre of the world. Christmas cards were made and sold in aid of the work, and food and blankets were collected for distribution to the lepers.

Mother Teresa took a personal interest in their activities and their talents. She expected very much more of them than a passing and superficial commitment, and was concerned to pass on to them the same spirit which she tried to instil into the Missionaries of Charity. In those days she would visit Shishu Bhavan, the children's home in Calcutta, every morning. She would go from one tiny baby to the next, and if she spotted one which was so frail or sick that it seemed likely to die that day, she would wrap it in a blanket and give it to one of the helpers to hold, with the instruction simply to love that child until it died. What mattered was that no child in her care should die without having experienced love. One morning Mother Teresa placed one of these desperately sick babies in the arms of one of the lay helpers. The helper held it and loved it until finally it died at 6 o'clock in the evening. She passed away the hours by humming Brahms's lullaby. More than thirty years later she would still retain the memory of how that tiny baby, weak as it was, pressed itself against her.

From Shishu Bhavan, Mother Teresa would go on to the home for the dying, taking one or two helpers with her to care for the dying. The first time one such helper went to Nirmal Hriday, she walked there alone with Mother Teresa. Sensing that the newcomer was nervous and apprehensive, before they reached the Kalighat, Mother Teresa stopped and said to her, "I don't want you to go to the home for the dying feeling sad. Pray and ask God to lift up your heart because whatever you see there, I want you to transmit joy." Mother Teresa knew that not everyone was equally well equipped to cope with the experience of being brought face to face with the poverty and suffering that contrasted so dramatically with the lifestyles of influential foreign business people in Calcutta. For some the home for the dying might well be the most wonderful place on earth; for others it was a strange twilight world with a touch of unreality about it; yet others were overwhelmed by the aroma of disinfectant which never quite disguised the smell of diseased flesh. For those unable to cope with touching the poor in Nirmal Hriday there were plenty of other tasks that were equally indispensable.

As far as the wider public was concerned, Mother Teresa's natural inclination was to allow the work, whatever form it took, to speak for itself. "Let them see your good works and glorify your father who is in heaven", she regularly exhorted her Sisters. Only at the insistence of Archbishop Périer did she accept the value of taking such opportunities to speak as presented themselves, and even then she had first to overcome her natural reticence. In the campaign for lepers Ann Blaikie supplemented Mother Teresa's public role by "announcing the work" on her behalf. It was a task which she would eventually undertake in countries all over the world.

In 1960, the Blaikies returned to England. As it transpired, so too did a number of other British helpers who had been prepared to follow the example of a little known nun, and if necessary to spend their time searching for new centres in the monsoon mud. Six such families settled within five miles of each other in Surrey, and within a week of her arrival in England, Ann Blaikie was once more caught up in the work of the Missionaries of Charity. Mother Teresa had written to John Southworth, the chairman of a leprosy relief charity that had been sending her money, to advise him to contact her friend in England for up-to-date information on the situation in India. Some six months later she actually visited England herself. She had been in the United States and was due to travel on to Germany. En route through London it was arranged for her to give a brief televised interview to form part of the evening news. From the offers of help which followed, what was known at the time as the "Mother Teresa Committee" was born, under the chairmanship of John Southworth, the vice-chairmanship of Ann Blaikie and with the support of other friends from India.

The focal point of the activities of these first UK helpers was a monthly meeting which began and ended with prayer and meditation, and which also organized material help for the Missionaries of Charity. Under the Child Welfare Scheme donors undertook to sponsor one of the orphaned or abandoned children in the care of the Sisters. People were encouraged to make bandages from old linen, to knit blankets and collect used clothing. Items suitable for India were sent to a number of collecting centres throughout the country and dispatched to Calcutta for use in the homes for the dying, the clinics and the children's homes. Each year newly designed Christmas cards were sent out to friends or placed on sale at the Mission for the Relief of Suffering shop in Knightsbridge. A sample medicine scheme dispatched free samples of medicine to the clinics in India, and money was raised through the collection and sale of used stamps and other similar enterprises. A newsletter was published at regular intervals to keep those interested in touch with current activities and with news from India. A limited amount of advertising was undertaken in those early years, but the principal way in which these helpers sought to enlarge their circle of members was through talks, illustrated with a film or slides, to schools and other organizations. Every encouragement was given to people living in different parts of the country to form groups of their own. As in India, so in England the number of people of good will increased steadily. The pattern for development in other countries was already set.

A visit by Mother Teresa to Great Britain in 1965 provided a catalyst for this growth. Mrs Blaikie, Mother Teresa afterwards reported to her Sisters, had been working very hard preparing for her stay. "I have been out so often I am just tired of meetings and talking," she told them, "but thinking of you all and our poor, it is worth doing it with Jesus and for Jesus." In 1968 she returned to London, and it was during this visit that she was interviewed by Malcolm Muggeridge for BBC television. Mother Teresa was very nervous in front of the camera and somewhat halting in speech. The interview was technically a disaster, so much so that the producers doubted for a while whether it was good enough for showing at all, except perhaps late at night. In the end it was put out on a Sunday evening, with extraordinary effect. Something about the woman whose answers to a highly professional interviewer were so perfectly simple and perfectly truthful that he had felt uneasy about keeping the programme going for the requisite half an hour, seemed to touch the nation. Malcolm Muggeridge had himself been profoundly impressed by her. Her entry into what he described as the "desolatingly familiar" setting of the studio was one which he would always remember – "It was, for me, one of those special occasions when a face, hitherto unknown, seems to stand out from all other faces as uniquely separate and uniquely significant, to be thenceforth for ever recognizable." Nevertheless, he had thought that with her, as with so many others, the camera would drain away whatever was real and alive in what it portrayed. In fact the response to the interview proved to be greater than he had known to any comparable programme, both in mail and in contributions of money for Mother Teresa's work. Letters poured in from rich and poor, young and old, educated and uneducated, all of them saying much the same thing – "This woman spoke to me as no one ever has, and I feel I must help her."

By 1969 the need had been felt to consolidate into a properly constituted organization the help and support that was increasingly forthcoming. As always, Mother Teresa had definite views about the role of this organization. Malcolm Muggeridge happened to overhear a discussion as to what it should be called. Someone suggested "Friends of Mother Teresa", but Mother Teresa broke in to say crisply that it was not friends she wanted but helpers. She had never met Gandhi but her respect for India's "Great Soul", who had made the plight of the pariah or untouchables his particular concern, manifested itself in not infrequent verbal references to him. Gandhi had once said, "I do not want to be reborn but if I have to be reborn, I should be born an untouchable, so that I may share the sorrows, sufferings and affronts levelled at them, in order that I may endeavour to free myself and them from that miserable condition." It was not on a passing whim that the leprosy centre at Titlagarh had been called Gandhiji Prem Nivas, the "Gandhi Centre of Love". Nor was it purely by chance that she elected to call the association of helpers affiliated to the Missionaries of Charity "Co-Workers". Mother Teresa chose the name as a tribute to one who had called his own helpers Co-Workers because they worked with him "for the brotherhood of man under the fatherhood of God". The term conveyed ideas of service, love and universality under God which would prove to be particularly appropriate.

On 23 March 1969 Mother Teresa went to Rome, partly with the intention of visiting her Sisters in their small convent in the Appia Nuova, partly to prepare the constitution of the new "International Association of Co-Workers of Mother Teresa". With her were Ann Blaikie, the chairman of the association, and her husband, who brought his legal skills to the compilation of the constitution. The vice-chairman, who was also present, was a Co-Worker from Germany, where news of Mother Teresa's work was already widespread thanks in part to an article in a publication called *Weltelend* which had powerfully depicted scenes from the Home for the Dying and the suffering of Calcutta's poor. In Rome Mother Teresa and this small team worked for several days on a draft constitution which would unite and reflect the diversity of nationality and creed which had from the very beginning characterized those drawn to help the Missionaries of Charity. Mother Teresa once estimated that for every Christian who helped her in India, she had ten non-Christians. The constitution had therefore to be worded in such a way as to appeal to people of good will everywhere: to Hindus, Buddhists, Christians and other faiths and denominations.

Mother Teresa was not one to theorize about ecumenism or different faiths or theologies. Nor would she generally spend time on discussion of such matters, but her interest, love and respect for individuals meant that she gave herself to them regardless of differences and was concerned not to hurt. There were times when proposals and ideas expressed in the language of the Roman Cath-olicism which she acknowledged was for her the "only way" could have been presented with greater sensitivity to non-Catholics. Even in 1991 a notice outside the chapel in the mother house stated with what some might consider unnecessary baldness that non-Catholics could not receive the sacraments; but such instances occurred most frequently out of ignorance that they might offend or exclude, and were generally adjusted when others drew attention to their possible effects. In this respect the requirements of non-Catholic Co-Workers at times had a role in tempering the language and approach to reflect the real universality of her heart.

Looking back on the preparation of the constitution of an associ-ation of which she would serve as international chairman and link for thirty-four years, Ann Blaikie also drew attention to the fact that they had had to take into account the social barriers which potentially divided Co-Workers in certain parts of the world: "the very rich and the poor who would not necessarily normally work together in acts of charity but who could be helped to do so by a charismatic constitution." The charismatic constitution submitted to Pope Paul VI on 26 March was possibly the first to affiliate an association of lay, not primarily Christian, people, to a Religious Order. It defined the association as consisting of:

men, women, young people and children of all religions and denominations throughout the world who seek to love God in their fellow men through wholehearted free service to the poorest of the poor of all castes and creeds, and who wish to unite themselves in a spirit of prayer and sacrifice with the work of Mother Teresa and the Missionaries of Charity.

Its professed aim was to help its members:

a) to recognize God in the person of the poor
b) to love God better through works of charity and service to the poor
c) to unite with the Missionaries of Charity and with each other throughout the world in prayer and sacrifice
d) to keep the family spirit
e) to foster aid between various countries and eliminate duplication of effort and aid for individual centres of the Missionaries of Charity

The Pope received the constitution and gave his blessing to those present and to the Order of the Missionaries of Charity throughout the world; and Mother Teresa could not resist taking the opportunity of offering him the service of her Sisters in Biafra and Vietnam. Shortly afterwards she received a letter of acknowledgement from Cardinal Agagianian, head of the Sacred Congregation of the Propagation of the Faith:

Reverend Mother, I wish to acknowledge receipt of and to thank you for the copy of the Constitution of the International Association of Co-Workers of Mother Teresa which you recently presented to this Sacred Congregation. This Sacred Congregation commends most highly the ideal which the Association offers to its members, namely union in prayer and sacrifice to the good works of your Institute and "wholehearted free service to the poorest of the poor of all castes and creeds". With every best wish for you, Reverend Mother, all the Missionary Sisters and Brothers of Charity and the members of the above mentioned Association, I remain, sincerely yours in Christ.

Adherence to the Constitution drawn up in Rome effected a unique bond between the growing "family" of Co-Workers throughout the world. Those who during the floods of 1968, for example, worked beside the Sisters in the foothills of the Himalayas, among the former inhabitants of a town submerged beneath six feet of silt, mud and water, were linked with those who in England quietly raised money for ambulance clinics to be shipped out to India. The woman who in the material affluence of Surrey set up the "Teresa Boutique", a charity shop selling nearly-new clothes, knitted garments and dolls to support the work of Mother Teresa, shared a common bond with those who, at the very heart of the turmoil, endeavoured to ensure that the Missionaries of Charity need not turn away a single refugee from East Pakistan because of lack of resources; and eventually with countless others throughout the world who shared in what was to be called the "Co-Workers' Way of Life".

In those countries where there were Sisters or Brothers, the Co-Workers frequently worked alongside them, supporting and complementing their labours, but there were countries where Co-Worker groups came into being prior to the arrival of Missionaries of Charity. In Finland, East Germany, Hungary, Poland, Czechoslovakia, the Soviet Union and the Arctic Circle, for some years there were individuals who sought to be Co-Workers in relative isolation. Mother Teresa was aware of their particular role and value as a presence of love and prayer, just as she was aware of the distinctive needs and potential failings of lay people living in the community at large. In March 1967 Mother Teresa had given an instruction to her Sisters that in future they were to say a particular prayer before leaving the chapel in the morning, after what she always referred to as Holy Mass. The use of the prayer was swiftly extended to the Co-Workers. It was one which struck right at the roots of any idea of self-congratulatory benevolence or of service, which was in fact a largely selfish meeting of some possibly unidentified personal need:

Make us worthy, Lord, to serve our fellow men throughout
the world who live and die in poverty and hunger.
Give them, through our hands, this day their daily bread,
and by our understanding love, give peace and joy.

To this she added an adaptation of the prayer of St Francis which was an expression of the concept of instrumentality, of God acting through an emptied self, which she saw as the inspiration and explanation of her own "achievements":

Agnes, aged ten, with her Skopje school friends.

ABOVE: 1924, taking part in a
Christmas Eve play.

RIGHT: Agnes (seated) with sister Aga and brother
Lazar in 1924.

ABOVE: Aga (with parasol) and Agnes visiting Nerezima.

RIGHT: Agnes (centre) in her 1928 graduation day portrait.

Agnes left for Ireland in September 1928, leaving this photograph with her aunt. A note read 'Dear Aunty, to remember me'.

ABOVE: The first photo of Sister Teresa, the novice in Darjeeling. It was taken on 22 February 1929.

RIGHT: A photograph of Mother Teresa taken in the 1950s and sent by her to the parents of one of her young Sisters as a gesture of affection and gratitude.

24 May 1931: Sister Teresa had just taken her first vows.

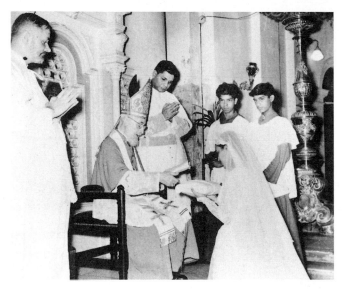

ABOVE: In the 1950s a young Missionary of Charity receives from Archbishop Périer her novice's habit. To the left of the Archbishop stands Monsignor Barber, then Vicar General of Calcutta. In the foreground is Father Celeste Van Exem.

RIGHT: Sister Agnes MC, a former pupil at the Loreto school in Entally and the first aspirant to join Mother Teresa at Creek Lane. (*Nachiketa Publications*)

BELOW: The Kalighat in Calcutta, where in what was once a resting place for pilgrims to the Kali temple, Mother Teresa created her first home for the dying. (*John Coo*)

ABOVE: Ann Blaikie speaking on behalf of Mother Teresa in March 1959 at the formal opening of the leprosy dispensary at Titagarh.

RIGHT: The chapel in the mother house at Lower Circular Road as it was in 1963.

On 26 July 1965 a group of Sisters arrives at Caracas airport, Venezuela, to initiate the first Missionary of Charity foundation outside India. On Mother Teresa's immediate right is Sister Nirmala, subsequently Superior of the contemplative Sisters and finally Superior General of the Missionaries of Charity.

LEFT: Mother Teresa with Brother Andrew, co-founder of the Missionary Brothers of Charity. *(Nachiketa Publications)*

BELOW: Mother Teresa in the Vatican with John and Ann Blaikie on 26 March 1969, on the occasion of the presentation of the constitution of the Co-Workers to Pope Paul VI.

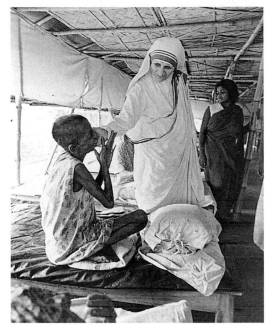

Mother Teresa 'touching the poor with her compassion' in temporary shelters erected by the Missionaries of Charity on otherwise unused corners of Calcutta's pavements. *(S. K. Dutt/Camera Press)*

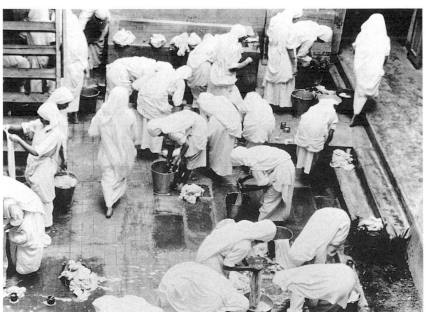

In the central courthouse of the mother house in Calcutta, the Missionaries of Charity do their daily washing in buckets. *(S. K. Dutt/Camera Press)*

ABOVE: In Africa a Missionary of Charity responds to a leper's appeal.

RIGHT: A Sister at work in the Missionary of Charity home for alcoholics in Melbourne, Australia.

Clasping in her arms one of the innumerable orphaned or abandoned children taken into the care of the Missionaries of Charity.
(S. K. Dutt/Camera Press)

Mrs Indira Ghandi in her capacity as chancellor of the Viswa Bharati University, conferring on her friend of many years the establishment's highest honour, the Deshikottama or Doctorate of Literature – 3 March 1976. (*Kumar Basak/Gamma/FSP*)

LEFT: Surveying the citation for the Nobel Prize, the 'gift of recognition of the poorest of the poor of the world', received in Oslo on 10 December 1979. (*Laurent Maous/Gamma/FSP*)

My brother— the only one left of the family is dying of cancer in the lungs— just days only — so pray for him. I was the one to tell him he had the cancer and that he would soon be joining the family in Heaven — very simple answer he gave — 'if you want to join the family you go — but I have no desire to do so now" He was so beautiful at the end when he said — Yes, I am ready to go — after his confession & the prayers together. Pray for him. As he has no soul— the family some will die with him.

Keep the joy of loving Jesus in your hearts and share this joy with each other and all you meet and pray for me.

God bless you
— Mother —

RIGHT: A letter written by Mother Teresa to a close friend on 14 February 1981.

ABOVE: A laboratory building in its five-acre grounds in Calcutta, donated by ICI and transformed by the Missionaries of Charity into a home for, among others, the mentally disturbed. From here also food and supplies are distributed to the hungry of the slums. (*John Coo*)

With President and Mrs Ronald Reagan, following a visit to the White House in June 1981. Behind her is Sister Priscilla, then Regional Superior in North America, and subsequently a Councillor and Secretary General. (*Associated Press*)

At the Rashtrapati Bhavan in New Delhi, on 24 November 1983, Mother Teresa thanks Queen Elizabeth II for her 'beautiful gift': the insignia of the Honorary Order of Merit. *(Associated Press)*

BELOW: Meeting Christ in the distressing disguise of the poor in Nirmal Hriday, Calcutta. *(S. K. Dutt/Camera Press)*

LEFT: Archbishop Desmond Tutu with a fellow Nobel prize winner in Paris on 30 May 1985, to discuss, at the invitation of French president François Mitterand, the current state of world human rights. *(Francis Apesteguy/Gamma/FSP)*

With Brother Roger and Marie Louise Sonaly, the orphaned Indian girl first cared for by the Missionaries of Charity and subsequently taken as the prior of Taizé's godchild to live close to him in France.

One of the many and varied visitors drawn to Calcutta by the presence of Mother Teresa, on 28 March 1990, Yasser Arafat, chairman of the Palestine Liberation Organisation, presents her with a cheque for $50,000. *(Associated Press)*

Prayer before the statue of the Virgin Mary in the San Gregorio convent in Rome, in May 1991, as Mother Teresa prepares to despatch Sisters and supplies to Romania.

Garlanded after the Indian fashion, Missionary of Charity Sisters are welcomed back to the Casilina convent in Rome after making their final vows on 24 May 1991. *(David Cobb)*

Diana, Princess of Wales with Sister Frederick and a group of Missionaries of Charity during her visit to Calcutta, 15 February 1992. *(Mail Newspapers/Solo Syndication)*

ABOVE: In one of the rare moments when the luminous smile abandoned her. *(MASU)*

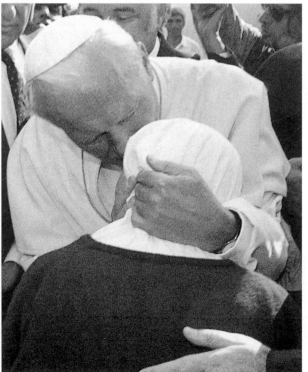

LEFT: On 25 April 1993, Pope John Paul II embraces Mother Teresa during his first visit to Albania, the country of her origins. *(Agencie France Press/Press Association)*

At a meeting in Antwerp on 8 May 1993, from left to right: Father Paul Chetcuti SJ, international spiritual adviser to the Co-Workers; Margaret Cullis, international link; Mother Teresa MC; Brother Geoff MC, General Servant of the Missionary Brothers; Ann Blaikie, former international link for the Co-Workers; Denise de Jongh, deputy international link. *(David Jarrett)*

LEFT: Jacqueline de Decker, Mother Teresa's sick and suffering 'other self', persuaded to pose in May 1993 in front of some of her numerous files, wearing the medal awarded to her by King George VI for war-time bravery.

RIGHT: The author put to work, cutting hair in the women's ward of Nirmal Hriday, the home for the dying in Calcutta. *(John Coo)*

LEFT: Mother Teresa walks with Diana, Princess of Wales, after receiving a visit from her on 18 June 1997, in New York. *(Associated Press/Bebeto Mattews)*

BELOW: Mourners look on as Mother Teresa is carried into the mother house in Calcutta on Saturday 13 September 1997, where she was buried after her State funeral. *(Associated Press/Bikas Das)*

ABOVE: Sister Nirmala, who succeeded Mother Teresa, smiles as she faces the media at a press conference in Calcutta. *(Associated Press/Saurabh Das)*

Lord, make me a channel of thy peace,
that where there is hatred, I may bring love;
that where there is wrong, I may bring the spirit of
    forgiveness;
that where there is discord, I may bring harmony;
that where there is error, I may bring truth;
that where there is doubt, I may bring faith;
that where there is despair, I may bring hope;
that where there are shadows, I may bring light;
that where there is sadness, I may bring joy.

Lord, grant that I may seek rather to comfort than to be
    comforted;
to understand rather than to be understood;
to love rather than be loved;
for it is by forgetting self that one finds;
it is by forgiving that one is forgiven;
it is by dying that one awakens to eternal life.

As in the case of the Missionaries of Charity, the relationship
between the Co-Workers and the poor was to be one which entailed
the surrender of the self in an encounter which was not one of
benefactor and humbled recipient but one based on the recognition
of the love of God for every individual. If God loved each person
then every meeting with another person involved the unique discovery of that which was the object of God's love in him, of that
which came to him from God. Such a discovery allowed no room
for condescension or for moral judgements, and took no cognizance
of the obsessive search for "concrete results". Mother Teresa called
upon those who lived in a world caught up in the race to be rich,
powerful and effective, to be aware of their own poverty, to make
themselves weak with the weak and not to seek to do big things but
only small things with great love. She saw the ease with which even
the most substantial cheque could be written for the abstract poor
of far distant lands, and she urged her Co-Workers not to give
from their abundance but rather to give "until it hurt".

In 1974 Mother Teresa undertook a tour of a series of European
countries: Malta, Austria, Switzerland, Germany, Sweden, the

Netherlands, Britain, Denmark, France. Her visits and her talks did much to confirm already existing groups of Co-Workers and to engender further interest. "You want to type letters," she told them, "you have to practise on a typewriter first; same thing – you want to give love to others, first, give love to your own children, your husband, your wife." As her appreciation of the poverty of affluent societies grew, she asked them to concentrate on discovering the poverty, be it material or spiritual, in their own neighbourhoods, on their own doorsteps, in their own homes:

Today, the poor are hungry for bread and rice and for love and the living word of God.
The poor are thirsty – for water and for peace, truth and justice.
The poor are homeless – for a shelter made of bricks, and for a joyful heart that understands, covers, loves.
The poor are naked – for clothes, for human dignity and compassion for the naked sinner.
They are sick – for medical care, and for that gentle touch and a warm smile.

Co-Workers were to endeavour to identify the need which was nearest to them and to meet it by giving of their time and their energy, and doing those apparently ordinary things which she had come to know contained the embryo of some secret promise. They were to pick someone a flower, bake them a cake, pay them a visit, show them a little love, because every act of love brought a person face to face with God. When St Teresa of Lisieux died and it was proposed that she should be canonized, Mother Teresa pointed out, there were those who were very doubtful about her eligibility: " 'For what will Holy Father canonize her?' they asked. 'She has not done anything.' And Holy Father wrote one sentence: 'I will canonize her because she did ordinary things with extraordinary love.'" In Mother Teresa's view the disintegration of society, the breakdown of world peace and all the misery and suffering which resulted from it, were attributable in no small measure to the loss of love and prayer in family life, and so she asked her Co-Workers to be witnesses of extraordinary love especially in the home:

Our Sisters are working around the world and I have seen all the trouble, all the misery, all the suffering. From where did it come? It has come from lack of love and lack of prayer. There is no more of that coming together in the family, praying together, coming together, staying together.

Speaking in a Carmelite Church in Dublin in 1979, Mother Teresa recalled an encounter with a boy with long hair:

The Sisters go out at night to work, to pick up people on the streets. They saw a young man there, late at night – lying in the street and they said, "You should not be here, you should be with your parents", and he said, "When I go home my mother does not want me because I have long hair. Every time I went home she pushed me out." By the time the Sisters came back he had overdosed himself and they had to take him to hospital. I could not help thinking it was quite possible that his mother was busy with the hunger of our people in India. Yet there was her own child hungry for her, hungry for love, hungry for her care and she refused it. Bring love into your home. If you really love God begin by loving your child, your husband, your wife. The old people, where are they? They are in some institution. Why are they not with you? Where is the crippled child? In some institution. Why is that child not with you? That child, young mothers and fathers, is a gift of God.

Co-Workers were to make their homes "centres of compassion" and "forgive endlessly". They were to smile even when they found it difficult to do so, just as she on occasions found it much more difficult to smile at her Sisters than at the poor. Though the feminist movement had largely passed her by, she did not view marriage altogether through the eyes of an idealist. Asked once whether she was married, she replied that she was married to Jesus, and sometimes she found it difficult to smile at him also. The practical woman in her knew that it was frequently women who were most readily at her disposal, and so she shrewdly paid particular attention to drawing their menfolk into the work. If it was the wives of Calcutta businessmen who were most active in their support for her, it was none the less to their husbands that she would write, thanking them for their lesser contributions. The women were expected to understand; and the men were undoubtedly charmed.

Even the most potentially cynical of husbands could be disarmed by her. The luminous smile and the directive: "You come to Calcutta and I put you to work", could reduce the most authoritative to meek and compliant submission.

In 1980 Mother Teresa would decide to make husbands and wives joint national chairmen, or "Links" as they would become known. It was a move which reflected more faithfully the kind of family unity for which she was urging Co-Workers to strive. It was also a very pragmatic step to prevent the kind of resentments which she was fully aware could arise when wives gave too much time and energy to something in which their husbands were not included. She was not always conscious of the disruption to "ordinary" lives that her personal requirements of people could make. The faithful sometimes found themselves spending nights on railway platforms, left painfully unaware that Mother Teresa's plans had been changed, or required to drop everything and follow at very short notice. She was discerning enough, however, to tell Co-Workers that they were always to give priority to their families over their Co-Worker meetings and other activities. For her, "love begins in the home" and "the family that prays together stays together" were far more than desirable clichés.

As the number of people involved in the international association of Co-Workers extended into the hundreds of thousands, the danger of it becoming more of a business and less of a family was also one of which Mother Teresa was aware. By 1979 there were some 800,000 Co-Workers scattered over five continents. In that year 2,194 bales of provisions were shipped from Great Britain alone. One million tablets of dapsone were dispatched monthly. So great a volume of material could not be handled without some degree of organization. Goods must be assembled at collecting centres, sorted, transported and deposited at the docks in such a condition that bales destined for India could be fumigated in accordance with trade stipulations. Accounts must be properly kept and audited, trade agreements must be scrutinized, and legal requirements must be met. The need for professional skills was apparently endless and the need for central co-ordination of all these skills was obvious.

Mother Teresa was nevertheless resolute that funds intended to alleviate suffering should not become absorbed by the supporting system. Even as she became increasingly internationally acclaimed, she continued to roll up her sleeves and scrub floors as required. Her work among the poor and the sick remained unaltered. Every hour absorbed by the demands of public life to which she allowed herself to be subjected for the sake of alerting the world to the needs of the poor, was in her heart of hearts resented because it diverted her from the works of love. This was the spirit with which she tried to imbue her Co-Workers. Over the years her insistence that the work must remain humble work and a work of love became more emphatic. In particular, she banned the fund-raising which had been recognized as necessary in the early days:

I want to make it very clear I do not want our Co-Workers to be involved in fund raising. It was necessary before for us to have Flag Days, Leper Days, Children's Days and all this. We had to do all this because nobody knew we existed but now the work has involved so many people that we just get – even in India where we never used to get anything before – we used to get about 20,000 rupees after working hours and hours – those who were in Calcutta they know how hard they had to work – now without even asking, without any difficulties we get quite a lot of money and help for the lepers. . . . Let us avoid publicity under that fund raising name because it has become like a target with other organizations and people are beginning to doubt, and so let us not give them a chance.

It was true that Mother Teresa's increasing fame attracted money from all kinds of sources. Each Christmas an anonymous donor would leave a wad of rupee notes in the crib outside a Roman Catholic Church in an English Cotswold town. Each year the donation increased by two hundred rupees, and each year the donor left clear instructions that it was to go to Mother Teresa in Calcutta. Who knew what acts of personal sacrifice made such gifts possible? Mother Teresa would tell the story of two young people who came to the mother house in Calcutta with a donation of sufficient money to feed a large number of hungry people:

We cook for many, many poor people and if we did not cook, maybe they would not eat. I asked the couple: "Where did you get so much money?"

and they said, "Two days ago we got married and before marriage we decided that we were not going to buy wedding clothes, we were not going to have a wedding feast. Instead we would give you the money to feed the poor." For me that was something extraordinary for Hindu high class people to do that, and it was a scandal in Calcutta but they said, "We love each other so much that we wanted to begin our life together by loving others, by making a sacrifice."

Mother Teresa was determined that money donated to the Missionaries of Charity was to be dealt with as effectively and simply as possible. Money sent to India could not be taken out of the country again. All finances not earmarked for India or specifically allocated to some other country were therefore dealt with in Rome. Only Mother Teresa could authorize the disposition of funds in these two places. Once the Sisters were established in a given country, Mother Teresa would usually withdraw all financial support. They were expected to become independent, responsible for their own upkeep and for works in their own neighbourhood. Only where self-sufficiency was impossible, as it would later prove to be in foundations opened in some of the poorer Eastern bloc countries, was support from the central funding sustained.

The Co-Workers' finances were handled similarly in India or Rome. They were, however, entitled to take some money out of the funds and to deposit it in a bank to earn interest for expenses only. The capital was then sent on. Even Mother Teresa was not exempt from external criminal elements. In January 1987 it was disclosed that cheques mailed to Mother Teresa in Calcutta and worth more than US $100,000 had been stolen from the post by thieves and cashed in Hong Kong, Singapore and other west Asian cities. "It is a terrible thing", Mother Teresa told the press in Calcutta. "Many of the senders are small children. They save and send with love to feed hungry children." For the same kind of reasons she made every effort to ensure that all money given actually went to the work.

Co-Workers had no offices and no paid help anywhere in the world. When it became cheaper to purchase ambulances in India than to buy them in England and ship them out, that was what was done. The newsletter, which began its life as a glossy pamphlet was reduced, at Mother Teresa's insistence, to typed sheets stapled together. Communication between Co-Workers was undertaken not on the official headed notepaper but on a motley selection of scraps of old paper and re-used envelopes guaranteed to baffle those unfamiliar with the system. "Collecting centres", despite the apparent grandeur of the name, generally consisted of a private garage, a vacant cellar, an unused corner of a church hall or simply someone's spare room. Transport took the form of any available means of locomotion which was cheap or free, including the backs of lorries driven by well-intentioned drivers heading for city markets or the docks.

Essential professional services were provided almost entirely by the miscellaneous talents of Co-Workers which meant, for example, that the Liverpool home for women could boast its own doctor, dentist and psychiatrist, all of whom, as Co-Workers, gave of their time and skills free of charge. The whole system, watched over by a series of links, operative at international, national and regional levels, and indeed by Mother Teresa herself, was to keep waste to an absolute minimum and to remain flexible in its openness to the particular needs of the moment. Items donated which were of no direct use to the Missionaries of Charity were passed on to others who could make better use of them. When special concessions were made for shipping between Belgium and South America, for example, the Belgian Co-Workers would assume a special concern for the requirements of the Missionaries of Charity in South America.

As funds became ever more readily available, Mother Teresa placed even greater emphasis on the Co-Workers' spiritual role, insisting that they were not to be Co-Workers of Mother Teresa but Co-Workers of Christ. The handwritten letters she sent them stressed the importance of finding time for the silence of the heart in which God spoke, for the deep spiritual life on which she had always seen the action as totally dependent. The call to a more prayerful role was not always easily understood and accepted by people more used to valuing "doing" rather than "being", and whose ideas of charity were inextricably interwoven with the active raising of money, but it was one on which Mother Teresa was uncompromising. The formation of the contemplative branches of the Missionaries of Charity was based on her continuing conviction that the work was simply not possible without prayer. So too was the desire she expressed in September 1974 to see each of her Congregation's houses "spiritually adopted" by one or more contemplative communities of other orders. Her hope was that these contemplative communities and enclosed Orders would by their prayers and their life of silence and renunciation uphold the Missionaries of Charity in their life of active service among the poorest of the poor. At her request, Father Georges Gorrée, chairman of the French Co-Workers, undertook the promotion of such a link and within a year approximately four hundred convents had accepted the idea of a form of spiritual "twinning" which entailed the special remembrance of their adopted convent of the Missionaries of Charity during their daily prayer and work.

By then another form of spiritual "twinning" was already well established. The same conviction of the need for spiritual support for the "active" work, combined with a belief in the particular potency of the prayers of the suffering, had given rise as early as 1952 to the Link for Sick and Suffering Co-Workers. It was an idea born out of a meeting in December 1948 with a Belgian woman who, like Mother Teresa, had come to India to devote her life to the poor. Jacqueline de Decker came from one of Antwerp's leading families. She was a graduate of the great Catholic university of Louvain, where she had specialized in sociology. She had also obtained a diploma in nursing and First Aid and, having felt since the age of seventeen that she had a vocation to serve India's poor, she had made plans with a group of like-minded lay people to use her skills in Madras.

Her first impulse had been to join the Missionary Sisters of Mary who also worked in India, but a brief stay in their convent in Belgium had convinced her that her vocation was to serve God in the world as a lay person. A tin of salmon opened in her honour had given her violent food poisoning and compelled her to leave after only one night. She took it as an intervention of Divine Providence. As it transpired, the war postponed her arrangements to sail to India. At a time when Antwerp was severely stricken and deserted by most of its doctors, Jacqueline de Decker remained to give invaluable medical assistance to the wounded, and displayed such

courage in helping the resistance movement that she was later decorated for her services. After the war, however, with the advice and
assistance of a Jesuit priest, Jacqueline finally left for India.

While Mother Teresa was still awaiting permission to leave the
Loreto Order, Jacqueline de Decker had already begun her work
among the poorest of the poor. The Jesuit priest who had urged
her to do medical social work in Madras died unexpectedly on 31
December 1946, the very day of Jacqueline's departure from Belgium. Consequently, when she arrived in India she found herself
with little financial and moral support. She was totally unprepared
for the poverty and suffering of the Indian people. Yet living alone
and on a pittance, she won the recognition and the affection of the
people with whom she worked. Jacqueline de Decker adopted the
Indian way of dressing and eating. She took her food sitting on
the floor and slept on the ground. She also made it clear that
she was prepared to help anyone in need, regardless of religious
commitment. There were times, however, when she was overwhelmed by a sense of isolation, and eventually a Jesuit priest in
Madras told her of Mother Teresa's plans for a life of service similar
to her own. She was advised to seek out Mother Teresa in Calcutta.
In fact Mother Teresa was in Patna undertaking her medical training course at the time, and so it was in the chapel at Patna that
Jacqueline de Decker finally found her, deep in prayer. Her first
sight of that kneeling figure was one which she would carry with
her for the remainder of her life.

Like Mother Teresa, Jacqueline would speak of an "inspiration
day" on which she received a second call from God. There is even
the suggestion that the calls heard by both women were identical
in their wording, but for Jacqueline de Decker also such experiences
were "hidden treasures". Her account of their first meeting would
be confined to a description of how they talked together and discovered that they "had the same ideal". Afterwards they worked
side by side in the hospital in Patna but then, at the end of
December 1948, Mother Teresa returned to Calcutta. Years later
Jacqueline de Decker would still have an address book for that
period in which she had entered the address from which all Mother
Teresa's first letters to her came: 14 Creek Lane.

Jacqueline de Decker's intention was to join Mother Teresa's new Congregation but her time in India had already revealed serious health problems. At the age of fifteen she had had a diving accident, and although at the time doctors had failed to identify the extent of the injury incurred, the heat and discomfort of India aggravated the problem. She needed to return to Antwerp for medical attention. In Belgium it was discovered that she was suffering from a severe disease of the spine and that in order to prevent paralysis she would have to undergo a number of operations. Gradually it became apparent that she would never be able to return to India, and that her total commitment to India's poor and diseased, and to what she had believed to be God's will for her, was not to be. The realization was initially a bitter one fraught with a sense of personal failure. The letter which came to her in the autumn of 1952, from the woman to whom she referred with affectionate disrespect as "just a little unknown nun", brought her renewed hope:

Today I am going to propose something to you. You have been longing to be a missionary. Why not become spiritually bound to our society which you love so dearly? While we work in the slums you share in the merit, the prayers and the work, with your suffering and prayers. The work here is tremendous and needs workers, it is true, but I need souls like yours to pray and suffer for the work – you'll be in body in Belgium but in soul in India where there are souls longing for our Lord, but for want of someone to pay the debt for them, they cannot move towards him. You'll be a true Missionary of Charity if you pay the debt while the Sisters – your Sisters – help them to come to God in body.

I need many people who suffer who would join us as I want to have (1) a glorious society in heaven, (2) the suffering society on earth – the spiritual children, and (3) the militant society, the Sisters on the battlefield. You can be in body in your country but a missionary in India, in the world. You must be happy, as you are chosen by the Lord who loves you so much that he gives you a part in his suffering. Be brave and cheerful and offer much that we may bring many souls to God. Once you come in touch with souls, the thirst grows daily.

Mother Teresa allocated to Jacqueline de Decker the task of offering joyfully a life of suffering and pain for her work, and in Belgium

Jacqueline undertook to become spiritually bound to the small Congregation in Calcutta. Even as she did so, however, the Missionaries of Charity were beginning to grow in number and Mother Teresa's vision of the Sick and Suffering as lives which would form "a burning light consumed for souls" grew accordingly.

In January 1953 she drafted the basis for the Link for Sick and Suffering Co-Workers:

I am very happy that you are willing to join the suffering members of the Missionaries of Charity – you see what I mean – you and others who will join will share in all our prayers, works and whatever we do for souls, and you do the same for us with your prayers and sufferings. You see the aim of our society is to satiate the thirst of Jesus on the cross for love of souls by working for the salvation and sanctification of the poor of the slums. Who could do this better than you and the others who suffer like you? Your suffering and prayers will be the chalice in which we the working members will pour in the love of souls we gather round. Therefore you are just as important and necessary for the fulfilment of our aim. To satiate this thirst we must have a chalice and you and the others – men, women, children – old and young – poor and rich – are all welcome to make the chalice.

In reality you can do much more while on your bed of pain than I running on my feet, but you and I together can do all things in him who strengthens me.

There will be no vows unless some get permission from their confessor to do so. We could get a few prayers we say, for you to say them also, so as to increase the family spirit, but one thing we must have in common – the spirit of our Society. Total surrender to God, loving trust and perfect cheerfulness – by this you will be known as a Missionary of Charity. Everyone and anyone who wishes to become a Missionary of Charity – a carrier of God's love – is welcome but I want especially the paralysed, the crippled, the incurables to join for I know they will bring to the feet of Jesus many souls. In our turn – the Sisters will each one have a Sister who prays, suffers, thinks, unites to her and so on – a second self. You see, my dear Sister, our work is a most difficult one. If you are with us – praying and suffering for us and the work – we shall be able to do great things for love of him – because of you.

Personally I feel very happy and a new strength has come in my soul at the thought of you and others doing the work with us, what would we not do, what can't we do for Him?

It was a letter written to a friend who Mother Teresa knew would understand her vision and the manner in which it was expressed, by one who, frequently blessed with certainties as she was, manifestly harboured no doubts that there would be others who would fulfil the kind of role she proposed. Mother Teresa herself was in fact linked not only to Jacqueline but also to two people in India: one a young girl called Agnes who was dying of tuberculosis in Patna but who "talked only of souls"; the other a boy named Nicholas who was crippled for life and unable to move. Nicholas's parents were very poor and he lived on the brink of starvation. "And yet", wrote Mother Teresa to Jacqueline, "the only time he weeps bitterly is when I do not visit him for a long time." It was on the strength of the prayers and offerings of these three that she professed to have survived some of the most arduous times of her life, at first alone and then with a handful of Sisters in the Calcutta streets. "Our Lord must have a good laugh", she confided, "when I attack him with the sacrifices of the three of you for souls. That is how I have been conquering his heart lately, so you see what power you have with God now as Missionaries of Charity."

*

The first ten Sisters were to be professed on 12 April 1953. They too would need the support of people who had a special "power with God". Recovering from one of a long succession of operations she would have to undergo, Jacqueline de Decker sought among her fellow patients and sufferers for those who would be prepared to pray for an adopted Sister, to write to her once or twice a year and, above all, to accept from the heart the mystery of suffering offered in faith and love for the work of a virtual stranger in a far distant land. Mother Teresa challenged them to see in the suffering that was more often an obstacle to faith, not meaninglessness and grounds for horror, but rather "a beautiful vocation". In a letter dated October 1954 she wrote:

What a beautiful vocation is yours – A Missionary of Charity – a carrier of God's love – we carry in our body and soul the love of an infinite thirsty God – and we – you and I and all the dear Sisters and the Sick and Suffering will satiate the burning thirst – you with your untold suffering, we with hard labour, but are we not all the same one – "as your Father in me and I in you", said Jesus.

By 1955 there were already forty-eight Missionary Sisters of Charity. There were also forty-eight Sick and Suffering links prepared to offer their pains for a "second self". Over the years Mother Teresa's message to Jacqueline de Decker and to all the other suffering links became no less fervent:

We the Missionaries of Charity, how grateful we must be – you to suffer and we to work. We finish in each other what is wanting in Christ. What a beautiful vocation is ours to be the carriers of Christ's love in the slums – your life of sacrifice is the chalice or rather our vows are the chalice and your sufferings and our work are the wine – the spotless host. We stand together holding the same chalice and so with the adoring angels satiate his burning thirst for souls.

My very dear children, let us love Jesus with our whole heart and soul. Let us bring him many souls. Keep smiling. Smile at Jesus in your suffering – for to be a real Missionary of Charity you must be a cheerful victim. There is nothing special for you to do but to allow Jesus to live his life in you by accepting whatever he gives and giving whatever he takes with a big smile.

There could be few who had touched and known the suffering of the world as Mother Teresa had. She knew the suffering of chronic disease, broken bodies and starvation, and the suffering of niggling aches and unshared sorrows, the suffering that arose from solitude or simply from the knowledge that all things in time must crumble and pass away. She knew the difficulty of acceptance and what it was she was really asking when she called upon the suffering to smile; but she had also witnessed a courage which far exceeded endurance, a joy which transcended pain and the manner in which suffering could be the medicine which deepened people's humanity. And she saw in all this the daily and universal repetition of a great redemptive passion. Deep in the hearts and bodies of humanity, to her Christ was actual and real, and for those prepared to perceive this reality suffering need be neither senseless nor solitary.

Fundamental to any understanding of the Link for Sick and Suffering Co-workers was an appreciation of the fact that it did not mean a desperate craving after healing but rather the constructive use of suffering. To Mother Teresa suffering was an essential part of the Christian way. "The following of Christ is inseparable from the cross of Calvary. Without our suffering, our work would just be social work, very good and helpful, but it would not be the work of Jesus Christ." "Suffering is not of God", she acknowledged. A sense of healing mission was central to Christ's understanding of himself and of the work that his disciples were to perform, but God, she believed, could be at work in the delays, no less than in the moment of release from sickness.

"Suffering in itself is nothing; but suffering shared with Christ's passion is a wonderful gift. Man's most beautiful gift is that he can share in the passion of Christ." "Suffering, if it is accepted together, borne together, is joy" – Mother Teresa's emphasis on suffering as a joy, a gift and a beautiful vocation could perhaps only be evaluated in the context of her daily encounter with the enormity of this world's suffering, of her understanding of human need and her belief in the mystery of Christ's passion. There were times when some found the language unpalatable. Her suggestion that suffering was "Jesus kissing you" provoked on one occasion the swift rejoinder, "Then would you please tell him to stop." But she was endeavouring to give voice to something which was rationally inexplicable though deeply rooted in her experience.

"Pope John XXIII, speaking on suffering, stressed the need to find a purpose in it. In the love of Christ there is no life without suffering", wrote one of the Missionary of Charity Brothers. "So we cannot escape it and we must do all we can to help one another find a purpose in it. If we can find a purpose for accepting his cross as Jesus Christ accepted his own then one will never feel alone." At its most fundamental the Link for Sick and Suffering Co-Workers achieved this end. An increasing number of suffering people were given a sense of purpose, and the Sisters and Brothers to whom they were linked found new strength and companionship in the knowledge that someone was praying specifically for them. Mother Teresa with almost pragmatic efficiency had brought together two perceived needs: the need for a kind of power house of prayer on the part of her Missionaries of Charity; and the need of the sick and suffering to find a meaning to their existence. Over and above this, however, many of the Sick and Suffering links became living witnesses to Mother Teresa's conviction that suffering could draw people closer to God. The letters of the Sick and Suffering bore such eloquent witness to her belief that "suffering begets life in the soul" that in 1983 Mother Teresa would take the unusual step of actually suggesting that they should be published. The reason she gave was less uncharacteristic: "It will help many people to love Jesus more."

In seeking an image to convey the interaction and interdependence at both the spiritual and the physical level of the Missionaries of Charity, the contemplative branches and the Co-Workers, Mother Teresa had recourse to the vision of the suffering Christ present in the world, which was so constantly with her. Speaking of the relationship between the Missionaries of Charity and the Co-Workers, before the foundation of the Missionary Fathers, she once told Ann Blaikie that they now had the five wounds of the crucified Jesus. The Contemplative Sisters were the wound in the right hand. The Contemplative Brothers were the wound in the left hand. The Missionary of Charity Sisters – the right foot; the Brothers – the left foot; and the Co-Workers – the heart. The contemplatives she saw as the hands because they joined in prayer. The active Missionaries of Charity were the feet because they went all over the world, and the Co-Workers were the heart because the heart of the world was the home and that was where the Co-Workers were.

The imagery is more or less meaningful according to individual taste and conviction; what must stand as the final recommendation of this corporate mission to the world at large was the fact that it worked, and it did so despite being made up of individuals susceptible to every human frailty. Among its members there were undoubtedly "hidden, unknown saints", but not all those committed to the shared task of "doing something beautiful for God" were spontaneously spiritual giants. The Co-Workers were perhaps more obviously than any other component part of the combined mission Everyman with his talents, his failings and his foibles, facing a challenge to sanctity in an ordinary world where the gods presenting themselves for worship were manifold and not always those of love. The Missionaries of Charity themselves, however, included simple, uneducated souls. It was not on the whole a Congregation which attracted intellectuals with complicated minds. Sometimes the Sisters' understanding of the spirituality for which Mother Teresa stood was limited, and sometimes they found themselves working in areas where they could receive little spiritual guidance in a way which cast yet another dimension on their commitment to poverty. There was always room for improvement, for growth in love and fidelity, and Mother Teresa did not shy away from promoting that growth where necessary. While the Congregation was still young and nearly all of the houses were made up for the most part of junior Sisters, Mother Teresa called those who were about to renew their vows to a strict examination of their religious life and service to the poor:

In many of our communities there is so much unhappiness and hurt created by you Sisters. If you were at home or in the world you would not dare to act this way. You would have to be very careful out of fear, lest you lose your job – or if you hoped to be married, nobody would marry you. You have just been professed and immediately you start with your health. I cannot eat – I cannot work – I cannot walk – I have a backache. These are some of the most common diseases of our young Sisters. Some of you do so little work that if you were to be paid, you would get nothing, and you have a vow to give wholehearted free service. Some of you have got into such a bad habit of answering back and creating disturbance in the community with the hope of being changed – so you go from community to community, as the young Superiors cannot control you. Many of you have cut down on your regular food, and are not ashamed to eat out of time in the houses you visit or in Shishu Bhavan or Nirmal Hriday – when people are actually dying of hunger. And yet Mother can work till all hours of the night, travelling by night and working by day. Is this not a humiliation for you that I at my age can take a regular meal and do a full day's work – and you live with the name of being poor but enjoy a lazy life.

If her Sisters did not want to strive for the goal of perfection she held constantly before them, Mother Teresa would gladly give them permission to go rather than have them remain as "handicapped religious" disturbing others who really wanted to live the life of a Missionary of Charity. She took her role as Mother to her young Sisters seriously, both from the spiritual point of view and from the point of view of their general and practical development. She even wrote to their parents asking that they pray for her that she might be able to help their children to become great saints. In time her approach would mellow a little, but even in the days when the requirement for strict formation was very much part of the process of passing on the "flame", her reprimands were always tempered with assurances that she did not call them to task in order to discourage them, and with statements of "Mother's" love:

for Mother loves you, as I love Jesus. Therefore I want you to be Christlike.

The whole, it seemed, was so much greater than the combined sum of its component parts and the achievements were unquestionably extraordinary. "In spite of all our defects," Mother Teresa would say, "God is in love with us and keeps using you and me to light the light of love in the world." The twenty-fifth anniversary of the erection of the Congregation of the Missionaries of Charity was marked on 7th October 1975, and there was much cause for celebration. As the silver jubilee of the Society approached Mother Teresa gave detailed instructions to Sisters and Co-Workers alike as to what should and should not be done to mark the occasion. On 7 October itself they were to "have a High Mass of thanksgiving and invite all our benefactors and our poor to join with us to say thank you to God for all he has done for us and for our Society these twenty-five years – through the intercession of the Immaculate Heart of Mary." What they were not to do was fund-raise in the name of the Jubilee, or spend money, "not one paisa". Nor were they to celebrate by holding concerts or giving speeches. There was to be no printing of brochures, pamphlets, photographs or pictures.

On 10 September 1975 she wrote a letter of appreciation to all those who had made the achievements of twenty-five years possible, beginning with a special word to the very first Sisters to join her in the upper room at Creek Lane:

After God and our Lady, Mother wants to thank each one of you for your constant fidelity and loyalty – especially for the blind trust with which you followed, without knowing if the Society will live or die. There was nothing to guarantee the future. All these years of hard labour with so much joy, all these years of love and service to the Poorest of the Poor – and it is with you all and through you all that Jesus laid the foundation of the Society on solid rock – humility and love.

She went on to address the others who had followed:

All you others: eleven hundred who have followed so generously in the footsteps of the first group – God love you and keep you to the end of your life, deeply rooted in his Heart.

All those loved Sisters who have spent a good part of their lives in the Society and for some reason had to leave – to each one of them God love you for the love you have given, for the work you have done with so much love, for the joy you have spread.

Also thanks for our Sisters, who, after finishing their work on earth, were taken home to Heaven to intercede for us.

She also thanked the Councillors, elected to share with her the internal authority of the Congregation, "who with so much fidelity and blind obedience have served the Society in spite of times when it was difficult to obey." She expressed her gratitude to the novice mistresses, postulant, aspirant and tertian mistresses who spent long hours teaching and instilling into the hearts of the Sisters the true spirit, and to the young Superiors who bravely bore the burden of the Society despite their age and inexperience.

She concluded:

During these twenty-five years, times have been joyful and hard. We have together worked for Jesus and with Jesus, always with Mary, the cause of our Joy by our side. Let us thank God for all gifts and promise we will make our Society something beautiful for God.

The Silver Jubilee celebrations went on for a month. Scattered throughout the world, over eleven hundred Sisters in some eighty houses of the Congregation joined in thanksgiving with the Co-Workers, the Sick and Suffering, the Brothers and those who offered their lives of contemplation in the seclusion of cloistered monasteries. In Calcutta, people who had travelled from five continents to assemble beneath the inscription "I thirst" in the chapel at Lower Circular Road joined in a Thanksgiving Mass attended by the Archbishop of Calcutta and the Governor of West Bengal. This was only one of a series of thanksgiving services which began on 28 September with worship in the American Holy Church of Nazareth and included services in the Methodist Church, the Catholic Church of the Most Holy Rosary, the Anglican Cathedral of St Paul's and the Mar Thomas Syrian Church. Prayers were offered with the Muslims, the Sikhs, the Parsis and the Jains. At the conclusion of a service held in the Buddhist temple, the head monk of the Mahabodhi Society presented Mother Teresa with two electric candles symbolizing her work, which he said would burn for ever. At the Assembly of God Church a packed congregation clapped and sang lustily beneath a banner bearing the words: "MC – 25 years – Christ's love lives on", and in the Jewish synagogue Mother Teresa was afforded the singular privilege of entering the "Holy of Holies". Mother Teresa looked on all the prayers that were offered throughout the world as "the best gift to God". What she saw as "another thing that is very wonderful" was the "way in which different religious bodies have accepted to have the prayer of thanksgiving with their people in their own places in Calcutta." Twenty-five years after the first handful of Missionaries of Charity had begun their life together in Michael Gomez's "upper room" the works of love being implemented across the continents had earned the acclaim of people of all world views. As Barbara Ward (Lady Jackson), a member of Britain's Pontifical Justice and Peace Commission, would conclude in her nomination of Mother Teresa for the Nobel Peace Prize: "In a world full of still bitter sectarian divisions, Mother Teresa has at least found one of the possible routes of reconciliation."

CHAPTER SEVEN

The Gift of Recognition

In the historic struggle between Galileo and the Church, Mother Teresa would have taken the side of the Church, the side of obedient faith against radical progress based on rational evidence. I once walked with her through the splendid corridors of the Vatican on our way to an audience with Pope John Paul II. For me, even with my relatively limited experience of the slums and the needs of the poor of the world, the experience raised many questions, obvious questions about the distribution of wealth and the churches' role in relation to the poor, questions which could perhaps be answered and dismissed but which were none the less very present. I looked at Mother Teresa as she made her way through the priceless assembly of paintings, sculptures and art objects, her rough sandals squeaking on the highly polished floors, and her mind appeared not to be troubled by the least interrogation. She seemed as at home in those corridors of beauty, power and wealth as she was in the bustees of Calcutta. Afterwards I discovered that she too had at one time not been so immune to the kind of questions which pursued me through what some regarded as the world's most spectacular museum. Her love of the poor might have brought her into conflict with the rich and the powerful, but then she had seen the poverty of the rich and the wealth of the poor, and the value of bringing rich and poor together. She did not condemn those who had many things. They were rich for a purpose. And if at times she was given to telling bishops that she would like to bring her poor into the splendour of their palaces, it did not make her any the less a faithful daughter of the Church. When she looked at the Vatican she saw the dedication and the faith that had gone into the creations of Michelangelo, Bernini, Fra Angelico, Leonardo da Vinci and countless others; and when she looked at the Pope she saw always the Vicar of Christ.

Her fidelity did not go unrecognized. At the end of June 1975 Mother Teresa was chosen as one of an eight-member delegation sent by the Holy See to the United Nations-sponsored World Conference of the International Women's Year, held in Mexico City. "Because the Church is everything to me and to you," she told her Sisters, "I have accepted to be sent to witness Christ's love for his poor in the name of the Church. So I will be away for about three weeks. I know that you will be praying for me and for one another that we do always what God and the Church expect." Speaking at the conference Mother Teresa emphasized the role of women in establishing world peace. "Love begins at home", she insisted. "If a woman fulfils her role in the home, if there is peace in her surroundings, there will be peace in the world. There is the part of a woman that no man can take – the power of producing, the power of love. . . . The greatness of women lies in their loving others, not themselves." She spoke of her experience in Calcutta and of the unknown, unwanted and unloved women of the streets. She appealed to the conference to realize that "the love of the unknown woman upholds the world".

Increasingly Mother Teresa was invited to take part in church congresses and other inter-church gatherings. The views she expressed on such occasions were in complete conformity with the traditional teachings of the Roman Catholic Church she represented, but she also had a way of cutting through the niceties of conventional expectation to speak very simply and sometimes outspokenly of the real needs she had encountered through firsthand experience. In 1976, as part of the Bicentennial Year celebrations of the founding of the United States, the Roman Catholic community decided to a hold a Congress on the theme of the Eucharist. Mother Teresa, who had been invited to Philadelphia to take part in it, turned potential theological abstractions into concrete experience. For her the Stations of the Cross were a living reality and she was eager that others should make the connection between Gospel teaching and the suffering of the world:

Today, in young people of the world, Jesus lives his Passion, in the suffering, in the hungry, the handicapped young people – in that child who eats a piece of bread crumb by crumb, because when that piece of bread is finished, there will be no more and hunger will come again. That is a station of the cross.

Indeed, the world was so full of such suffering, of hatred and disharmony that there was certainly no room for disunity between Christians. Mother Teresa believed in Christian unity also because she believed that it was important that Christians should stand as a light for the world. Gandhi, she was fond of pointing out, had once said that if Christians lived their Christian life to the full there would be no more Hindus left in India. Christians should be Christlike. They should be recognizable by the fact that they loved one another. She was in full accord with the vision of reconciliation which in 1940 had inspired Roger Schutz, the son of a Swiss Protestant pastor, to found the ecumenical community at Taizé in France. At a time when Europe was torn asunder, the man who was to become Brother Roger had asked himself why such conflict should exist between people in general but particularly between Christians. He had established a community in which members of different Christian denominations would live together what he called a "parable of communion".

In the autumn of 1976 Mother Teresa visited Taizé, and, despite the fact that she spoke no French and Brother Roger spoke very little English, they found a mutual understanding based on common compassion and commitment. It was the kind of understanding which, according to Brother Roger, worked best when they were alone together. "In many respects they are very different," commented one of his Brothers, "but there is between them an indefinable something which operates at the level of the heart." Together during that visit Mother Teresa and the Prior of Taizé composed a prayer:

> *Oh God, the father of all,*
> *You ask every one of us to spread*
> *Love where the poor are humiliated,*
> *Joy where the Church is brought low,*

And reconciliation where people are divided . . .
Father against son, mother against daughter,
Husband against wife,
Believers against those who cannot believe,
Christians against their unloved fellow Christians.

You open this way for us, so that the wounded body of Jesus Christ, your Church, may be leaven of Communion for the poor of the earth and in the whole human family.

In that same year Brother Roger and a number of other Taizé Brothers spent a period of time in the slums of Calcutta, living in a hovel and sharing the life of the poorest of the poor near where Mother Teresa had first begun her work. Brother Roger remembered with obvious affection how Mother Teresa undertook all the necessary organization. She arranged for them to receive the reserved sacrament and provided the wooden tabernacle in which it could be kept in their slum house. In the morning she joined them for prayer. She also extracted a promise from the Prior of Taizé that in Calcutta he would wear his white habit all the time, as a visible witness to the love of God in the world. Normally the Brothers did not wear their robes when working, but in Calcutta Brother Roger agreed to wear his habit everywhere. In return Mother Teresa took his measurements for a lightweight robe and stitched at least part of it herself.

"We are both of us challenged", they wrote together, *"by the suffering of the modern world. Confronted with all that wounds humanity, we find the division between Christians unbearable. Are we ready to set aside our separations, freeing ourselves from our fear of one another? When people differ, what use is there in trying to find who was right or wrong?"*

In Mother Teresa the desire for unity, the outreaching of the heart did not express itself in any non-conformity to orthodox Roman Catholicism at the level of worship and church practice. For all her other expressions of solidarity with the Indian culture, the form of worship used by the Missionary of Charity Sisters remained very

Western by comparison with some others in India who sought to express Christianity in terms which would make it more accessible to the local people. In an ashram in the south of India, on the banks of the sacred Cauvery River, Dom Bede Griffiths, an English Benedictine monk, had adopted the life of a sannyasi. In the temple there, Christian worship was expressed in forms and symbols meaningful to the Indian culture and potentially enriching to Christianity itself. The ashram had become a centre of prayer and meditation to many who sought the universal and eternal truth at the heart of all religions. Mother Teresa sometimes sent her Sisters there for brief retreats. I once chanced upon a group of them, after a Christian service in which, as in Hindu temples throughout India, the worshippers had marked their foreheads with sandalwood paste. Sandalwood, a very precious wood which spreads its fragrance even when cut with an axe, had been used to signify the grace of God. The Sisters were at first, at least, taken aback, even confused, for it was not Mother Teresa's way to use the symbolism of Hinduism to express the Christian message.

Yet her orthodoxy and her insistence on disciplined adherence to the "rules" coexisted with an emphasis on the primacy of love and the assertion that religion was a matter for individual conscience. "My religion is everything to me, but for every individual according to the grace God has given to that soul." Her comment to one journalist seemed to summarize her attitude: "God has his own ways and means to work in the hearts of men and we do not know how close they are to him, but by their actions we will always know whether they are at his disposal or not."

In 1978 a bill entitled, with shades of Orwellian "doublespeak", "the Freedom of Religion Bill" was proposed in the Indian parliament. Its ostensible aim was to prevent conversions to Christianity by "force, fraud, inducement or allurement". These terms were so loosely applied, however, that Christian worship and usual church activity might well be taken as contraventions of the law. The suggestion of divine displeasure alone was tantamount to "force" while "inducement" included the hope of salvation. This bill formed part of a government campaign to discourage the activities of foreign missionaries. Already no foreign missionaries were permitted in tribal areas along the north-eastern border such as Nagaland or Arunachal Pradesh, and many had been expelled or refused extension of their stay in India. As far as India's fifteen million Christians were concerned, the bill was an attempt to put the stamp of respectability on discriminatory legislation already enacted in Arunachal Pradesh. It provoked a strong reaction from church leaders. In such circumstances Mother Teresa did not hesitate to use the influence that increasing recognition was giving her. She wrote an open letter to the elderly Prime Minister, Morarji Desai:

Dear Mr Desai and Members of our Parliament

After much prayer and sacrifices I write to you, asking you to face God in prayer, before you take the step which will destroy the joy and the freedom of our people.

Our people, as you know better than I – are God-fearing people. In whatever way you approach them, that presence of God – the fear of God, is there. Today all over the country everybody feels insecure because the very life of freedom of conscience is being touched. Religion is not something that you and I can touch. Religion is the worship of God – therefore, a matter of conscience. I alone must decide for myself and you for yourself, what we choose. For me the religion I live and use to worship God is the Catholic religion. For me this is my very life, my joy and the greatest gift of God in his love for me. He could have given me no greater gift.

I love my people very much, more than myself, and so naturally I would wish to give them the joy of possessing this treasure, but it is not mine to give, nor can I force it on anyone. So also no man, no law, no Government has the right to prevent me or force me, or any one, if I choose to embrace the religion that gives me peace, joy, love.

I was told that Gandhiji had said: "If the Christians would live their lives according to the teaching of Jesus Christ there would be no more Hindus left in India." You cannot give what you do not have.

This new move that is being brought before Parliament under the cover of freedom of religion, is false. There is no freedom if a person is not free to choose according to his or her conscience. Our people in Arunachal are so disturbed. All these years our people have lived together in peace. Now religion is used as a deadly weapon to destroy the love they had for each other, just because some are Christians, some Hindus, some Tribals. Are you not afraid of God?

You call him ISHWAR, some call him ALLAH, some simply God, but

*we all have to acknowledge that it is he who made us for greater things:
to love and to be loved. Who are we to prevent our people from finding
this God who has made them – who loves them – to whom they have to
return?*

*You took over your sacred duty in the name of God – acknowledge
God's supreme right over your country and her people. It was so beautiful.
But now I am afraid for you. I am afraid for our people. Abortion being
allowed, has brought so much hatred – for if a mother can murder her
own child, what is left for others to kill each other? You do not know what
abortion has done and is doing to our people. There is so much more
immorality, so many broken homes, so much mental disturbance because
of the murder of the innocent unborn child. You don't know how much
evil is spreading everywhere.*

*Mr Desai, you are so close to meeting God face to face. I wonder what
answer you will give for allowing the destruction of the life of the innocent
unborn children and destroying the freedom to serve God, according to
one's choice and belief. At the hour of death, I believe we will be judged
according to the words of Jesus who has said:*

> *I was hungry, you gave me food*
> *I was thirsty, you gave me to drink*
> *I was homeless, you took me in*
> *I was naked, you clothed me*
> *I was sick, you took care of me*
> *I was in prison, you visited me*
> *truly I say to you, for as much as you did it to these the least of my
> brothers, you did it to me.*

*Gandhiji has also said: "He who serves the poor serves God." I spend
hours and hours in serving the sick and the dying, the unwanted, the
unloved, the lepers, the mental – because I love God and I believe his
word: "You did it to me." . . .*

*Mr Desai and Members of Parliament, in the name of God, do not
destroy the freedom our country and people have had to serve and love
God according to their conscience and belief.*

Mother Teresa went on to urge Mr Desai not to "belittle our
Hindu religion by saying that our Hindu poor people give up their

religion for a plate of rice", and to cite a few very practical examples of ways in which she had "made it a rule to co-operate with the central and state government". The letter was characteristic in many ways: in its close identification with the Indian people, in its courageous determination, in its directness of approach which had no reservations about reminding the Indian Prime Minister that he would soon be meeting his maker, in the views it expressed on the life of the unborn child, its emphasis on religion as a matter of individual conscience and in its personal commitment to Roman Catholicism in the context of a tolerant understanding.

To this tolerant understanding many people in India had manifestly responded. The national link for the Co-Workers in India was a Hindu. Indeed, the work of the Missionaries of Charity had attracted a number of Hindus to such a point that steps were taken towards the creation of a Hindu Order of "nuns" who would lead the same life as the Missionaries of Charity based on similar vows. In the Indian culture, as one Indian Sister pointed out, if you were religious you looked above all for a person of prayer. Mother Teresa was such a person and there was much about the life of the Missionaries of Charity with which Hindus could readily identify. A search was instigated for ways of expressing the basis of the Missionaries of Charity in Hindu terms. Hinduism had the concept of chastity and renunciation of the world in Brahmachari. It also had the concept of Dardran Narayan meaning "God in the poor", by which the offering of any service to the poor was a service to God. Gandhiji, as Mother Teresa knew well, used to say that he who served and loved the poor, served and loved God. The primary obstacle to young Indian girls becoming Hindu Missionaries of Charity proved to be a very practical one: the fact that the life would offer no security and require a separation from their families. The Missionaries of Charity had no providence fund or pocket money, no means by which they could support their relatives. The idea of Hindu Sisters had never been totally rejected but the fact that there were also a number of Indian monasteries in Calcutta which offered a very similar way of life had also worked against it. Young Muslim women had also expressed an interest but in their case, family opposition was invariably too strong.

Mother Teresa was non-discursive by nature. Her spirituality was not a question of thinking, reasoning and logic, but of transcending rational thought. She did not come to know God through clear images and careful argument nor with the eyes of the body, but with that intuitive inner eye which concerns itself with the ultimate truth. It was possible for some to find in her spirituality elements of both Buddhist and Hindu mysticism, to detect for example in her desire for continual "oneness with Christ" the path which the Buddhist mystic treads towards "nirvana", the realm of enlightenment where he becomes one with the One; to find in Mother Teresa's self-detachment – the process of emptying herself of self – a parallel with the Buddhist "samadhi" with its emphasis on silence, emptiness, the void and the cessation of desire. In a sense, however, such an exercise was unnecessary, for if the mystical element may be said to have entered into religious experience, where religious feeling transcends its rational content, when the hidden, non-rational unconscious elements prevail and determine the emotional life and the intellectual attitude, then it had entered into the experience of Mother Teresa, and at the level of the mystical it is arguable that barriers which exist at the intellectual, rational and emotional level necessarily diminish in importance.

Certainly it seemed that there was in Mother Teresa something which people of a wide variety of faiths could value and to which they could respond. Christians referred to her as a saint. Some more accustomed to the Hindu mode of thinking chose to see in her the "reincarnation of Jesus", Muslims acclaimed her as an "evolved spirit", and people of all religious beliefs and denominations were prepared to recognize her as a "holy person". In the words of India's President Giri, Mother Teresa was "among those emancipated souls who have transcended all barriers of race, religion, creed and nation". The very existence of the extended family of the Co-Workers, compiled as it was of men, women and children of all creeds, colours and castes was powerful evidence of this fact.

The coexistence of Mother Teresa's insistence on disciplined adherence to Roman Catholic orthodoxy with the idea of religion as a matter for individual conscience might seem as uneasy and even contradictory as that of her public protestations of tolerance with the desire she constantly expressed in private to satiate the thirst of Christ for souls. They found a mysterious harmony at the level of the non-rational and the hidden, and at the level of action. Asked once for his impressions of Mother Teresa, the Muslim President of India, Dr Zakir Husain, chose to recount how Mother Teresa had picked up the abandoned children and the dying in Calcutta. He told the story of how Hindu fanatics had wanted to turn her out of the pilgrims' rest home but had not been prepared to do what she and her Sisters were doing for their own dying Hindus, let alone for suffering Muslims or Christians. He elected to conclude his answer with terminology more readily associated with Christianity: "In your lexicon I believe this woman is a saint." Dr Zakir chose to answer with a concrete example of what the Missionaries of Charity had done. Actions were, according to Mother Teresa, the evidence of faith. It was in actions, not words, that faith was at its most universally articulate. Actions, like love, spoke even to those who would not subscribe to any religious view.

Mother Teresa's actions became the focus of a growing interest on the part of the world's public and media. She was at first painfully uncomfortable in front of cameras, to such a point that she claimed that for every photograph taken of her a soul should be released from purgatory. Yet there was in her also the conviction that God's work should be known, and if that was the case, then with St Paul the world was entitled to ask, "How can it be known if it is not announced?" Coupled with this understanding there was her natural reluctance to hurt or disappoint by rejection. There was also the desire to co-operate with journalists and writers in an attempt to draw from them the fulfilment of the vocation she saw as theirs: namely, to write something beautiful for God.

Recognition expressed itself most tangibly in the form of numerous awards which came not only from the Church but from the international community at large. The 1962 Magsaysay Award for International Understanding, which had enabled Mother Teresa to buy the children's home in Agra, was only one of many prizes and honours which were bestowed on her over the years. Earlier that same year she had received the Padma Shri (Lotus diffusing radiance), India's second highest award, from the President of India, Dr Rajendra Prasad. When news of the President's intention reached her Mother Teresa consulted Archbishop Dyer: "Your Grace, as I am a nun, I suppose I should not travel to Delhi to receive the honour?" The Archbishop, however, directed her to go: "Mother, you will go to Delhi for the investiture ceremony. In bestowing this medal upon you the President certainly means to honour all our Sisters who spend themselves in works of charity all over the country." She went and received the longest applause of all from the distinguished gathering. Jawaharlal Nehru, who was present for the occasion, sought out the object of his continuing admiration to congratulate her in person. In January 1971 Pope Paul VI had once more demonstrated his support for Mother Teresa's work by presenting her with a cheque worth £10,000, given by the Vatican as the first Pope John XXIII Peace Prize. Mother Teresa accepted it "unworthily" and allocated it to the construction of a leper colony in Madhya Pradesh on land donated by the Indian government. On 15 October 1971 the Joseph P. Kennedy Jr Foundation presented her with an award in Washington. It took the form of a heavy glass vase engraved with a figure of St Raphael and inscribed with the increasingly familiar words: "To Mother Teresa, whose struggles have shaped something beautiful for God."

In November of the following year it was once more the turn of the Indian government, this time to give her the Nehru Award for international understanding. The citation said that she had rightly been called "one of the most impressive manifestations of charity throughout the world". It further stated that she had inspired a large number of devoted people all over the world to work with her in the service of the destitute, the uncared for and helpless members of society. In 1973 Mother Teresa became the first recipient of the Templeton Prize for Progress in Religion. She was chosen out of a total of two thousand nominations by a panel of judges representing the major religious traditions of the world, including Christianity, Judaism, Buddhism and Hinduism.

When, in 1974, the Prime Minister of the Yemen Arab Republic invited Mother Teresa to bring her Sisters to his country, he assured them of his personal protection and presented her with a "Sword of Honour". She accepted it as a token of good will but afterwards could not contain her sense of humour: "Imagine, a sword to me!" It was by no means the only somewhat unlikely tribute. "Would you consent to be our FAO Ceres? We would be moved if you

agreed", wrote Mr R. Lloyd of the Food and Agriculture Organization of the United Nations on 25 September 1973. To this Mother
Teresa replied in December: "Thank you for your kind letter.
Kindly forgive the delay. I have never heard before of FAO Ceres
Medals. I am grateful to you, to the British Medallist and everyone
at FAO for suggesting me to feature on your medal. I accept only
if it will be for the glory of God and the good of the poor. God
love you for all the love you have given to the people of the world
and in gratitude for the great work you have shared with our people,
my acceptance is a small token." So, in recognition of Mother
Teresa's "exemplary love and concern for the hungry and the poorest of the poor" the United Nations Food and Agriculture Organization struck its Ceres Medals in March 1975 with Mother Teresa
representing the Roman goddess of agriculture.

The traditional views on the role of women which Mother Teresa
had expressed at the International Women's Year Conference in
Mexico City in June 1975 were widely publicized in the United
States. They were well out of step with those expressed by many
others at the conference and in the world at large, who were seeking
a speedy and revolutionary change in the role of women. Yet they
appeared to do little to diminish her general popularity. Mother
Teresa was in fact awarded the Voice of America's International
Women's Year Pin for her work for the poor in India. Nominations
had poured in for her special mention on the Voice of America
Breakfast Show. On 23 October she became a recipient of one
of the first Albert Schweitzer International Prizes awarded at the
University of North Carolina, Wilmington. The very next day she
addressed a Spiritual Summit Conference in New York. She had
been selected to speak for Christianity as one of five spiritual leaders
representing the great religions of the world. Two days after that
she was honoured at the National Shrine of the Immaculate Con-
ception in Washington, when Cardinal O'Boyle, Chairman of the
Shrine's Committee, presented her with a monetary gift on behalf
of the thousands of visitors to the shrine.

On 2 November 1975 more than seven hundred people attended
a special ceremony at St Francis Xavier University in Antigonish,
Nova Scotia, at which the increasingly famous Missionary of
Charity Sister in a white sari with a blue border was awarded an

honorary Doctor of Laws degree. In his invitation to Mother Teresa to accept this honorary degree, the Rev. Malcolm Macdonnell, the President of the university, gave voice to his understanding that her life and dedication had little room or time for such worldly honours, "But it is that very realization that makes all of us very keen on having you visit us. Not only do we need the blessing of your presence but the teachers and all of us are as poor as the people to whom you are giving your life although our need and poverty are of a different kind. In every walk of life inspiration is needed and we are no exception."

In India on 3 March 1976 Mrs Indira Gandhi, in her capacity as chancellor of the Viswa Bharati University, conferred on Mother Teresa the establishment's highest honour, the Deshikottama (Doctor of Literature) scarf in recognition of her significant contribution to the cause of suffering humanity. "She is tiny to look at," Mrs Gandhi commented about the recipient, who had been flown in by helicopter for the occasion, "but there is nothing small about her."

June 1977 brought Mother Teresa an honorary Doctorate of Divinity from the University of Cambridge. There were those who could not fully appreciate the appropriateness of bestowing such an honour on a woman of limited academic achievement, but when she spoke in the University Church it was packed. People listened with a kind of breathless intensity as she spoke of love and compassion, and of the suffering and privation in the world, and of how, whoever and wherever they might be, it was within their power to help, with love and fellowship and, according to their means, material aid. Later that year members of the International Register of Chivalry and of the *Unione Cavaleria Cristiana Internazionale* met in Milan and Rome for the Italian ceremony of the presentation of prizes of the *Cavalieri dell'Umanita*. Mother Teresa found herself alongside astronaut Neil Armstrong as a newly appointed "Knight of Humanity".

So the list of honours and awards lengthened. In India the Missionaries of Charity had earned themselves a position of general respect. Whereas other Christians and foreigners undertaking work to relieve the suffering of the poor were accused of giving disproportionate emphasis to the problem of India's poverty, and experienced difficulties with the renewal of visas and other attempts at

THE GIFT OF RECOGNITION 163

obstruction, Mother Teresa was regarded by many as a national heroine. The Indian government granted her all kinds of visa privileges and customs exemptions. Innumerable concessions and marks of appreciation, such as free travel on Indian Railways, facilitated the progress of her work. Mother Teresa once asked the Government of India to let her serve as a stewardess on the Indian airline so that she could keep in touch with her various Missionary of Charity homes without using money that could otherwise be spent on the poor, but in 1973 Indira Gandhi gave her a free pass on Indian Airlines, thus depriving other prospective passengers of the services of an extremely unusual stewardess.

Mother Teresa herself maintained a certain ambivalence to the privileges and honours that were heaped upon her. She accepted them but did so with a profound sense of her own unworthiness, and an insistence that she did so only on behalf of the poor. The prizes were not for her. They were for "her people". Money was accepted because the poor of the world were so desperately in need of it, and she underwent the presentation ceremonies attached to honorary degrees because she realized that they gave her an opportunity to reach out to those who would not otherwise hear the message of the rejected. "I don't know why universities and colleges are conferring titles on me. I never know whether I should accept or not; it means nothing to me. But it gives me a chance to speak of Christ to people who otherwise may not hear of him." Her confidence in public speaking had grown along with the conviction that Archbishop Périer had been right in advising her to pass on to audiences weighed down by news of violence and despair a message of hope. Mother Teresa never set out to talk about her work or about the history of the Missionaries of Charity. Her aim was always to touch the hearts of those to whom she spoke with a spiritual message, to bring them the Good News. She never prepared a speech no matter how large or sophisticated the audience or "important" the occasion, other than with prayer. She once told Father Van Exem that prior to speaking she would go into the chapel and stay there for ten minutes, and then she knew exactly what to say. Afterwards, with academic scarves draped incongruously over her darned knitted cardigan, she would simply make the sign of the cross and start to speak about poverty, about the need for God and for the love of the neighbour people could see, without which, she maintained, it was impossible to love the God people could not see. Incidents from her work were told and retold to demonstrate a simple message. On the receipt of the Templeton Award Mother Teresa informed the large audience which included the Duke of Edinburgh:

In one of the places in Melbourne, I visited an old man, whom nobody ever knew that he existed, and I saw his room, in a terrible state, and I wanted to clean his house, his room, and he kept on saying "I'm all right". But I didn't say a word. In the end he allowed me. There in that room was a beautiful lamp which had been covered with dirt for many years. I asked him: "Why do you not light the lamp?" – "For whom?" he said. "No one comes for me, I don't need the lamp." And I asked him: "Will you light the lamp if the Sisters come to see you?" He said, "Yes, if I hear a human voice, I will do it." And the other day, he sent me word: "Tell my friend the light she has lighted in my life is still burning." This is the people that we must know. This is Jesus yesterday and today and tomorrow, and you and I must know who they are.

Her speech was always simple, sometimes ungrammatical, often repetitious, but it came straight from the heart. The great and the humble were treated alike for in Mother Teresa's eyes they were all children of God and worthy of respect. She did not compromise the rules of the Society for the sake of the grandeur of social occasions. Certain concessions relating to where the Sisters could eat had been made in 1967. They could eat when at meetings with other religious or in a parish when other religious ate, and in the houses of their parents and grandparents, but the general rule of not eating or drinking in individual houses still stood. It applied also to the plushest of occasions, even though Mother Teresa's rigour in applying it was sometimes misconstrued. Years later, in 1989, when three Missionary of Charity Sisters attended a lunch at which Princess Diana presented the Women of the World awards in London's Grosvenor House Hotel, they retired to a separate room to pray and drink water "out of respect for the poor". Princess Diana was reported by a Royal aide not to have been offended but the popular press tried to imply otherwise. When, at the reception for the Templeton Award the champagne was flowing liberally, Mother Teresa would as usual accept only water. The message was whispered down the line from her hosts to those at work in the kitchens that a glass of water was needed for Mother Teresa. Eventually it appeared – in a crystal glass on a silver tray but it was water none the less. Nor was there any adjustment of attitude or language in relation to social standing, any more than there was any compromise on the expression of her religious faith. Even the receipt in 1979 of what some regarded as the ultimate accolade, the Nobel Peace Prize, would prove no occasion for exception.

That was not the first year in which she had been nominated for the prize. Ever since interviewing Mother Teresa on television, Malcolm Muggeridge had been in some profound way impressed and touched by her. He had, not without a certain difficulty, persuaded her to subject herself to a BBC camera crew for the purpose of making a television programme about herself and her work. "Let us then", she had finally said, "use the occasion to do something beautiful for God." In the spring of 1969 he returned to the Calcutta he had known as a journalist in the nineteen-thirties. He had only five days in which to do the filming. Mother Teresa was nervous to the point of asking one of her Sisters to accompany her for moral support. The home for the dying was so dimly lit that it seemed impossible to film it. Nevertheless the film crew persevered, and when the film was finally processed the interior appeared to be bathed in a soft and beautiful light, while the outside shots were dim and confused. "The home was overflowing with love," Malcolm Muggeridge said, "and the love was luminous. God's invisible omnipresent love. A miracle." He called the film *Something Beautiful for God*, wrote a book using the same title, and became an active campaigner on behalf of Mother Teresa's work. He was also among those who lobbied support for her nomination for the Nobel Peace Prize. Those supporting her candidacy in 1972 included Mr Lester Pearson, the former Canadian Premier and earlier Nobel Peace Prize winner, Lady Jackson, a member of Britain's Pontifical Justice and Peace Commission, and members of the provincial curia of the Hospitaller Order of St John of God.

In response to this first nomination of Mother Teresa as a potential Nobel Prize candidate, word came back from Oslo asking for some elucidation of her work for peace. Had she stopped a war? Initiated peace negotiations? Organized pacifist demonstrations, or helped to abate the alleged population explosion? Drafting an answer fell to Malcolm Muggeridge: "I tried to explain how, by dedicating her life wholly to Christ, by seeing in every suffering soul her Saviour and treating them accordingly, by being, along with her Missionaries of Charity, a sort of power-house of love in the world, she was a counterforce to the power mania, cupidity and egotistic pursuits, out of which violence, individual and collective, in all its forms, comes."

Mother Teresa had spoken out for peace on a number of international platforms. On 18 October 1971 she had joined Jean Vanier, founder of the l'Arche communities for people with handicaps, to speak on the "Secret of Peace" in Toronto. She had spoken there, as she did elsewhere, about the peace which began with a loving word and a smile, but not everyone could make the connection between those small domestic gestures and an international peace-promoting role. In 1972 the Prize went elsewhere. It did again in 1975 when Shirley Williams, then Secretary of State for Consumer Protection in the British Government, and Maurice Strong, executive director of the United Nations Environment Program, Senator Edward Kennedy and Robert McNamara, head of the World Bank, added their support to a nomination which they hoped would be further strengthened by the fact that it was "International Women's Year". In fact when news of her nomination reached the press, letters of support poured in from the five continents in a manner which some thought may have made the Norwegian committee feel placed under undue pressure.

It was inevitable that Mother Teresa should come to hear of the lobbying on her behalf. "It will come only when Jesus thinks it is time", was her reaction. The Missionaries of Charity had none the less calculated that the prize money would provide the funds necessary to build two hundred houses for lepers, "so our people will have to do the praying". In 1977 Lady Jackson discreetly resubmitted her nomination of Mother Teresa. Only finally, on 17 October 1979, however, was the news announced that the £90,000 award was to go to the woman at whose hands "the most wretched have received compassion without condescension". Hordes of journalists invaded the mother house in Calcutta. "I am unworthy," the recipient said, "but thank God for this blessed gift for the poor." Plainly embarrassed by the whirring television cameras, she added firmly, "And now I'm going to hide somewhere." Her unwillingness to be unkind to any part of creation was put severely to the test. "Last night it was like vultures had descended", she confided next morning. Then she caught herself: "But even vultures can be beautiful."

On 8 December 1979 she stepped on to the tarmac of Oslo's international airport into a temperature of ten degrees below zero, accompanied by Sister Agnes and Sister Gertrude. The Nobel Committee had sent her two extra tickets and she had elected to take with her the two first to join the Congregation as "a mark of love and gratitude to all our Sisters of the first group for having the courage to join when there was nothing". They were offered heavy coats and fur-lined boots to protect them against the cold, but Mother Teresa politely refused them. It was only at the insistence of the Nuns of St Joseph, with whom the Sisters stayed while in Oslo, that the three Sisters from Calcutta agreed to wear woollen socks with their sandals. The usual celebratory banquet was cancelled at Mother Teresa's request. She said that she would rather the money was used for those who were really in need of a meal, and the £3,000 earmarked for it was duly added to the prize money, together with a further £36,000 raised by Norwegian young people.

Photographers and journalists pursued her from the moment she arrived in Oslo until the moment she left. It was a rigorous schedule which began as soon as she landed, with a reception held for her by the Indian Ambassador to Norway. Among the nearly one thousand guests awaiting her there were the Norwegian Foreign Minister, the Chief Justice and members of the royal household. Also awaiting her was an international press corps larger than she had ever previously had to confront. Questioned as to why she had decided to come to receive the Nobel Prize in person, she made the point which would become the leitmotiv of her public statements in Oslo. Mother Teresa was grateful for the gift that would provide housing for the homeless and for leper families, but she was especially grateful for the "gift of recognition of the poorest of the poor of the world". "I am myself unworthy of the prize. I do not want it personally. But by this award the Norwegian people have recognized the existence of the poor. It is on their behalf that I have come." On Sunday, 9 December, a morning service was held at St Olaf's Catholic Cathedral, an afternoon Mass was celebrated in the chapel of St Joseph's Institute, and in the evening there was an ecumenical service at the Domkirche, the Lutheran Cathedral in Oslo. Afterwards, as members of the congregation stepped out into the chill darkness of the Norwegian night, they were handed flaming torches to carry. A torchlight procession of several thousands made its way through the streets of Oslo to the Norwegian Mission Society where the Lutheran women's association had prepared a supper for five hundred people in the mission hall.

On 10 December 1979, in the presence of King Olaf V, Crown Prince Harald, Crown Princess Sonja, and numerous other dignitaries, Mother Teresa accepted the gold medal and the money, as she had accepted all other honours, "unworthily" but "gratefully in the name of the poor, the hungry, the sick and the lonely". Also present for the occasion were her brother Lazar and his daughter Aggi, Bishop Nikola Prela, the Albanian Vicar-General of Skopje, and a number of Co-Workers, including Mother Teresa's two "other selves" Ann Blaikie and Jacqueline de Decker.

Even in the Aula Magna of the University of Oslo, with the eyes of the world upon her, Mother Teresa did not deviate from her practice of speaking without notes. Before delivering a speech prepared only with the sign of the cross she called upon her audience to recite the Prayer of St Francis, and in the name of peace all those present – Roman Catholics, Lutherans, Anglicans, Greek Orthodox, Baptists, Methodists and those who had forgotten how to pray, joined in the words: "Lord, make me an instrument of thy peace that where there is hatred I may bring love." As Father Van Exem would afterwards comment: "Only Mother could have got away with it."

From the podium of the Great Hall, a figure in a simple cotton sari and sandals reminded her exalted audience that they had been created to live God's gift of peace. God had made himself man to proclaim the good news and that news was peace to men of good will. She went on to explain: "I feel the greatest destroyer of peace today is abortion, because it is a direct war, a direct killing, direct murder by the mother herself." She spoke of the poor as very great and wonderful people who needed not pity but understanding love. She spoke of the smiles she experienced on the faces of dying people, and of the four-year-old Hindu boy who had given up his sugar allowance for three days so that Mother Teresa's children could have it. She also told of how she had once been taken to an old people's home in Europe:

I saw that in that home they had everything, beautiful things, but everybody was looking towards the door. And I did not see a single one with a smile on their face. And I turned to the sister and I asked: "How is that? How is it that these people who have everything here, why are they all looking towards the door? Why are they not smiling?" And she said: "This is so nearly every day. They are expecting, they are hoping that a son or daughter will come to visit them. They are hurt because they are forgotten."

Finally Mother Teresa called upon the people of Norway to love, to share and to smile:

I think that this is something, that we must live life beautifully, we have Jesus with us and he loves us. If we could only remember that God loves us, and we have an opportunity to love others as he loves us, not in big things, but in small things with great love, then Norway becomes a nest of love.

The message relating to the life of the unborn child in particular was potentially an unpopular one in a country which had recently made state-financed abortions readily available. Mother Teresa made no compromise on her convictions for the occasion. At the informal reception that replaced the ceremonial banquet she took, as always, only a glass of water, but she had a smile for each one of the thousands she encountered. Those who knew well that such events numbered among Mother Teresa's greatest trials, so much so that she saw them as furthering her path to heaven, remarked upon her serenity throughout. As it transpired, the awarding of the Nobel Peace Prize to Mother Teresa proved to be one of the least controversial of those prizes. In the previous year the Nobel Prize for Peace had been given to Menachem Begin, the Prime Minister of Israel, and the Norwegians had been so concerned about possible attack from international terrorists that the ceremonies had had to be transferred to Oslo's ancient fortress. No such precautions had been necessary for Mother Teresa. Instead, the proceedings passed off without the slightest incident to mar the celebrations. The potentially unpopular message seemed to do little to detract from the popularity of the medium, perhaps because Mother Teresa lived the Christianity she talked about. She had been living it before she described it and before she became famous for it. The occasion spoke of many things, not least of how faith was indeed at its most articulate in action, of the achievements of those who aspire to nothing, and of the recognition that the works of love were the works of peace.

On Tuesday 11 December all the papers in Oslo carried pictures of Mother Teresa on their front pages. One Norwegian journalist wrote in *Aftenposten:* "How good it is to experience the world press for once spellbound by a real star, with a real glitter, a star without a wig, without a painted face, without false eyelashes, without a mink and without diamonds, without theatrical gestures and airs. Her only thought is how to use the Nobel Prize in the best possible way for the world's poorest of the poor."

From the moment she became "Mother Teresa, the Nobel Prize-winner", the attentions of the press were rarely to abandon "the saint of the gutters" altogether. If she had hoped to leave them behind in Oslo, she was to be disappointed, for India, despite opposition from some anti-Gandhian extremists, was waiting to show its appreciation of a national who had won international recognition.

Mother Teresa did not return directly to India. A request had come through from the families of American hostages held in Iran for her to intercede personally on their behalf and appeal for their release. Mother Teresa, by her own admission, knew little of the political complexities of the problem. The active demands of her life left her little time to read newspapers or hear the news, but she responded to an obvious human need by going to the Iranian Embassy in Rome and asking to speak to the Ayatollah either on the telephone or in Iran itself. The Iranian Embassy gave the new Nobel laureate no response at all.

As a token of India's appreciation, however, in February 1980 Mother Teresa became one of only three Indians ever to have been honoured with an official reception within the ramparts of Delhi's historic Red Fort. The other two recipients were Nehru and Indira Gandhi. The function was organized by a Hindu organization in recognition of her receipt of the Nobel Prize, and was attended by all the dignitaries of the capital: the Prime Minister, cabinet and government officials, diplomats and businessmen. After the usual felicitations and addresses, Mother Teresa rose to speak. She told the story of a leper who had rung the doorbell of the mother house a few days previously. Her tale was a clear indication of the perspective from which she viewed her international acclaim:

It was a leper shivering with cold. I asked him whether he needed anything from me. I wanted to offer him food and a blanket to protect himself from the bitter night of Calcutta.

He replied in the negative. He showed me his begging bowl. He told me in Bengali: "Mother, people were talking that you had received some prize. This morning I decided that whatever I got through begging today, I would hand over to you this evening. That is why I am here."

I found in the begging bowl 75 paise (2 pence). The gift was small. I keep it even today on my table because this tiny gift reveals to me the largeness of a human heart. It is beautiful.

The leper's small gift she kept on her table; the Nobel medal she had temporarily mislaid at the reception following the ceremony. After some searching it was found among the coats in the entrance hall.

There were to be numerous other honorary doctorates and awards. In the Rashtrapati Bhavan, the presidential palace in Delhi, the President of India, Neelam Sanjiva Reddy, gave her India's highest civilian award, the Bharat Ratna or "Jewel of India". Not least among the numerous other honours was the Gold Medal of the official Soviet Peace Committee, on the receipt of which Mother Teresa promptly said that she was keen to send her Sisters to the Soviet Union. On 20 June 1985 at the White House in Washington, President Reagan presented her with the United States' presidential Medal of Freedom, calling her a "heroine of our times". Ronald Reagan said that the award was usually given to US citizens "who've done our country proud" but that, as was demonstrated by Mother Teresa, "the goodness in some hearts transcends all borders and all narrow nationalistic considerations."

Books about her life and work appeared in a multitude of languages. Malcolm Muggeridge acknowledged that the translation of *Something Beautiful for God* into more and more languages was a source of particular pride and satisfaction to him. Some of the other books were written without Mother Teresa's consent; some with. Most seemed to touch the lives and hearts of people in a way which Mother Teresa could value. She would not read what was written about her, but even whilst insisting to her Sisters that the growth of public attention imposed upon them the obligation for even greater humility, seemed gradually to come to terms with the importance of "announcing the Good News" and to recognize that the use of her example and of her words could lead, even sometimes unwittingly, to a realization of spiritual truth. She did not herself write, except letters to her Sisters, to her Co-Workers and to friends. The message remained unchanging, the wording simple in the extreme but often possessed of a spontaneous rhythm and lyricism, even beauty:

Today, once more, when Jesus comes amongst his own, his own don't know him! He comes in the rotten bodies of our poor: he comes even in the rich choked by their own riches. He comes in the loneliness of their hearts, and when there is no one to love them. Jesus comes to you and me and often, very, very often, we pass him by.

Joy is prayer – joy is strength – joy is love, joy is a net of love by which you can catch souls.

Today, more than ever, we need to pray for the light to perceive the word of God, for the love to accept the will of God, for the way to do the will of God

God is the friend of silence. If we really want to pray we must first learn to listen, for in the silence of the heart God speaks.

The fruit of silence is prayer,
The fruit of prayer is faith,
The fruit of faith is love and
The fruit of love is silence.

Let us not use bombs and guns to overcome the world. Let us use love and compassion. Peace begins with a smile.

Mother Teresa's use of language was as unsophisticated as her taste in religious art, her love for small plastic statues of the Virgin Mary or prayer cards depicting the bleeding heart of Jesus. Rhythmic catchphrases were easily remembered and therein lay a very practical value. She liked, for example, to take a person's hand and ask him or her to repeat after her, as she counted off each finger: "You did it to me." To her there was value in the mere act of repetition. Prayer did not consist of many words but in the simple turning of a heart towards God. Similarly, all words were useless unless they "came from within". Her own words, drawn as they deliberately were from prayer and silence, bore witness to her belief that the value of words, like the value of a small plastic statue, lay in the manner in which they could point beyond themselves to a reality that was infinitely greater. It was by this means that they became "beautiful". So it was that often her co-operation with a project would depend upon her sensing in its author the recognition of that principle, the principle of doing something only for the glory of God, which could in turn dissolve the contours of the familiar and change it into something rich and challenging.

At the international chapter of the Co-Workers held in Rome on 15 and 16 May 1982, Mother Teresa gave her permission to two young American sisters, Ann and Jeanette Petrie, to make a film about her life and work. The film crew accompanied her on some of her travels to Beirut, to the United States and elsewhere. The resulting documentary film, entitled *Mother Teresa* was shown five years later at the United Nations General Assembly Hall. Mother Teresa herself was in New York to address a capacity audience of a thousand diplomats and dignitaries who had gathered in the United Nations building to mark the fortieth anniversary of the Organization. From a large screen hanging over the General

Assembly podium, images flashed through the hall of the hungry of Guatemala, the deformed of Beirut and the dying of Calcutta. It was an appropriate forum for the premiere of a film about a woman whom Ann Petrie referred to as a "citizen of the world". In fact the film won worldwide acclaim. In July 1987 it was awarded the Soviet Peace Committee Prize during the Fifteenth International Film Festival held in Moscow. It was after the film had received standing ovations and repeat screenings at the festival that an invitation was extended to Mother Teresa by the Soviet Peace Committee and the Russian Orthodox Church to visit the Soviet Union. The film did much to bring the work of the Missionaries of Charity, and thus the "Good News", to the knowledge of many throughout the world who would not necessarily have been prepared to read a book about them, or who would not have access to such books. It even found its way to Cuba's Ninth International Film Festival, and an adapted version was circulated throughout the country.

The path of another and rather different film proposal was to run less smoothly. In December 1982 Mother Teresa signed a formally witnessed agreement granting to the French writer Dominique Lapierre and his wife, also called Dominique, exclusive permission to undertake a motion picture portraying her life and the work of the Missionaries of Charity. Dominique Lapierre was co-author with Larry Collins of a series of best-selling books, including a celebrated work about India's independence, *Freedom at Midnight*. Research for that book marked the beginning of a deep attachment to India for Dominique Lapierre, and his subsequent epic story about the people of Calcutta, *City of Joy*, brought him into contact with, among other less well-known "saints" in the city, Mother Teresa and the Missionaries of Charity. The experience inspired him to make a deep and lasting commitment to humanitarian work in India, and transformed his life. He had also, later, been deeply impressed by Richard Attenborough's film *Gandhi*. This, combined with the influence he had seen exerted by a French film about the life of St Vincent de Paul, had convinced him of the particular power of film to convey a spiritual message to an audience which would be unlikely to read religious books.

In fact his aspiration was to reach even those audiences which would be unlikely to watch a documentary for, as time would show, even a documentary as laudable and successful as that made by the Petrie sisters could lack what television controllers regarded as peak viewing time appeal. The film made by Anne and Jeanette Petrie was not shown on the United States television network at peak viewing time. French television broadcast it at 10.30 p.m. after cutting it to two-thirds of its original length. British television also only showed it in its reduced form. It was for this reason that Dominique Lapierre wanted to make a film with a fictionalized story which would none the less accurately portray the spirit of Mother Teresa. He regarded the making of a film in which the message of Mother Teresa's life would be brought to audiences throughout the world by an actress as an apostolate to which he was called and, after two years of consideration, Mother Teresa responded to his conviction, placing only one condition upon their agreement:

Mr and Mrs Dominique Lapierre will be free to conceive, write, produce and direct their motion picture in the manner they choose, as long as their work will serve the cause of the poorest of the poor.

Difficulties were to arise, however, both in connection with the script and with the choice of actress to play the part of a woman whom an increasing number of people regarded as a living saint. The requirements of people financing what they hoped would be an enormous and popular box-office success, and those of Mother Teresa – whose concern was primarily spiritual, whose emphasis was on small things with great love and whose attitude to truth left no room for compromise for commercial ends – were perhaps inevitably not easily reconciled. The difference of interests was further aggravated by press reaction, when, for example, it became known that Glenda Jackson had been approached to play the part of Mother Teresa. Journalists did not fail to highlight the incongruity of an actress who had played "steamy roles" in *Women in Love* and *A Touch of Class* taking the leading role in the life story of a "saintly nun". In fact it was afterwards deemed more appropriate to find a relatively unknown actress to play the part. What was essentially a conflict between the need to convey the message of

Mother Teresa in the kind of popular terms which would ensure box-office appeal – a need which Dominique Lapierre saw as justifiable, because it was precisely at people who would not learn of her message in other ways that the film was aimed – and Mother Teresa's reticence to see the truth altered in any way for the sake of commercialism, would continue for several years.

"No need to add things for the public", she wrote to the Lapierres in August 1989. "It is true I do not know anything about films – but this I know, that we must give to the public the true and beautiful gift of God: Our Poor." At Easter 1988 she had withdrawn her original permission of 1982. On the strength of Mother Teresa's disapproval of the film the Indian Government, ever sensitive about the focus of international eyes on the poverty of India, had declined to give the film company the requisite permission to film in India for what had by then evolved into a telefilm entitled *In the name of God's Poor*. The Lapierres, however, succeeded once more in convincing Mother Teresa of their sincere intention to make a film for "the greater glory of God and the good of the people". Mother Teresa duly wrote to Rajiv Gandhi, and the Indian Prime Minister responded by giving his assurance of the Ministry of Information and Broadcasting's official clearance. Mother Teresa required that certain changes be made to the script, and in Calcutta in August 1990 Father Gaston Roberge SJ, having read the revised version, confirmed that these changes had been made in both letter and spirit. Yet Mother Teresa was once again to withdraw her permission and the impasse continued.

There was hurt on both sides. On Mother Teresa's part because "The permission I had given you was given based upon my own misunderstanding of your intentions. I mistakenly believed that anything that would be written would be a factual account of our work and our life as Missionaries of Charity, for the honour and glory of God, and that it would serve the cause of the poorest of the poor." Her reservations were undoubtedly also underlined by the fact that publicity arising from Dominique Lapierre's best-selling book about the birth and development of AIDS, *Beyond Love*, had drawn unwelcome and inaccurate attention to the Missionary of Charity Sisters' work with AIDS patients in the United States.

On the other side there was a sense of injustice and disappointment that a formally signed and witnessed agreement could be treated with such an apparent lack of appreciation of the realities, both in relation to the means by which the message should be expressed and in relation to the practical and financial problems resulting from Mother Teresa's changes of attitude. Mother Teresa, constantly on the receiving end of requests for her presence, authority for books and other similar appeals, and surrounded as she inevitably was by people who admired and respected her, perhaps did not fully realize that the fact that a film depicted her life would not automatically guarantee its showing to the kind of audiences which were a far cry from a gathering of diplomats and dignitaries at the United Nations building. It was made quite clear to Dominique Lapierre that network television in the United States was not at all attracted to the idea of a saint. A compromise was necessary and he felt that he had found it. When Mother Teresa requested changes, those changes had been made. The suggestion that when even then she withdrew any previous permission she was "only acting in the interest of the poorest of the poor" was not one readily understood by someone who believed wholeheartedly in Mother Teresa and in his own call to convey her message to the world. Father Van Exem, having read the script, believed the film was destined to do immense good. The project also had the declared support of the Vatican, but Mother Teresa continued to display what was for her rare, perhaps even unique, reluctance to accord with Vatican wishes.

Mother Teresa's relationship with the Vatican became an ever closer one. During one of her early visits to St Peter's, Pope Paul VI had accidentally referred to her as Mother Teresa of Delhi. Much as she might sometimes yearn for anonymity, the chances of that happening now were infinitesimally small. An indication of the esteem in which Pope John Paul II held Mother Teresa came in October 1980, when she was invited to address the World Synod of Bishops in Rome. The Synod was on the theme of the Christian family in the modern world. The Pope had let his concern about the breakdown of family life be known to her and she manifestly shared his views on contraception, abortion and the duty of the Church to reaffirm the commandment "Thou shalt not kill", even to the point of joining in demonstrations by the Movement for Life in Italy. As it happened, when she addressed the Synod, Mother Teresa was moved to call for greater holiness on the part of priests. Undaunted by the august gathering of churchmen confronting her, she impressed upon them their role in promoting spiritual values in the life of the family.

There was between Mother Teresa and Pope John Paul II clearly a relationship of reciprocal personal respect and affection. To the eyes of the general public this was particularly apparent when in 1986, during Pope John Paul II's visit to India, Mother Teresa showed him round the home for the dying in Calcutta, on what she described as the happiest day of her life. When the Pope arrived straight from Dum Dum airport in his Rover Popemobile, Mother Teresa stepped into the vehicle to touch his feet but he blessed her with a kiss on the forehead and a hug. Mother Teresa introduced him to the head *sevayat* of the adjacent Kali temple, and then took him to a dais erected in his honour where she garlanded him. The Pope took off the garland and placed it round her neck, and the large crowd which had gathered to greet him cheered. John Paul II spent almost three-quarters of an hour in Nirmal Hriday, feeding some of the occupants, pausing beside the low cots to hold the face of a suffering person in his hands, blessing them. He paid rich tributes to Mother Teresa's work among the poor: "For the destitute and the dying Nirmal Hriday is a place of hope. This place represents a profound dignity of every human person." As for Mother Teresa, she saw his presence as a real gift of God: "He touched the very life of everyone here. He blessed and touched everybody. We are very happy to have the Holy Father touch our poor."

Apart from any considerations of personal regard, however, the role of a universally acclaimed Nobel prize winner of unquestionable orthodoxy and fidelity as an ambassadress for the Roman Catholic Church was obviously of value. It was, moreover, a role which a woman who had consistently urged her Sisters to pray that everything they did would be for the greater glory of God and his Church, would willingly assume. Mother Teresa was not so ingenuous that she did not realize that her presence alone was enough now to focus the eyes of the world on a particular need, that sometimes she could tread where other leaders in the Roman Catholic

Church could not, and that the high public profile, however personally painful, gave her a capacity to influence.

Because of her presence an increasing number of prominent
people came to Calcutta and found themselves either figuratively
or literally touching the poor. Shortly after the Pope it was the turn
of the Archbishop of Canterbury to visit Mother Teresa, but it was
not only churchmen who were drawn to her. The visitors who sat
waiting to see her, while in the courtyard of the mother house the
Sisters bustled and washed and went about the business of their
day, ranged from filmstars like Gina Lollobrigida to international
cricketers. "Cricket?" Mother Teresa enquired of one such visitor
as she mimed an overarm action. "Is it played this way? Or is it this
way?" Her arm attempted a baseball swipe. She told the Derbyshire
and England cricketer, Bob Taylor, that she and he were both
equally serving Christ. "You must play this game of yours simply
to the best of your ability, for if you are doing your best you are
pleasing mankind and thus you too are doing God's work." From
her, as the cricket writer Frank Keating would afterwards point
out, the suggestion had not the slightest corniness. John Craven,
with the filmcrew for *Newsround Extra*, was another to find his
way to the mother house and be moved by the sight of nuns
kneeling in the dust, washing in a bucket the spare habit which
they would wear next day. In December 1980 Prince Charles spent
time with Mother Teresa, watching the Sisters prepare food for
more than seven thousand people, meeting some of the children in
her care. The Prince was visibly moved by the plight of one tiny
baby who had been found in a slum gutter. "I will pray for you,"
Mother Teresa told him, "so that the love and compassion you
have for the poor and the needy grows and you are able to serve
them better." In 1985 Princess Ann visited Shishu Bhavan, Calcutta. Mother Teresa treated her royal visitors with exactly the
same natural warmth as she approached the lepers who came to the
door of 54A Lower Circular Road.

In the light of the attention which was focused upon her, it is
hardly surprising that there were times when she appeared to take
it for granted that she would have the centre of the stage, times
when she would assume that a letter from her would be enough to
halt the publication of a book or guarantee it sales, that her inter-

vention alone would be enough to resolve a problematic situation. Yet she had always the interests of the poor and the suffering at heart. The assertion, heard with ever-increasing frequency, that she was a living saint was consistently countered with the claim that every human being was called to be a saint. "Holiness", she continued to respond to such suggestions, "is a simple duty for you and for me." Meeting the hunger of the world for love was also something which she saw as a simple duty, and that hunger she insisted was present in everyone: "People throughout the world may look different, or have a different religion, education or position but they are all the same. They are all people to be loved." Above all, fame did nothing to alter the interest, respect and love she had for individuals, regardless of their nationality, standing or creed.

On 24 November 1983 at the Presidential Palace in Delhi, Queen Elizabeth II presented Mother Teresa with the insignia of the Honorary Order of Merit, an insignia which would eventually find its way onto a statue of the one whom Mother Teresa considered really deserved it, the Blessed Virgin. Having handed Mother Teresa her personal award, the Queen was momentarily taken aback and obviously touched by the kindly attempt of an elderly woman to put her at her ease, for after thanking Her Majesty for the "beautiful gift", Mother Teresa enquired, "And how is your grandson, Prince William?"

CHAPTER EIGHT

Works of Peace

If there had been an evolution in the work, Mother Teresa saw it retrospectively in terms of a "deepening in love". The Missionaries of Charity had seen both the suffering of "their people" and their greatness, and their own love had deepened accordingly. In personal terms for their foundress that process called for ever greater reserves of energy at a time when her physical strength was beginning to falter. Often she would quote the words of St Augustine: "Fill yourself first and then only will you be able to give to others", and as always she applied the principle to her own life. It was as if, as one close observer put it, "she ran on prayer". Drained, exhausted and empty after a schedule which would have daunted much younger people, she would retire to the chapel and emerge after an interval manifestly revitalized, "filled" and ready to continue God's work. So it was that her energy and achievements belied the frailty of one whom the Loreto Sisters had felt required special treatment because of her health. Considering the conditions under which she lived, her constitution had proved to be remarkably resilient. She herself considered her "robust health" one of God's great gifts to her. As her Sisters pointed out, however, it was difficult to determine the real extent to which she underwent pain and suffering because she never spoke about how she felt. Joy was the impression she left with those who met her, but joy was, as she often said to others, "the mantle that hides a life of self-sacrifice".

There had been times when she had fallen ill from sheer exhaustion. She suffered from malaria, which would flare up in times of particular stress. In 1964 she was involved in a car accident in Darjeeling during which the vehicle in which she had been travelling was forced to stop abruptly. Mother Teresa's head smashed into a metal fixture attached to the windscreen and she was badly cut. She was given nineteen stitches at a nursing home in Darjeeling. That evening Indira Gandhi, who happened to be in that hill station, called at the hospital to express her concern, but as soon as Mother Teresa discovered the cost of treatment she had retreated swiftly to the Missionary of Charity children's home in Darjeeling. On more than one occasion, she had experienced some injury before embarking on a long journey. For one who believed so profoundly in the relationship between offered pain and creative growth such occurrences were accepted as something more than accidents. A few days before she left for Australia in 1969 she fell out of bed, and hit her arm so badly that a bone protruded from her forearm. A doctor told her she should not travel but she insisted on doing so. He therefore strapped her up in extensive bandages. The bandages, however, impeded her more than the injury. They were subsequently removed and she managed to continue – with a smile.

By the early nineteen-eighties her eyesight was obviously deteriorating. The rounded back and stoop of her later years was caused by spondylitis. More significantly, in 1974 she suffered a slight stroke but it was not until 1981 that doctors diagnosed a heart condition. The diagnosis occurred almost by accident. At the time Mother Teresa was travelling in the United States with a senior Sister who would subsequently become one of the councillors who together with the Superior General had responsibility for exercising internal authority over the Congregation of Missionary of Charity Sisters. Mother Teresa had really gone to a doctor to talk to him about someone else, but while she was there she was persuaded to have a check-up. Afterwards the doctor came out and told Sister Priscilla that Mother Teresa had a bad heart condition. He also asked her not to tell Mother Teresa he had informed her, because Mother Teresa wanted her condition kept a secret. Later she told Sister Priscilla that she wanted to die on her feet and to continue her life exactly as previously. She felt, she said, that Jesus was asking this of her and she had never said "No" to Jesus.

As early as April 1970 Mother Teresa had divided the Missionary of Charity houses in India into five regions, each with a regional Superior. The big question which must be concerning her Sisters then, Mother Teresa had decided without the least awareness of any irony, was "If all the work is done by the Regional Superiors, what will Mother do?" She answered her own hypothesized query: "Mother will pray that you will become saints, and so fulfil her promise. Also I will be able to stay longer with our Sisters outside India and establish the Society." The latter task had become an ever more demanding one. In 1981 alone the Missionaries of Charity opened eight more foundations in India and seventeen others in America, Europe, Africa, Australia and Asia, including a house in Tokyo. In April of that year Mother Teresa visited Japan at the invitation of the Japan Family Life Association to give her support to a Declaration on Reverence for Life. Her hectic schedule also included a walk through the streets of the Sanya district of Tokyo, a neighbourhood renowned for the number of alcoholics who congregate there. One month later, on 24 May, the Bishop of Tokyo blessed a new house of the Missionaries of Charity in Tokyo.

The fiftieth anniversary of Mother Teresa's vows as a religious was on 24 May 1981. Not only at the mother house in Calcutta, but in over two hundred houses of the Missionaries of Charity, the day was celebrated with prayers and thanksgiving. Groups of Co-Workers around the world joined in services and hours of prayer. The special Golden Jubilee Mass, however, which Mother Teresa was due to attend in the Calcutta mother house, had to be moved to the morning of 19 May because of unexpected changes in Mother Teresa's schedule, one of them being a call by the Vatican to attend meetings on abortion in Italy.

Shortly afterwards Mother Teresa was asked to take part in a symposium of the American Family Institute in Washington DC. It was a potentially political occasion attended by various congressmen and senators opposed to abortion. Mother Teresa had always insisted that she knew nothing about politics, and that political methods of bringing about change were for others. As early as 1972 when the Bangladesh government had asked her to take care of the girls who had been "used" by the Pakistan army, she had shown her Indian Sisters the way of political neutrality. Yet if she steered a course of non-identification with political causes it was not always because she did not know or understand their implications, but rather because she believed that to be the Church's way. On this occasion, as on many others, she refused to be drawn, stating simply that she was not there to mix in politics but to support life.

With her Sisters she had always taken the line that the heads of countries knew their duty. The role of the Missionaries of Charity was not to discuss the rights and wrongs of their policies but to pray that they would fulfil their duty with justice and dignity. This did nothing to impair her capacity to make friends of those who did hold political views, or indeed her ability to affect rival world leaders to the same extent. The fourth of June 1981 saw Mother Teresa visiting Ronald and Nancy Reagan at the White House. It was not long after an attempt had been made on the United States President's life, and she informed him that his suffering would bring him closer to Jesus and to the poor. Afterwards the international press reported how, when President Reagan had been asked what he had said to his guest, he had replied simply, "I listened".

The meeting at the White House was followed by the inauguration of a foundation for destitutes and drug addicts in Harlem. A few days after that Mother Teresa was in the communist-controlled German Democratic Republic to open a foundation there. In the same month twelve thousand Rotarians listened attentively in Brazil as she addressed the seventy-second Rotary International Convention. "It is not your money but your time we need," she told them, "we want all of you to donate YOURSELVES to the poor people. . . . I think that all of you and I myself should start sharing what we have got. This attitude would certainly beget a better understanding between nations."

The following month took her to Corrymeela, an Ecumenical Peace Community in Northern Ireland, to talk on peace to people suffering on both sides of the violent conflict. If, as Mother Teresa firmly believed, all works of love were works of peace, then her life was a constant expression of her peace-making role, but there were occasions when her insistence on the unifying power of an awareness of the constant loving presence of an all-forgiving God was more explicit than others. The gathering in Corrymeela was one of them. Her next major public engagement was another. From the Hill of Harmony, as the Gaelic word Corrymeela means, Mother Teresa flew to London for the public "launching" of an international prayer for peace. So strongly was her name associated with the prayer, so energetically did she encourage Co-Workers and others to use it, that its authorship was frequently attributed to her. In fact it was composed by an Indian, Satish Kumar, who called it a peace mantra, but it was Mother Teresa who led the reading of the prayer aloud in St James's Church, Piccadilly, where the congregation included a throng of journalists and photographers attracted by her presence:

> Lead me from death to life,
> from falsehood to truth;
> Lead me from despair to hope,
> from fear to trust;
> Lead me from hate to love,
> from war to peace;
> Let peace fill our hearts, our world, our universe.

On 3 July 1981, a date recorded by Mother Teresa as the first Friday of the month and thus a day of special devotion to the Sacred Heart, Lazar Bojaxhiu died of cancer of the lungs in Palermo, Italy. In February that year, Mother Teresa had written to a friend asking for prayers for him:

I was the one to tell him he had the cancer and that he would be joining the family in Heaven – very simple answer he gave, "If you want to join the family you go – but I have no desire to do so now."

When the time came Mother Teresa was unable to be with him, but she would afterwards write from Kathmandu of how he had died at peace:

He was so beautiful at the end when he said, "Yes, I am ready to go" – after his confession and the prayer together. Pray for him as he has no son – the family name will die with him.

In her own case the desire to die in action seemed to bring even greater perseverance in her vocation. On 7 December 1981 Mother Teresa was in Calcutta to receive a cheque from the Vice Chancellor of Calcutta University. Only three days later she was in Italy to receive an honorary Doctorate of Medicine from Rome's Catholic

University. "Abortion", she announced on receiving it, "is nothing but the fear of the child – fear to have to feed one more child, to have to educate one more child, to have to love one more child. Therefore the child must die." In all she opened twenty-six houses that year, eighteen of them outside India, and she endeavoured whenever possible to accompany her Sisters when a new foundation was to be begun, when another tabernacle was to be given to Jesus. In September she was sent to Australia by Pope John Paul II. She had hoped to have some time to devote to the training and guidance of her Sisters, but in obedience she set off for Australia for further meetings, talks and interviews.

In her absence responsibility was left in the hands of a Maltese Sister, Sister Frederick, who served as Assistant General. Mother Teresa urged her Sisters to give her the same love, trust and obedience they gave to her. "Do not be afraid. Only trust and obey and you will be all right." Still she guided them to greater understanding love and even more generous service:

What we must do is to have and to put into the work greater love and more generous service.
– If it is the school, then the calling of the children and the preparation of your school work and Sunday School must be done with greater care and thought for the children.
– If it is first communion or marriage classes, with greater faith and conviction of what you teach – after much real preparation and knowledge of what the Church is teaching today. In preparing families – especially the fidelity of married life and the sinfulness of abortion, the importance of natural family planning as a sign of greater love.
– If dispensary work, go in time and do not leave before you have attended each person. In giving medicine, give with respect, do not humiliate the poverty of the poor by giving with harshness and being in a hurry.
– If with the lepers – what love, what tender compassion, what tender courageous love you need. If you pray you will be able to do so with faith . . . and if you believe, the fruit of that faith is love and compassion. They need your understanding love full of patience and thoughtfulness.
– If at Nirmal Hriday – the living tabernacle of the suffering Christ – how clean your hands must be to touch the broken bodies, how clean your tongue must be to speak the words of comfort, faith and love. For many

of them it is their first contact with love and it may be their last. How much you must be alive to his presence, if you really believe what Jesus has said, "You did it to me".

– If in Shishu Bhavan where life begins, how much of that tender loving love and touch you must put into the work. How much you need to pray the work – not just do the work. It may be doing it for something instead of doing it for somebody. Right there we must protect the unwanted child.

– Especially we must take care of our big girls – in their hunger for love and in their rejection they are inclined to give trouble sometimes. The work with them is more difficult than with the lepers, but they are Christ in his distressing disguise. Help them to pray, pray with them, go among them as one to serve and not as one to be served. Never use the words, "You have been picked up" or "You are a bad girl", etc. She like you and me has been created by the same loving hand of God, for greater things, to love and to be loved – therefore my sister, my brother.

– If visiting the families, with how much delicate respect and dignity must you do this work – how much you need Our Lady's example. When visiting her cousin, she went there with Jesus as the handmaid of the Lord – not to gossip, not to find fault, not to hurt but to serve. Jesus has taught us. Before he could give his body to his disciples, he had to wash their feet. Also make sure your visits bring peace, joy and unity. Out of respect for the poor do not eat or drink outside when visiting the rich or the poor. Come praying, pray with them, leave the place praying.

In his old age Father Van Exem would say of Mother Teresa that over the years the spirit of prayer and the kindness he had first noticed in her had grown. She was, he said, a real mother to her Sisters. Even as their numbers exceeded a thousand she knew each one. She might not remember their names but she knew their faces and their personal circumstances. Distances might reduce the frequency with which she could be physically present to them but she was still very protective of them, and when they got into difficulties it was still Mother who sorted them out. In 1981 the Sisters in Bangladesh were found by the authorities to be in breach of some of the country's complex regulations. Mother Teresa immediately boarded the first plane to the capital of Bangladesh. She was met at the airport by the Indian High Commissioner and the local Roman Catholic Archbishop, and arrangements were made for her to call on President Zia. She told him his customs were complicated and troublesome, whereupon he ironed everything out to her satisfaction, and the Sisters remained to continue their work.

April 1982 took her again to Japan, this time to Nagasaki, to the site of the explosion of the second nuclear bomb on 9 August 1945. It was there that on 26 April she appealed for prayer, "We must all pray that no human hand will ever again do what has been done here", and recited another peace prayer:

> *Eternal Father, in union with the suffering and Passion of Christ which is being relived at every Mass – we offer you the pain and suffering caused by the atomic bomb in this place to thousands of people, and we implore you, Eternal Father, to protect the whole world from the pain and suffering nuclear war would bring to the people of Japan and the whole world, already filled with so much fear and distrust and anxiety among the nations. Eternal Father, have pity on us all.*

Mother Teresa had seen famine and death and suffering in a multitude of forms, but she had not to date been subjected directly to the devastation of war. On 10 August 1982, however, shortly after she had made a visit to London and Glasgow, Pope John Paul II chose to send her to Beirut as a demonstration of his solidarity with the war victims there. Mother Teresa attended Mass in the Pope's private chapel at Castel Gandolfo and then set off on a journey which involved a seventeen-hour sea crossing from Cyprus in a battered steamer. She arrived in Beirut at a time when the bombing and shelling were at their worst. The Sisters' house in East Beirut was no more than five miles from the primary target area. There were snipers everywhere and the destruction was nightmarish.

The Petrie Productions' documentary film would record for posterity the stand Mother Teresa made there, in defiance of churchmen and the voices of reason, to convince them of the possibility of going into West Beirut to rescue the victims of the violence and of the importance of doing so irrespective of the small numbers that might be helped in this way. With the patience of one who had manifestly had to make this point on many occasions, she informed them that if she had not picked up the very first dying person from the streets of Calcutta, the forty-two thousand retrieved from the city's streets to date would also have died alone and neglected. Mother Teresa would pray for a cease-fire and there was no doubt in her mind, despite all arguments and sound advice to the contrary, that there would be one. She had brought with her a large Easter candle with an image of the Madonna and Child on it. At 4 p.m. while the bombing was still at its worst she lit it, and at 5 p.m. suddenly all was quiet. On 12 August Mother Teresa went into the war-torn Western section and brought out thirty-eight mentally and physically handicapped Muslims aged between seven and twenty-one. Some of the staff had fled, and patients were already said to have died of starvation in the badly shelled mental hospital in the southern Palestinian neighbourhood of Sabra. Prior to their evacuation the children had huddled on soiled rubber mattresses, two to a bed, with too few staff to feed or wash them. Above all they were terrified. Mother Teresa went amongst them, comforting and reassuring them. She took command and the thirty-seven were placed in a convoy of cars provided by the International Red Cross and taken to the Mar Takla convent in mainly Christian East Beirut. There she instantly set about organizing the supplies necessary for their care.

Two days later Mother Teresa again crossed the Israeli-controlled checkpoint to evacuate another twenty-seven children. Before her arrival no one had been very keen to take these children, but slowly other people began to respond. Neighbours began to bring food and clothing. Other religious, government officials and doctors arrived to offer goods and services. One of the Red Cross officials who admitted quite candidly that his initial reaction to Mother Teresa's presence had been that a saint was not what he needed most, afterwards acknowledged that he had been astonished at the efficiency and energy which went hand in hand with her spirituality. She was, he said, "a cross between a military commander and St Francis". All the same, Mother Teresa's experience of man's inhumanity to man had left her in a state of bewildered incomprehension: "What do people feel when they do these things? I don't understand. They are all children of God. Why do they do it? I don't understand."

On 19 August she left for Mexico via Athens for a meeting with "the rich of the world". The Easter candle she had lit in Beirut burned out the night before she left. En route to Mexico Mother Teresa asked her Sisters, if they had an Easter candle, to light it in front of the statue of the Virgin in thanksgiving. She also asked them to pray, together with the Holy Father, that Jesus would be brought into the family lives of the rich she was about to meet. The demands for her were apparently insatiable. In that same year, 1982, Mother Teresa attended an international chapter of Co-Workers in Rome which brought together representatives of the Co-Workers from more than thirty countries as far afield as Iceland, Lesotho, Mauritius and Zimbabwe, looking to her for guidance, inspiration and approval. She addressed a gathering in Assisi for the close of the eight hundredth anniversary of the birth of the saint whom she maintained had "taught us how to pray". She was present at a Right to Life Convention in St Louis, an anti-abortion rally in Glasgow and a news conference in Dublin organized by the Society for the Protection of the Unborn Child, and she also addressed an anti-abortion rally at the National Stadium. She laid the foundations for the Sanjay Gandhi and Family Welfare Centre in Churhat and the Gauhati Shishu Bhavan, the sixth in North-East India. On her seventy-second birthday she inaugurated a Home for the Poor in Caracas, Venezuela. Moreover, these were only some of the more public events in a life essentially devoted to the poor and the hidden. "Let the poor eat you up", Mother Teresa would tell her Sisters. The process of allowing the works of peace and the requirements of the poor of the world to eat her up went on. Nor did the early part of 1983 show any relenting of the pace. There were times when in their eagerness for her presence people, even her Co-Workers, did not seem to realize that she was human.

On 2 June 1983, however, Mother Teresa fell out of bed in the Rome convent of the Missionaries of Charity at San Gregorio on the Coelian Hill, and hurt her foot. She was admitted to the Salvator Mundi Hospital, an establishment especially devoted to the religious community in Rome and run by the Sisters of the Divine Saviour. After only two days she insisted on returning to the convent, but several days after that her foot began to cause her acute pain. Doctors and associates and those around her, including the Pope, knew that exhaustion was a strong factor in her illness. She was urged to return to the hospital, and finally, when Pope John Paul II himself telephoned her to say, "the whole world needs you, so please enter the hospital and rest", she agreed.

Officially it was given out that a minor heart condition and aphthae in her mouth were the reason for her stay in hospital under the supervision of Dr Vincenzo Bilotti, a respected Roman heart specialist, but undoubtedly the need for enforced rest and a nourishing diet were also strong considerations. The enforced stay in bed, the first ever period of rest since she heard the call within a call in 1946, came just in time. Mother Teresa was told that if she had not fallen she would almost certainly have suffered a heart attack. To her this was yet another manifestation of the tender concern of a loving father. She was convinced it was her guardian angel who had pushed her. In hospital she was put in a room marked "Strictly no visitors". A plain-clothes police officer was posted at the exit to the lift to her floor. Only the Missionary of Charity Sisters and the hospital priest were allowed access to her. For a while she was obviously in pain but she declined to take the painkillers prescribed for her, telling her doctor that she wanted to offer up her sufferings to God. Gradually her strength returned and her visitors then included the King and Queen of Belgium. Prayers were offered from all over the world, and bouquets poured in from, among others, the President of India. Mother Teresa's spirits rose. She was particularly delighted when on 10 June President Reagan sent her seven roses, because on that day seven new foundations of the Missionaries of Charity were opened in various parts of the world.

In a room adorned with a large picture of Jesus and a small statue of the Virgin and Child, Mother Teresa wrote a four-page meditation on the text of St Matthew 16:15 "Who do you say I am?" The meditation, which she would afterwards share with her Sisters and Co-Workers, expressed in characteristic terms the totality of her relationship to Jesus, concluding with the lines, "Jesus, I love with my whole heart, with my whole being – I have given him all even my sins and he has espoused me to himself in tenderness and love. Now and for life I am the spouse of my crucified Spouse." "Let us be ready for anything that God may decide for us", she told her Sisters, but by the end of June it was clearly apparent to Mother Teresa that Jesus in the distressing disguise of the poor still needed her to continue the work. When Dominique and Dominique Lapierre visited her on 26 June she admitted to having pains in her back, but she was already making plans for visits to Germany, Belgium and Poland and possibly the USA. She was full of appreciation for all the prayers, sacrifices and letters. With continued prayer she was convinced she would soon be all right, but there were those close to her who prayed that the doctors would tax her patience to the full.

On 4 July she left the Salvator Mundi Hospital, thereafter went briefly to the Gemelli Hospital, where she was given a final examination with the advanced equipment available there, and was then released into the medical care of Sister Gertrude. She had been assured that she would live for another thirty years provided she obeyed the rules, which included the directive that she should no longer lift children up in her arms. The fall had meant cancelling a visit to the British Isles in June. "We realize", wrote the national link for the Co-Workers in Great Britain, following Mother Teresa's period in hospital, "that no longer should she be expected to undertake big public engagements as before."

Mother Teresa remained in Rome for a short period, still weak but by no means idle. Her first move on leaving hospital was to place before the Sacred Congregation for the Doctrine of the Faith a proposition which had evolved out of Father Joseph Langford's approach to her in 1978, for an international movement of priestly renewal. Father Langford's hope was that priests and ministers might share, within the context of their own priestly vocation and ministry, in the charism of renewal which he saw as having been given to the universal Church through Mother Teresa. The movement's fundamental aim would be personal priestly renewal lived out in three fundamental areas: a deeper prayer life, simplified lifestyle and ministerial charity. In 1979 Father Langford had met Mother Teresa in New York to suggest that she start a branch of the Co-Workers for priests. Her response then, as so often, had been, "Write to me and we'll see", so he had written her a ten-page letter, to which he had received no reply. One-and-a-half years later, however, she was in Haiti on her way to Calcutta when suddenly she changed her plans and sent word via the Sisters for him to meet her in New York. There she told him that while she was in Haiti she had felt very strongly that it was God's will for her to begin something for the ministry of priests. They had therefore spent four days together in the contemplative house in the Bronx, writing the first draft of the statutes of what would be the Priest Co-Workers of Mother Teresa. It was from the Bronx that Mother Teresa had flown to Rome to the Synod on the role of the Christian family in the modern world, and that was why, when she stood up to address the gathering of bishops and cardinals, instead of talking specifically about family life she had told them that if they wished to help Christian families they must provide holy priests. In the words of Father Joseph Langford, "She had come from Haiti with this volcano inside her and it was still with her when she got to Rome."

The synod lasted a month. By the time it had finished Mother Teresa and Father Langford had taken the constitutions for the Priest Co-Workers to Pope John Paul II. The Pope gave the proposal his very personal encouragement by expressing his wish to be considered "the movement's first member", and the Priest Co-Workers began, initially in a very small and disorganized way but eventually spreading to some sixty countries.

At the same time, however, since Mother Teresa had asked him to write down his proposals in 1979, Father Langford had been reflecting upon the possibility of a nucleus of priests who could dedicate themselves on a full-time basis to living out Mother Teresa's message by wholehearted and joyful priestly service to Jesus present in the poorest of the poor. He had broached the subject with Mother Teresa in 1979. She had said neither "Yes" nor "No", and the idea of having "something parallel to the Missionaries of Charity for Priests" remained with him as the Priest Co-Worker movement grew and expanded throughout the world. Finally, when Mother Teresa was in hospital in June 1983, Father Langford felt the time was right to present the idea to the Sacred Congregation for the Doctrine of the Faith. He visited Mother Teresa and found her in agreement.

As soon as she was discharged, they approached the Sacred Congregation together. The suggestion was given whole-hearted endorsement, but this was not enough for Mother Teresa. On 20 July they went to Castel Gandolfo to raise the proposition with the

Pope himself, who gave it a verbal "Yes". Still this did not satisfy Mother Teresa. She left Rome for Poland and on her return went once more to see the Pope. On this occasion it was to be a private audience, and Father Langford could not accompany her. She asked him therefore to jot down a brief note as an aide memoire. He roughed out a few handwritten points on a slip of paper, about how this nucleus of priests would live together, work together for the poorest of the poor and spread Mother's message, and Mother Teresa duly folded it up like a handkerchief and put it into a bag. Later she presented the same scrap of paper to John Paul II with a request for his blessing. It was not the practice for the Pope to sign anything, but on this occasion he thought for a moment and then wrote on Father Langford's handwritten notes: "With my blessing, John Paul II, 17 August 1983." The author of the notes was waiting in the Sisters' convent at San Gregorio for the outcome of the meeting. Without saying a word to him, Mother Teresa went first to the chapel to pray and then motioned him into the "parlour". Still without speaking she reached into her bag, pulled out the crumpled piece of paper and unfolded it before him with the one word of triumph: "Look!"

From there she went to New York to ask Cardinal Cooke for permission for what was then called the Corpus Christi Fraternity to begin in his diocese. The Cardinal provided a house in the South Bronx and established the fraternity as a Pious Union. Father Langford obtained exclaustration from the Congregation to which he had previously belonged, and together with two others formed the fledgeling Congregation which began on 1 October 1983. As yet it was essentially a loose community of priest Co-Workers but during that first year in the South Bronx other priests began to come to the house, and the feeling grew that they wanted to live the life of a religious community structured in a similar way to the life of the Brothers and Sisters.

In October 1984 Mother Teresa summoned Father Langford to Rome again. By a synchronization of thought which he saw as providential, it was she who put the suggestion to him: "Father, I have been praying all this year and I feel your people should be a religious community." Once again the Vatican raised no objections, and as they flew back to New York together all that remained to

be a settled was the actual name of the new community. Mother
Teresa was seventy-four years old. Out of deference for her age
Father Langford was reluctant to ask her to assume the responsibility of beginning another branch of the Missionaries of Charity. She
looked very tired and he left her to sleep, but when she opened a
book to read, he began tentatively in an attempt to avoid pressuriz-
ing her: "Mother, I understand that we can't be Missionaries of
Charity. . . ." "Why not?" came the swift rejoinder. At thirty-seven
thousand feet she decided everything, and on landing the news was
immediately announced to the small community in the South
Bronx. The Missionary of Charity Fathers, which Mother Teresa
described as "something so beautiful and so wonderful", began
officially on 3 October 1984. "We have now MC Fathers in New
York", Mother Teresa would later relay the news. "They are really
the gift of God."

In that same year Mother Teresa decided to ask the considerable
number of doctors among her Co-Workers to form a special medical branch. In 1982 a group of doctors in Rome working in various
Sisters' establishments had begun to assemble once a month for
prayer and reflection. Together they had explored ethical and spiritual problems relating to medical practice, with particular attention
to the emergent problems of abortion, euthanasia, birth control,
sexual disorders, drug problems, alcoholic addiction, mental health
and diseases due to poverty in many developing countries. At intervals Mother Teresa had attended these meetings at the Missionary
of Charity house of San Gregorio, sharing with the physicians her
own insights and encouraging them to give their time and professional commitment to the service of the Missionaries of Charity
and the people they worked with in Rome. "Because the sick, the
lonely, the disabled come to you with hope, they must be able to
receive from you tender love and compassion", she told them. "The
sick and suffering don't need pity and sympathy; they need love
and compassion." She spoke to them of the spiritual value of doctors
trying to help the suffering, and in July 1984 a letter was sent out
to Co-Workers throughout the world, urging that doctors in the
various countries should not pursue purely material goals but give
some of their time to helping to improve the lot of the poor. Mother
Teresa appointed Dr Francesco Di Raimondo, senior physician at

the Lazzaro Spallanzani Hospital for Infectious Diseases in Rome, and his wife Gabriella, as international links for the Medical Co-Workers. The association would include not only doctors, nurses, pharmacists and others professionally committed to health care who had volunteered their services to help the Missionaries of Charity in various parts of the world, but also medical people who wished to develop in their own practice a different manner of seeing, touching and speaking to the sick, "a manner which gives confidence and hope to all, even when the sickness is serious and death inevitable." The doctors could be of any faith. What mattered was that they shared in the spirit of Mother Teresa and in an approach based on the belief that medicine was a blessing given by God, and that sick people were to be respected before God and man. Within four years the network of Medical Co-Workers had spread worldwide.

Despite Mother Teresa's physical frailty, despite the fact that her familiar stoop was becoming more pronounced and that she ran a temperature virtually every morning, the work was still expanding in other respects also. By the end of 1983 she had been obliged to appeal to existing foundations to spare some of their Sisters because there were 130 outstanding applications to open new houses. Her unflagging enthusiasm for initiating new foundations had a profoundly spiritual motive. In 1978, having celebrated a series of Silver Jubilees, Mother Teresa announced that the Congregation would now celebrate the "Jubilee of Jesus" by opening twenty-five houses, "that means twenty-five chapels with tabernacles where Jesus will be". Each time the Missionaries of Charity opened a new house the first thing they did was place in it a tabernacle, a chalice and a ciborium. "Each time we open a new house, Jesus becomes present in that house, that locality." By February 1979 Mother Teresa could announce her congratulations to Jesus on his Silver Jubilee with the news that the congregation had indeed opened twenty-five tabernacles in his honour in places as far afield as Caracas, El Salvador, Manila and Liverpool. The Jubilee offering might have been completed but the desire to bring the presence of Jesus especially to those places where he was least known was insatiable.

Essentially, as she would insist, the work undertaken and the spirit in which it was carried out was the same everywhere, but the fact that an increasing number of Missionary of Charity houses was being opened in communist countries was both deeply meaningful to her and a particular tribute to the way in which the most daunting walls crumbled at the onslaught of her persuasive powers. It seemed that she had only to tell the most sceptical and atheistic authorities in the quietly determined way she had that she wanted to bring God's tender loving care to their people, and the way would open, and if a first attempt did not succeed she kept on telling them. In the case of communist countries the determination was further endorsed by long-standing personal aspirations.

On 28 March 1978, nearly eight years after Mother Teresa's brief visit at the invitation of the Red Cross, she returned to Yugoslavia, this time at the invitation of the Catholic bishops there. In fact there had been Co-Workers in Yugloslavia since 1976, and the Archbishop of Zagreb told Mother Teresa when she arrived in his diocese that he was proud to be one of them. Here as in other Iron Curtain countries, Co-Workers had been quietly translating and circulating literature about Mother Teresa for some time. Her fame and her message were already widespread. She was accompanied during her visit by Father Gabric, the Croatian Jesuit priest from Calcutta whom Mother Teresa had wanted in the early days to take over the leadership of the Missionary Brothers. Together they spoke to crowds in many Yugoslavian towns including Skopje, the city where she was born. "You can hardly imagine what this visit of Mother means for our country", Father Gabric afterwards told the Sisters. "One eighty-year-old lady told me, 'Now I'll die peacefully'." As for Mother Teresa, she managed, despite over forty years without real practice, to speak Serbo-Croat and Albanian, with Father Gabric at her side serving as a dictionary.

News of her arrival spread like wild-fire. This time when she visited Skopje she was given an official welcome by the mayor, who congratulated her on the award of the Nobel Prize. She visited the graves of those who had died in the 1963 earthquake, and looked round the reconstructed city. The places she had known as a child had been destroyed. The Church of the Sacred Heart had gone, and there was no longer any trace of her father's grave in the cemetery. "It may look completely different," she pronounced on seeing the town's new commercial quarter, "but it is still my Skopje."

Crowds came to meet her wherever she went. The churches were so packed that special bodyguards had to be appointed to prevent her from being crushed. "People are really full of faith", Mother Teresa reported with excitement. "Trials have purified and strengthened them in their faith – thank God." She added that the people of Yugoslavia were anxious to have the Missionaries of Charity in their midst, "so pray if this be the will of God."

One year after her visit the Missionaries of Charity opened a house in Zagreb, and a year after that Mother Teresa returned with four Sisters to open a house in Skopje itself, telling the local people, "You gave one person. I bring back four." One of the four Sisters she sent was Albanian. Of the others one was Maltese, and two were Indian. The "convent" consisted of just three rooms. The Sisters visited and cared for the elderly, the blind, the lame, the crippled and the poor all over the city. "There are very few Catholics," one Sister reported back, "and we visit all groups including gypsies. There is so much to say about our people. They are very lovable. Our old people are so beautiful. Many consider us their daughters and when we delay, they ask, 'Where were you, my daughters? Have you forgotten your Mama?' We have an old blind woman who takes care of a grandson. She says, 'If it was not for the Sisters, I would never see tomatoes and peppers and all these fresh vegetables and fruits.'" The Sister also wrote of how to many "material-minded" people the Sisters riding bicycles and wearing saris seemed crazy, and there were undoubtedly times when the attempt to care for those people who were not aware of the world-famous activities of a former citizen of Skopje was not easy.

A house in East Berlin, one of the twenty-six opened in 1981, was the next of Mother Teresa's foundations behind the Iron Curtain. Again, a request had come from the local bishops, and as always the work began in a small way, with the Sisters living in a flat in a poor neighbourhood, from where they went out to visit the sick and the lonely. Two years later, in December of 1983, another house was opened in East Germany, this time in Karl Marx Stadt. For Mother Teresa the poverty of the people of communist countries was extreme, for they were deprived of that most vital of all riches: the knowledge of the love of God for all men. Her own ill health could not be allowed to stand in the way of endeavours to meet that need.

On 14 April 1984, during a visit to the Vatican to give a talk on youth activities, she informed Cardinal Agostino Cassaroli that she had set her sights on China. It was an ambition which she had been harbouring for some years. In 1969, during the private audience in which the Constitutions for the Co-Workers were presented to the Pope, she had quietly asked Pope Paul VI to pray for her to go and start a foundation in the world's most populous country. By the time she declared her intentions to Cardinal Cassaroli she had already been to the Chinese Embassy in New Delhi to offer the services of her Sisters. An official at the embassy had asked whether she had been sent by the Pope. His response was a cautious one but he later went to see the work of the Missionaries of Charity for himself. After visiting the home for the dying he offered his support: "If I can do anything to help you, please let me know." Paving the way to enter China would prove to be a protracted process. Difficulties arose not so much on account of the government. The communist authorities told Mother Teresa that they had no poor in China, because in China the government looked after the poor, whereupon Mother Teresa informed them that she was delighted to hear that they had no poor but that she thought perhaps there might be some people who were disheartened and in need of a little encouragement. She and her Sisters would like to bring hope to the discouraged. That much the Chinese government was prepared to allow them to do.

There was little doubt in Mother Teresa's mind that once in China she would find material poverty. She had not expected to find such poverty in Tokyo but the Sisters had delved it out. It was spiritual food which the Missionaries of Charity saw as their primary gift to China, however. For this reason Mother Teresa was anxious to send a priest with her Sisters, and it was in this connection that delays arose. There were those who wanted her to take a priest from the pro-government patriotic wing of the Roman Catholic Church in China, but the Patriotic Church did not recognize Vatican authority. Mother Teresa insisted on the Sisters' right to have the priest of her choice.

As it transpired, Mother Teresa visited Poland instead in 1984 at the request of Cardinal Josef Glemp who had visited her in Rome shortly after she came out of Salvator Mundi Hospital and invited her to Warsaw. On her return to Rome she was obliged to spend a few more days in hospital. Only the occasional word she let drop indicated the limitations imposed on her by her weakened heart. The doctors had told her that she must avoid climbing stairs unless it was absolutely necessary. She was beginning to accept that she could not herself undertake all the visits to the Sisters overseas. Her Assistant General, Sister Frederick, toured the foundations in Central and South America on her behalf that year, but Mother Teresa still managed to travel the length and breadth of India, visiting the various Missionary of Charity houses, bringing news and encouragement, and still wanting to scrub floors and clean bathrooms. When violence erupted in India following the assassination of Mrs Indira Gandhi on 31 October 1984, Mother Teresa dispatched several Sisters to work among Sikh refugees. "We began by cleaning latrines," she would afterwards explain, "and this is something that opened people's hearts."

Mother Teresa made a point of attending the cremation of the woman whom she had continued to call friend even when allegations of corruption were being made against her. "May her soul live in peace for ever", she prayed aloud at Indira Gandhi's cremation pyre at the burning ghat on the banks of the Jumna River in New Delhi. Afterwards, as the British press were swift to point out, India might have been mourning a second great lady had it not been for a rather unlikely alliance. Mr Kinnock and Mr Steel were among the throng of dignitaries boarding official buses after the ceremony, when they spotted the diminutive figure of Mother Teresa in the path of one of the departing vehicles. Mr Steel grabbed one arm, Mr Kinnock the other, and the pair whisked her from beneath the wheels. She was saved to continue her works of peace, tending the wounded, comforting the widowed and feeding the hungry in the makeshift camps where Sikhs had taken refuge from the repercussions of the murder of Mrs Gandhi by a Sikh member of her bodyguard.

By Christmas, Mother Teresa was deeply concerned about the famine in Africa, so much so that on Christmas Day, despite the

WORKS OF PEACE   201

fact that she was running a fever, she left for Ethiopia. On her arrival she announced that she had "come to serve", and set about visiting the five Missionary of Charity houses in that country and organizing famine relief centres. In Addis Ababa, she met Bob Geldof, the rock singer and brain behind a chart-topping record which raised more than £6,000,000 for famine relief in Ethiopia. Bob Geldof was there to discuss with aid officials how the money made by the record "Do they know it's Christmas?" should be spent. Mother Teresa accepted a copy of the disc and told the singer: "What you do I could not do, and what I do you could not do. But as long as it is clear in your heart and your mind, then it is God's will to see us through." Bob Geldof afterwards said that he was flattered to have met her because she was the "living embodiment of moral good".

On 20 January 1985, at the invitation of the Patriotic Church, Mother Teresa at last set foot in China for the first time. Travelling on an Indian diplomatic passport, she arrived on a flight from Hong Kong, having spent the previous few days visiting Macao and Taiwan. Already there were houses in Macao, Korea and Hong Kong. The government had provided Mother Teresa with a building in Hong Kong in which to begin another Nirmal Hriday. A house was ready and only awaiting the arrival of four Sisters in Taipei, and Mother Teresa had decided that the time had come for some Missionaries of Charity to start learning Chinese. Like English and Spanish in the West, she saw Chinese as being the language in which to proclaim the Good News in the East. The initiative for the invitation to China had come originally from her. She was only the second influential Roman Catholic to receive one, the first having been Cardinal Jaime Sin of the Philippines, but she wasted no time before publicly expressing the hope that her Missionaries of Charity would one day bestow on the sick and the poor of China the kind of "tender love and care" which the state could perhaps not provide. Asked if she had brought any message from the Vatican to the estranged Chinese Patriotic Catholic Association, she replied firmly and unambiguously, "No, I'm coming from Calcutta." Her four-day stay included a visit to a home for the aged in a Peking commune and a tour of a factory for handicapped workers, where she wrote in the visitors' book the words which invariably preceded her signature, "God bless you all". She also met the Chinese leader Deng Xiaoping's paraplegic son, Deng Pufang, who said he was an atheist and debated with her God's role in his work on behalf of the handicapped. It was a celebration of the Eucharist by a priest in his eighties who, Mother Teresa deduced, must have been ordained before the separation of the Chinese Patriotic Church, which had most impact on her. It was a very cold weekday morning and there was a conspicuous lack of young people present but the church was packed: "The Holy Mass is still offered in Latin, the old way. The people still pray the Rosary during Holy Mass but I have never seen anywhere such an attitude of adoration and humility on receiving Holy Communion."

Mother Teresa usually stayed in a convent when travelling, if not one of the Missionary of Charity houses then at least one belonging to some other religious order. The state-approved Chinese Church, however, had a few nuns but no surviving convents. Mother Teresa's first visit to China was thus a very rare occasion on which she found herself comfortably installed, much against her natural inclinations, in a brand new high-rise hotel.

CHAPTER NINE

A Quiet Storm

Four million leprosy patients treated through the mobile leprosy clinics by the year 1984; the provision of weekly dry rations to 106,271 people and cooked food to 51,580 through the relief centres; the admission of 13,246 to the homes for dying destitute and the successful discharging of 8,627 of those who might otherwise have been left to die; the reception of 6,000 children into the 103 Shishu Bhavans – these were the kind of statistics which Mother Teresa frequently had at her finger tips, and which she would cite with pleasure as irrefutable evidence of God's achievements in spite of man or woman's ineptitude. In many people's terms all this, not to mention an invitation to China, would have more than justified a pause for rest or at least to draw breath, but for Mother Teresa every achievement was just one small progression on a long, long road. She was never still. She never sat back to savour one little breakthrough, and her principle of meeting needs as they arose remained unaltered. She was a woman who saw at once a person's immediate urgent need and went to meet it in a simple and direct way. If she encountered a starving child she would not make a survey or set up a study course. Instead she would go at once to get milk for the child by the shortest possible route, and frequently more long-term care would follow in her train.

In 1985 she received a letter from a patient of Dr Richard Di-Gioia a physician in Washington DC, who cared for a number of the area's AIDS sufferers. The patient in question was not himself an AIDS sufferer, but he described to her the suffering of those who were, in words which evidently struck a chord of recognition. In the pain, the anguish and the rejection of the growing number of people afflicted with AIDS, she saw once more Christ in his distressing disguise. The need had been brought to her attention and she went to meet it as swiftly as she could. In June of that year, during a visit to Washington, she made a point of responding to the letter writer's request that she visit AIDS patients at George Washington University Hospital. Escorted by Dr DiGioia, she greeted each patient personally, enquired about their families, and suggested that they pray. She asked many questions about AIDS, about how the epidemic started, what caused it, how it was diagnosed and whether there was a cure. Asked after Mother Teresa's visit whether his patient's letter had mentioned that the disease had primarily stricken gay men, Dr DiGioia said that he did not know, but he added that he thought more Christians should take a lesson from her example and act rather than be judgemental.

Mother Teresa did indeed act. In December she worked what the press described as a "miracle in Manhattan", a miracle which "jolted the imagination of America". In the brash and sometimes irreverent community of Greenwich Village on the sophisticated East side of Manhattan, she set about opening a hospice for those people whom many regarded as the final flotsam of the permissive society, the victims of AIDS whose family and friends had shunned them, leaving them to face an inevitable and agonizing death alone. The "miracle" began with a visit to New York's Sing Sing prison and an encounter with Antonio Rivera, Jimmy Matos and Daryl Monsett, three tough young prisoners serving sentences for crimes of violence. Mother Teresa met them in their cells and was immediately spurred into action by the plight of the men who, after repeated abortive attempts to have them transferred, faced a painful and isolated death behind bars. "In God's name, please let these men die in peace", she pleaded with New York's Governor Cuomo, and Mario Cuomo, who had previously turned down similar appeals, found himself signing a release order within twenty-four hours. The three were immediately transferred to a Manhattan hospital to await places in a new hospice which Mother Teresa was set upon providing.

Mother Teresa's particular gift for opening doors was brought into full play. She was by no means as politically naïve or as unfamiliar with the ways of the world as it sometimes suited her to appear. She knew she had an ability to draw out a chivalrous passion to defend her interests, and was not above using it. Although per-

haps more by a kind of innate shrewdness than calculated deliberation, she also had a way of involving the right influential people
and making them feel they were specially chosen instruments for a
divine purpose. As a spokesman at the Gay Men's Crisis Centre in
Manhattan pointed out at the time, countless hours and money had
been spent trying to spotlight the plight of AIDS victims, but then
a small woman came halfway round the world from India, and in
her own quiet but unswerving way brought them the focus they
needed in a matter of days.

To the support of Governor Cuomo for the release of the three
AIDS sufferers in Sing Sing, Mother Teresa added the leverage of
Mayor Koch, who announced that he felt like "a blessed instrument
to be the vehicle for making this request". He could not believe
that anyone could say "No" to her. The Roman Catholic Primate,
Cardinal John O'Connor, was equally impressed. Together that
Christmas Eve they found themselves in the company of Mother
Teresa for the opening of New York's first AIDS hospice in the
rectory of a Greenwich Village church. Christmas had seemed to
her a particularly appropriate time at which to open a house for
those who found no welcome elsewhere, for those who were being
rejected even by their own families: "This is the time when Jesus
is born to joy and love and peace, so I wanted them to be born to
joy and love and peace." She achieved her objective. Christmas in
the Sisters' liturgical and spiritual calendar was "a time to welcome
Jesus, not in a cold manger of our hearts but in a heart full of love
and humility, in a heart so pure, so immaculate, so warm with love
for one another". To the public at large Mother Teresa insisted:
"We are not here to sit in judgement on these people, to decide
blame or guilt. Our mission is to help them, to make their dying
days more tolerable." In fact, as one long-standing friend and Co-
Worker was to point out, it is doubtful how detailed an appreciation
Mother Teresa really had of the activities which in some cases had
led to the contracting of AIDS. There was everything to suggest
that the excesses of the San Francisco bath-houses, for example,
might have occasioned in her something of the personal distaste of
many others of her generation, background and calling, but in a
sense such attitudes were irrelevant. They paled into insignificance
beside the overriding requirement to love. She was meeting yet

another form of poverty. She saw the victims of AIDS as the lepers of the West, as people whom others might condemn as "unclean" but who like everyone else were in need of love. So it was that in a speech to the National Council for International Health she defined the greatest pain for AIDS victims as being "the pain of the heart – of being unwanted and unloved, thrown away by society."

The professed objective in the creation of the "Gift of Love", as the New York hospice was called, was very much that of Nirmal Hriday in Calcutta: to assist people to die in peace and in the knowledge that they were loved. The home which could provide such care for some fourteen men had little in the way of sophisticated equipment. Consequently many of the men in fact died in hospital, but often the Sisters, who became their companions in what could be a protracted and painful process, were instrumental in helping them to come to terms with the approach of death. The building had its chapel, dominated as always by a crucifix and the words "I thirst". The five Sisters who worked there had Mass and the Rosary daily. There was also periodic religious instruction for those who wanted it. Mother Teresa herself made no attempt to disguise her joy when those who had frequently lived for many years estranged from their creator found faith in the redemptive message of the one in whose Passion she believed they were sharing. She would speak with joy of one such man who had been obliged to spend some time in hospital. He had looked upon her as his friend and asked to speak to her in confidence: "What did he say after twenty-five years of being away from God? 'When I get the terrible pain in my head, I share it with Jesus and suffer as he did when he was crowned with thorns. When I get the terrible pain in my back, I share it with him when he was scourged at the pillar, and when I get the pain in my hands and feet, I share it with him when he was nailed to the cross. I ask you to take me home. I want to die with you.'" Mother Teresa obtained permission to take him "home". She took him to the chapel where he "talked to Jesus" as she had never heard anyone talk before: "so tenderly and full of love". Three days later he died at peace.

Mother Teresa was well aware that the capacity of the Sisters' love to transform was not easy for everyone to understand. Inevitably, as in the case of Nirmal Hriday, Calcutta, the Missionaries of Charity here were susceptible to the allegation that they were setting out to convert the vulnerable. It was a potential criticism of which the Sisters were conscious, and which they set out to counter-act by insisting that spiritual instruction and worship were strictly voluntary. Conversion was only for those who asked for it.

Another difficulty which the work with dying AIDS patients encountered, in common with the work with the dying destitute of Calcutta, was opposition from the people who lived in its vicinity. This had proved an obstacle in the search for a suitable location for "Gift of Love" in New York. It became a more enduring problem in the case of a second home for dying AIDS victims and people with other terminal illnesses which was subsequently opened in Washington DC. On Friday, 13 June 1986 Mother Teresa had a meeting with the United States President, Ronald Reagan, at the White House. It was only a short meeting but the President gave her his encouragement for a plan to open a second centre in America for the victims of AIDS. "We are looking for a nice place where the people can come and receive love and also remove their loneliness", Mother Teresa said afterwards. "I told Mr President I would do the praying, and he will have to do the work." In fact it was the Most Reverend James Hickey, Archbishop of Washington, who invited Mother Teresa to open a new convent which he saw not so much as a hospital or hospice as a "loving home where persons with AIDS and other terminal illnesses could find the care, com-passion and peace they deserve as children of God". It was to be a place for the forgotten, the abandoned and the homeless who faced a terrible illness alone. Unlike the Gift of Love home, it would have the capacity to accommodate women and children as well as men.

As soon as Mother Teresa telephoned the Archbishop to accept his invitation, a vigorous search for the best location began. The requirement was for a home with some measure of privacy and comfort for the Sisters and their guests, and a place which could be made available quickly. They were also sensitive to the fact that the ministry they proposed could raise a variety of community issues. Finally, they thought they had found the right place at the old St Joseph's home, a sizeable red brick building formerly used as a convent, orphanage, school and the offices of Catholic Chari-ties. By a unanimous vote the Board of Catholic Charities supported the decision to offer Mother Teresa the building and twelve acres of grounds, set in a leafy middle-class suburban enclave. The convent, it was made clear, would not be a medical facility, hospice or community residence facility, but home for a religious community reaching out to the suffering and homeless victims of terminal illnesses. Georgetown University Medical Center joined with the Archdiocese in offering assistance to the Sisters. Its help included health screening and medical care of the residents. Hospitals, community clinics and other groups could make referrals of people needing a caring home to the "Gift of Peace", with the referring agencies continuing to provide medical care. Catholic Charities worked with community leaders and neighbourhood residents to share plans for the convent and reassure them on issues of neighbourhood concern.

At the announcement of the proposal at a news conference on 21 August 1986 Archbishop Hickey released letters from the Surgeon General of the United States and the Director of the National Institute for Infectious Diseases, welcoming the convent and stressing that it posed no health risks for the surrounding community. The nearest home was actually four hundred feet from the convent. Only those who made a significant effort to reach it would have contact with the residents. Yet it seemed that the fear of AIDS transcended all attempts to inform and educate about the disease. Despite repeated assurances that AIDS had been shown to be transmitted only through intimate sexual contact, through infected needles or through the exchange of blood, some neighbours remained fearful that the virus could be transmitted through the air. One resident of the neighbourhood even protested that a used Kleenex tissue could fall out of the rubbish, blow into her garden and be picked up by her daughter, who might then contract the disease. The day after the August announcement two hundred angry house owners gathered at a community meeting to register their objections. Apart from fears of potential health hazards, there was also a concern that the neighbouring property prices would slump. Others disapproved of the fact that the home should be caring for gay men at all. "AIDS comes because of immoral acts", protested one churchman. "Why is it doing charity work to bring them in?"

But the Sisters did bring them in. "Gift of Peace" opened on

8 November 1986. Most patients arrived by ambulance from area hospitals or their homes in the final throes of Acquired Immune Deficiency Syndrome, the as yet incurable virus that killed most victims within two years of diagnosis. Some were suffering from dementia, which was found to be increasingly affecting AIDS victims. Nearly all were very much alone in their suffering, and nearly all were far too weak even to walk up the stairs, let alone roam beyond the extensive grounds of Gift of Peace. Those people whom local residents were alarmed to see waiting at bus stops were people suffering from other terminal illnesses.

The fears occasioned by the presence of AIDS patients in what some saw as an unregulated medical facility foisted on them under false pretences by the Archdiocese of Washington and the city government, persisted. Some neighbours remained unconvinced by the argument that this was not a hospice, that the property had a charitable use designation and did not therefore require "rezoning", or that since it was not a medical facility it did not require a licence. The Sisters' attempt to bring love and care to those suffering with AIDS would remain fraught with difficulties. When it was not an appeal to the zoning board it was the alleged breach of various fire regulations that threatened the existence of the home.

Not everyone was opposed to its aims, however. The Co-Workers, volunteers and other lay people with professional expertise found a role in helping to unravel the red tape; part of the building was allocated to Missionary of Charity Tertians and the process by which the Sisters established themselves was likened by one Co-Worker to the camel of popular fable who first put his nose in the tent and then before long the entire camel was in. Meanwhile Mother Teresa continued to spread her message that AIDS should be seen as a "sign that God wants us to open our hearts and love one another".

The Gift of Peace was a place with strict rules and a religious atmosphere. The walls there, as in other Missionary of Charity houses, were hung with coloured pictures of saints and the Pope. Visitors were usually only permitted between 4 and 5.30 p.m. Radios were allowed but television was not. The occupants were not required to take part in the Sisters' worship but, like the Gift of Love, it was not a place for people who wanted to entertain friends and pursue this world's distractions. Nor was the life one to which everyone readily adjusted. There were those who preferred to end their days elsewhere, but there were also those who experienced, in the Sisters' care, the strange beauty of coming to terms with death.

In the Gift of Love home in New York there was one man who had used drugs in Vietnam "to ease the strain". After the war he continued using drugs. He also received "hundreds" of blood transfusions while on kidney dialysis. He did not know by which means he had contracted AIDS. "But with my drug record they blame it on the drugs", he said. "I blame nothing. I don't think I would ever have come to God without this. They would have found me on the street." He had seen many others die before him: "In the end they ask for Christ. They say, 'Oh God have mercy!' In the end they grasp the peace." The man in question had met Mother Teresa at the house. She was "like a quiet storm that will shake you", he maintained. "She says little things – but from them come oak trees."

The work with AIDS patients grew. In June 1988 another Gift of Love was opened in San Francisco, and in March 1989 Addis Ababa, Ethiopia also received a similar "gift". In December 1989 an AIDS home was begun by the Sisters in Denver, Colorado. When the AIDS crisis erupted in Los Angeles county the Brothers there were particularly touched by the fact that even some doctors and nurses were refusing to work with people suffering from AIDS. To one Brother in particular, who was physically very demonstrative, the idea that people might refuse to touch another human being who was sick and in need was horrifying. He started up a day care facility in Oakland, the first of its kind in the country, designed to provide a welcome not only for the AIDS sufferers themselves but also for those who were close to them, their families and people who tried to care for them. It was to be a haven to which they could come and find rest and support. There came a point, however, where the Brother in question, knowing that he could be called away at any time and wanting to ensure its continuation, felt it best to hand over responsibility for the centre to a board of directors. The Missionary Brothers would continue to show their concern for the plight of people with AIDS in very practical ways, visiting them in prison, giving support to those who cared for them. The Medical

Co-Workers were also called upon to be particularly sensitive to the needs of those suffering from the "leprosy of the West".

"Plant love in the world and it will grow" – Mother Teresa took the words of St John of the Cross to heart and endeavoured to live their message in places where others were sometimes too fearful of potential complexities. On 8 July 1986, at the invitation of Cuba's Roman Catholic Episcopal Conference, she arrived in Havana for talks with the Cuban President, Fidel Castro. Two days later she announced to a packed church in the suburb of Regla that she was happy to share the good news that very soon her Sisters would be coming to Cuba. The success of her venture was seen as a thaw of relations between Havana and the Vatican.

In October 1986, shortly after the opening of the Gift of Peace home in Washington, she undertook a tour of East Africa. She was deeply concerned about the famine situation in the Sudan, and planned to set up a centre in the south to care for some of the victims. In Khartoum she offered prayers for the victims of the three-year-old civil war in southern Sudan, and then flew on to Dar es Salaam, Tanzania. From there she was due to visit Kenya where her Sisters were working among destitute and other needy people in the Mathari Valley, one of the poorest areas of Nairobi. As the light aircraft gathered speed to take off from the rough airstrip at Hombolo near Dodoma in central Tanzania it slewed into the crowd lining the runway, killing five people. "We were praying the Rosary," Mother Teresa afterwards described the experience, "but all of a sudden the plane instead of going up went among the Sisters and the people, who had come to see us off. In less than fifteen minutes all was over – five lay dead – two wounded. Three children, the manager of the leprosy centre and our Sister M. Serena covered with blood – all dead."

It was a gruesome accident. At least one of the dead had been decapitated by the plane's propellers. Mother Teresa herself accompanied the two children and her Sister to hospital, where they were pronounced dead. Apart from the dead, two other Missionary of Charity Sisters were wounded. Mother Teresa attended the funeral of Sister Serena and was deeply affected by the experience. The press reported her as saying, "My coming is behind the accident". To her Sisters she spoke of those days as being full of pain and suffering, but also of deep gratitude to God for those who had been spared and for the love and care that had been shown to them by the Bishop and many other local people. There was talk of abandoning the rest of her tour but the terrible suffering of southern Sudan was calling to her, and she was intent upon enlisting help from the Tanzanian people and sending four Sisters to the area worst affected. As it transpired, she flew on to Tabora where she attended a ceremony at which seven Missionary of Charity Sisters took their first vows.

Her itinerary for the remainder of October and November alone included Rome on the 26th, Assisi on the 27th and 28th, professions again in Rome on the 29th and 30th. Cuba on the 2nd, San Francisco professions on the 9th and 10th. By 15 November she hoped to be in Calcutta. In fact on 7 November she was still in Cuba on her second visit to that country in five months. Since 1959 church membership and activity had dwindled under the communist government, but Fidel Castro had recently expressed an interest in improving government relations with the Roman Catholic Church. He had allowed a meeting of Cuban bishops, and the bishops had been to the Vatican for an audience with Pope John Paul II, but Mother Teresa's visits were also a part of the demonstrations of improved relations.

The travelling was not all hardship. Even in her old age Mother Teresa acknowledged with girlish pleasure that she had "an itch to travel". It was, however, taking its toll, and in 1987 Mother Teresa actually cancelled at short notice the visit she had planned to make to Japan. In an unprecedented step she suggested to the Sisters in Tokyo and the national link for the Co-Workers that they tape-record a telephone message to the people she would have seen in the course of her tour. She knew how disappointed they would be, and only serious physical disability could ever have kept her away. On 28 March her voice, which according to Sister Leon MC sounded "pained, almost excruciatingly so", conveyed her deep regret:

Dear Japanese people,

I have been looking forward to come to you all. As you know, I am suffering from heart and I found that I will not be able to make the

journey and do the work there during these days. That's why I had at the
last moment to cancel my going to Tokyo. I would have loved to be with
you all but I think physically I will not be able to to do it. But my message
to you all is that God has a special love for the people of Japan.

And the message is to love one another as God loves each one and this
love begins at home. The family that prays together stays together and if
you stay together you will love one another as God loves each one of you.

This is my prayer for you that through this love for one another, you
grow in the love of God.

God bless you and keep you in his heart.

Undeterred by what proved to be a temporary setback she still
managed to journey to San Francisco to attend the first profession
of ten novices, to New York, to Austria, to Poland for more professions, to Africa, to the Soviet Union to visit the survivors of the
Chernobyl disaster and to receive the Gold Medal of the Soviet
Peace Committee, and on more than one occasion to Rome. May
1987 brought an announcement from the Vatican which must have
given her particular personal satisfaction. The pert suggestions to
senior churchmen that she would like to bring her poor into some
of their imposing buildings had apparently paid off. In a radical and
historic step to show the support of the Vatican for the poor, Pope
John Paul II authorized the building of a shelter for some of Rome's
estimated five thousand down-and-outs. The Pope had seen the
city's vagrants and jobless immigrants sleeping under the archways
and outside the shops and offices near the Vatican City, and was
undoubtedly touched by their plight, but there were those close to
Mother Teresa who were convinced that it was she who had sown
the seeds of the idea. The Pope gave the task of supervising what
the Vatican chose to call a "hospice" to Mother Teresa. A new
building, designed by a leading Italian architect, Angelo Malfatto,
providing beds for seventy-four sick and homeless people, and food
for thousands more, was to be constructed in an unused courtyard
near the Vatican's Holy Office. "All tramps and vagabonds are
welcome regardless of their religion", a Vatican official announced.
"We do not want people sleeping under the arches of Tiber bridges
or at railway stations. People of all faiths – and those of none – will
be welcomed in." Mother Teresa, for her part, acknowledged

herself delighted that the Holy Father had given the Missionaries of Charity a place in his home to welcome the sick and the poor. Construction of the building to be known as "Dona de Maria", "Gift of Mary", was soon under way.

Not long afterwards Mayor Edward Koch of New York suffered a minor stroke, and was much surprised when suddenly Mother Teresa stopped at his home for a "sick visit". Mother Teresa herself had only recently undergone eye surgery to remove a cataract in St Vincent's Hospital, New York, but neither this nor the multitude of other demands made on her time could be allowed to prevent her from making such impromptu demonstrations of her concern. "I had heard you were sick and I came to comfort you", the Mayor quoted Mother Teresa as saying. "I am well now," he told her, "so come on in."

While still recovering from her own operation she rushed to the assistance of people affected by the earthquake which rocked the India–Nepal border region on 21 August 1988, killing an estimated eight hundred people and leaving many more homeless and without resources. November that year saw her in South Africa. After many years of anticipation and delays, she finally set foot in a country fraught with political tension, to be met with an ecstatic welcome. South Africa was a country in which it was difficult in the extreme to avoid alignment with any particular political standpoint, but Mother Teresa managed it. As South Africans ranging from Mrs Harry Oppenheimer and Archbishop Tutu to the humblest of township residents, people from right across the political, social and racial spectrum, pressed to see her, she fielded with consummate skill suggestions that her mission was politically inspired, making it clear that her invitation had come originally from Roman Catholic Archbishop George Daniel: "I did not know that apartheid or something like that existed. I never mix up in politics because I do not know. But what I know is that we are a religious congregation and the invitation was sent and answered by us because we want to give our love in action." To her colour was irrelevant and she was not afraid to say so. "White, black, green, yellow, whatever, you are all children of God, created for greater things, to love and to be loved."

She chose Khayelitsha, a vast black township sited on an expanse

of windswept sand dunes outside Cape Town, as the location for
the four Sisters she intended to leave to meet whatever need might
manifest itself, and she chose it not, she insisted, because the people
there were coloured but because they were poor. On Wednesday,
9 November Mother Teresa prayed to St Joseph that she would
find a convent for her nuns in Khayelitsha, and by lunchtime her
prayer had been answered. We met completely by chance that day
in the sand-strewn roads that divided up the monotonous rows of
rudimentary housing constructed to accommodate the more fortunate members of Cape Town's rapidly expanding coloured population. The less fortunate found unofficial accommodation in
improvised shacks and shanties not so very different from the
improvised dwellings of the Calcutta slums.

"Are you writing something beautiful?" Her age and the
unexpected circumstances of our encounter did nothing to impair
her extraordinary gift for remembering faces. "And you, Mother.
Are you opening a house?" She told me that the Sisters would be
moving into what had been a home for the elderly owned by the
Catholic Welfare Bureau. They would move in that very evening
and spend the night there. Eventually she would like a little more
land to build a place for the sick and the dying, but for the moment
the Sisters' needs had been met. Of the four Sisters she left there,
two were Indian, one was British but had spent the first nine years
of her life in South Africa, and the fourth was from Rwanda.
Together in the coloured township of Khayelitsha they would bear
quiet witness to the harmony which could exist between people of
different races. It had all happened with a speed which others saw
as extraordinary but which Mother Teresa took for granted. The
sight of her being driven in haste through the township in a
"combi" van brought obvious joy to people living on the brink of
gang warfare and political faction fighting. She left behind her a
wake of sand and of smiles.

Her message, as she went on to Port Elizabeth, Durban and the
impoverished Winterveld area north of Pretoria, that if people
deepened their faith in prayer they would see "there is no religion,
no caste, no colour, no nationality, no riches and no poverty" was
widely pronounced to have been balm for the wounds of a troubled
country. There were those who were disappointed that she had not

been prepared to criticize the enforcers of apartheid and those who tried to place a political construction on some of what she said. She told the story of how once when torrential rains lashed the streets of Calcutta, she had taken a little rice on a plate to a Hindu family she knew to be without money or food:

And the woman disappeared immediately and she came back with only half what I had taken on the plate. I asked her, "What did you do with the rice?" She replied, "I have shared what you gave me with a Muslim family and they are our neighbours." That woman knew her neighbours' need. It did not matter that they were Muslim, or that her own family were very hungry. That is giving until it hurts.

If there was a political message in the story she told, it was one of harmony and human togetherness based on sharing. "Unlike so many do-gooders," commented the *Cape Times*, "she did not sit on foreign sidelines condemning people or a situation in this country. She came in person, identified herself with those most in need of compassion, and set up a mission to help them. This has always been her method, ever since she started her first hospice in the slums of Calcutta. Her saintly credentials are so universally respected that they silence even the most rabid radicals – for once no one questioned a famous international figure's decision to visit South Africa."

By the time she left South Africa on 15 November 1988, Mother Teresa was already making plans for a second house in the Winterveld area. Her next stop was to be Nairobi. Those who flew with her over the African bushland were privileged to see her with her face pressed to the windows of the aircraft, spotting the wild game beneath her with all the interest, energy and enthusiasm of a child. What was it that enabled her to continue? Often she would say: "It is the joy of giving, the joy of bringing love into people's lives that keeps us all going."

On 8 December came an invitation from the Soviet Peace Committee in Moscow to come to the USSR to sign an agreement for a new foundation. She arrived in Moscow at 11 p.m. on 15 December, tired but manifestly delighted to be there. Next day a car was placed at her disposal to attend Mass in the chapel dedicated to Our Lady of Peace, and afterwards talks began with the Peace Committee. Consent was immediately given for four Sisters to start work at once in Moscow, but Mother Teresa wanted to bring in four more for Armenia. The earthquake of 7 December had caused the death of an estimated fifty-five thousand people in Armenia. More than ten thousand people were being treated in hospital and many more had been left homeless. Their need was something that Mother Teresa could not ignore. On the 17th she managed to meet many of the people of Moscow, who knew of her presence because Soviet television had reported her arrival and, much to the satisfaction of one of the Missionary of Charity Sisters who would afterwards form part of the foundation in the Soviet capital, had focused for more than five seconds on Mother Teresa's hand, tightly clutching her rosary. Next day she boarded a plane for a three-hour flight to Armenia, presenting the crew with a small statue of the Virgin Mary which they fixed to the controls next to the pilot. She was welcomed to Armenia by the Vice President of the Armenian Peace Committee and then taken to the residence of the Armenian Patriarch, who abandoned an important meeting with his bishops to welcome Mother Teresa with great warmth and invite her to stay in his house. Mother Teresa was swift to take the opportunity to ask his permission for a Catholic priest to come to Armenia also and he gave his consent subject to the government's agreement. That afternoon Mother Teresa visited a hospital where children injured in the earthquake were being cared for. She spent time with each child, praying over them and giving them miraculous medals. For people who had lost everything and sometimes everybody they had loved, her presence alone was a source of renewed hope.

At noon on the 19th, after Mass celebrated in a chapel in the Armenian Patriarch's residence and a visit to a hospital packed to overflowing with injured people, Mother Teresa was received by the Soviet Prime Minister, Mr Nikolai Ryzhkov, who was visiting Armenia together with the Foreign Minister and the head of the Armenian Communist party. "I have brought no gold or silver," she told them, "but I hope to offer the help of my voluntary workers in the continuing process of relief and rehabilitation." Mother Teresa emerged from the meeting beaming broadly. She had received permission to bring four more Sisters to Armenia and for a Catholic priest to accompany them to provide for their spiritual needs. It would be the first time that a Catholic priest had come to Armenia for seventy years. Immediately afterwards Mother Teresa left the Armenian capital Yerevan for a five-hour car journey to Leninakan, a city which had been totally destroyed by the earthquake. The road as she approached the city was lined on either side with coffins stacked in piles. Rescue crews were still in the process of searching out the injured and the dead from the rubble. Mother Teresa made a careful study of requirements and from there it was back to Moscow on the 20th, where in an interview with Moscow television she expressed the intentions of her Sisters in the simplest unchanging terms: they would come only to "give tender love and care".

The very next day four Sisters arrived from Rome. Mother Teresa welcomed them at the airport with obvious joy and took them to their new home, a hospital which would provide them with accommodation in the form of three rooms – one for a refectory, one for a dormitory and one for a chapel – until they could find a house.

Two days later two more Sisters arrived from Rome together with an Australian priest, and the day after that, on Christmas Eve, two Sisters were due to arrive from India but, having erroneously been put on an Air India flight to Amsterdam, they did not in fact turn up until the 27th. In the meantime Mother Teresa and her handful of Sisters celebrated their first Christmas in another "land of their dreams". Mother Teresa signed an agreement in Armenia relating to the work of the Missionaries of Charity and remained long enough to settle her Sisters in, but on the 29th she was back in Moscow where next day she had a meeting with Mr Chazov, the Minister of Health. Mr Chazov expressed his gratitude to the Missionaries of Charity for coming to the Soviet Union. He informed Mother Teresa that he was an atheist, but to her unbridled delight told her that he would pray for her and her Sisters. "The 31st", wrote one of the newly arrived Sisters from Moscow, "was rather calm. Mother could finish some of her letters."

Asked once why she did not rest more, Mother Teresa said simply: "There will be plenty of time to rest in eternity. Here there is so much to do. . . ."

CHAPTER TEN

Passing on the Mantle

On 11 April 1990 it was announced to the world that Pope John Paul II had accepted the resignation of Mother Teresa as Superior General of the Missionaries of Charity. It was not the first time that she had hoped the electoral body of the Society, always guided by the Holy Spirit, would entrust its leadership to someone else. According to the constitutions of the Missionaries of Charity consecrated by the Holy See, the "Chapter General" made up of regional delegates themselves elected from the various foundations of the Congregation throughout the world, met every six years to elect its Superior General. The constitutions also stated that the Superior General could be elected for a second but not for a third time without the special approval of the Holy See. In the case of Mother Teresa the Vatican had repeatedly waived the two-term regulation because she was the founder of the Congregation. There were those who believed that she had deliberately held on to her position and had done so for too long. In fact Mother Teresa had on the occasion of several previous elections privately expressed the wish to be relieved of her position, although always within the context of submission to the will of God. The Society was not hers, she insisted, nor was it the Sisters'. It belonged to God and therein lay its security.

The very first Chapter General, made up as it was then of the Sister Superiors and a deputy from each house, met for the first time in 1961. Even at a time when the outcome might reasonably have been taken for granted, Mother Teresa directed her Sisters to prepare themselves carefully for the responsibility of election with daily prayer that they might know and do the things that were pleasing to God. At the request of Archbishop Dyer, Father Van Exem was present at the 1961 election to ensure the validity of the voting undertaken by secret ballot. Every single vote was for "Mother", with the exception of one: Mother Teresa's own vote which Father Van Exem advised should be kept secret even from the remainder of the "electoral college".

Preparation for the 1967 Chapter General began a year in advance. Already in October 1966 Mother Teresa was laying the spiritual foundations for a gathering which she hoped would bring much fruit. Spiritual preparation involved a special concentration on humility in thought, word and action. For three months before the Chapter each Sister was required to make at least five sacrifices of real charity. At each Mass the first intention after the intention for the Church was to be for the Society. All their prayer and work were to be offered daily for the Congregation with a particular supplication to the Holy Spirit "by whose wisdom it was created, and by whose providence it was governed". In 1967 Father Van Exem was absent from Calcutta when the Chapter General was held but the outcome was conclusive. In 1973 once again the Chapter was prefaced with much prayer and preparation. On that occasion Archbishop Picachy confided to Father Van Exem his conviction that there would be a substantial number of votes for someone other than Mother Teresa, but Father Van Exem remained unconvinced and, sure enough, when the voting took place, once again there was only one vote for anyone other than "Mother": Mother Teresa's own vote which was once again kept secret.

In 1979 Father Van Exem was in Kidderpur at the time of the ballot, but shortly before the election a number of Sisters came to him to report that Mother Teresa was insisting that she was too old and ill to continue. She was certain that among the many wonderful Sisters in the Society there was one who could easily take her place and she had made no secret of this conviction. She had even gone so far as to say that she believed it would be for the greater glory of God, the good of the Society, every individual Sister and the poor, that they vote for a Superior General from among the Senior Sisters. Indeed so vigorously was she spreading this message that Father Van Exem was obliged to write her a letter warning that if she continued to pressurize her Sisters in this way the election would be invalid and she would have to reassemble the voters from all over the world and hold another Chapter. "So I got a sweet little note saying 'The Sisters are completely free. They can vote for anybody.' That was the end of Mother's canvassing."

Mother Teresa did not canvass any more. In this as in other things she was obedient to the man who had been her spiritual director for so many years. By the time the Chapter General met again in 1985, however, to elect the Superior General and six councillors, her age and state of health was really lending weight to her personal inclination. By then inevitably outside attention was being drawn to the question of who might be a suitable successor to one with such considerable personal charisma, spiritual gifts, capacity for work, travel and organization. Mother Teresa's duties and responsibilities included representing the Society officially before the ecclesiastical and civil authorities, a task which involved considerable paper work and administrative ability. By the constitutions of the Congregation she was both its guiding spirit and its fighting arm. Speculation began in the press. An article in *India Today* by a journalist in Calcutta looked closely but inconclusively at a number of Senior Sisters as possible candidates.

Mother Teresa herself, despite any wishes she might have harboured to relinquish some of the responsibility she carried, had always made it clear that she left the question of her successor to the Divine Providence which had never yet failed the congregation: "God will find another person, more humble, more devoted, more obedient to him and if it is God's will the Society will go on." She answered any fears the Sisters themselves might have relating to the future of a Congregation in which she had been so staunchly, so tenderly and for so many years "Mother", with the reassurance that God had brought them together for some good and that he would guarantee its future provided they put no obstacles in his way. Prior to the election she called them to deep prayer, to purity of heart, openness to the Holy Spirit and the desire only to do with great love what must be done for the glory of God and for his Church. Asked by the press in 1985 whether she intended to seek re-election she would say only that "God's will must be fulfilled". Privately she thanked those without whom she could not have done what she had done in the course of the past thirty-five years, manifestly believing that a new Superior General would be found. The

Sisters prayed for the light to know the will of God, the love to accept it and the courage to do it, and they re-elected Mother Teresa.

Her physical condition obliged her to delegate more and more of her daily responsibility to the second tier of leadership, the elected councillors, but the central burden was still very much hers. In June 1989 she visited Budapest in the company of five Sisters. In July she returned to Calcutta but then left for Peru, Switzerland and Albania. In Albania the film *Mother Teresa* was being shown for the first time, and in mid-August Mother Teresa made a brief and relatively discreet visit, at the invitation of Albania's President, to seek out her mother's grave and to explore the possibilities for a future foundation in the homeland from which she had been so painfully separated for so long. The visit brought her a very personal satisfaction and joy. Full of excitement and renewed zeal, she was back in Calcutta in time for the Society Feast on 22 August.

The message was being brought home to her nevertheless that such a strenuous schedule demanded a degree of physical strength which she no longer had. On the evening of 3 September she was overcome with fatigue and nausea, and experiencing pain in her stomach and heart. The high fever she was running went on through the next day, and on 5 September she asked to receive the sacraments of the sick, after which she was admitted to Woodlands nursing home in Calcutta. There it was found that she had a blockage in her heart which was functioning on only one valve. On 8 September her condition took a turn for the worse. This caused great concern throughout the world. From Rome Pope John Paul II sent her a message of personal concern: "Informed of your sudden illness, I hasten to assure you of my prayers and spiritual closeness. At this time, commending you to the intercession of Our loving Mother Mary, Help of the Sick. I cordially impart my special Apostolic Blessing as a pledge of strength and comfort in Our Lord and Saviour Jesus Christ." And from her sick bed in India Mother Teresa responded immediately: "I am offering all for you." Messages of sympathy also came from India's President, R. Venkataraman, as well as Prime Minister Rajiv Gandhi. Dr Vincenzo Bilotti, the Italian heart specialist who had previously tended to her, flew from Rome to treat her and she was fitted with a temporary, external pacemaker to control an irregular heartbeat. The condition was described as a worsening of her chronic angina. It was also discovered that malaria parasites had contributed to her illness.

At times her condition would improve; at others she was in considerable pain and discomfort. Not far from the Woodlands nursing home one of her Sisters was dying of cancer. Sister Premila had asked to spend her last days with the Sisters who worked in Nirmal Hriday and who now lived in accommodation above the home for the dying. She died on 25 September 1989, offering her suffering for Mother Teresa. The Missionaries of Charity in general prayed for a miracle to restore their "Mother". Prayers were offered by Co-Workers throughout the world, and Ann Blaikie flew out to Calcutta to visit her friend of so many years. Old age had rendered Mother Teresa more demonstrative: "She just put out her arms and gave me the biggest bear hug I have ever had in my life and then we both burst into tears", Ann recalled. "Then she said, 'My suffering has brought all the world to prayer'."

Finally, after more than a month of treatment, doctors were hopeful of Mother Teresa's complete recovery. When Rajiv Gandhi visited her in hospital he found her talking and cheerful. Not for the first time, however, she was warned that she must reduce her globe-trotting. Her niece Aggi, who had come to Calcutta to be at Mother Teresa's bedside, even offered to give up smoking if she would do as the doctors told her. As for Mother Teresa herself, she had one all-absorbing prayer: "Jesus, please tell your Mother to make Mother all right so that she can take you to Albania."

It was to a Missionary of Charity house in Park Street that Mother Teresa was first released on 14 October, because the mother house was overcrowded and the presence of visitors and the sound of the constant ringing of the bell would disrupt the rest that was so essential for her complete recovery. She was given a room adjacent to the chapel but she also had the reserved sacrament with her, as she had done in hospital. One month later she returned "home" to be greeted by Sisters and novices lining the approach to the mother house, singing the Magnificat and ringing bells. The reprieve was only temporary, however. On 29 November she was rushed back to Woodlands nursing home after acknowledging that she was suffering from severe dizziness. This time she underwent an operation to fit a more permanent pacemaker. After the operation she was her usual cheerful self. She left the hospital on 11 December, and Christmas saw her attending midnight Mass and enjoying tea and cakes with the Sisters. After that it was more or less "business as usual". On 28 March Yasser Arafat, President of the Palestine Liberation Organization, joined the list of callers at the mother house in Calcutta. He invited Mother Teresa to the Holy Land and asked her to open "Death with Dignity" homes in Bethlehem and Jerusalem, promising her US $50,000 for the work.

Shortly afterwards, however, Mother Teresa wrote to Rome asking permission to step down and to have the 1991 Chapter brought forward by a year. On 11 April 1990 the Pope, who had always taken such a personal interest in Mother Teresa's welfare, was said to have agreed "reluctantly" in recognition of her physical condition. When the news became public Monsignor Pennacchini, speaking on behalf of the Vatican, said that Mother Teresa had submitted her resignation for health reasons and was happy to turn over the reins to "younger hands". Mother Teresa herself said that she had resigned in the interests of her Congregation which needed to be run efficently: "To me, the work and the cause of my mission is more important than any individual." The announcement came as a shock to some. People all over the world regretted the necessity but few begrudged her the prospect of a well-earned rest.

The issue of the successor became a more vexed one. "The Sister chosen to succeed her faces a humanly impossible task", the British Catholic newspaper *The Universe* commented. "Tensions and differences within such a vast enterprise are likely to emerge. It may well be the final contribution of this amazing and saintly woman to prepare her Missionaries to carry on effectively after she has finally departed."

As the 1990 Chapter approached, Mother Teresa wrote a letter to her entire family – Sisters, Brothers, Fathers, Co-Workers.

This brings you my prayer and blessing for each one of you – my love and gratitude to each one of you for all you have been and have done all these forty years to share the joy of loving each other and the Poorest of the Poor.

Your presence and the work you have done throughout the world for the glory of God and the good of the Poor has been a living miracle of love of God and yours in action. God has shown his greatness by using nothingness – so let us always remain in our nothingness – so as to give God free hand to use us without consulting us. Let us accept whatever he gives and give whatever he gives and give whatever he takes with a big smile.

As the days of the General Chapter draw near my heart is filled with joy and expectation of the beautiful things God will do through each one of you by accepting with joy, the one God has chosen to be our Superior General. Beautiful are the ways of God if we allow him to use us as he wants.

It was a letter of great gratitude, acceptance and serenity. She was satisfied that such preparation as was required for the Missionaries of Charity to carry on effectively was already there in the spirit and the Constitutions which represented the word of God for them. They had but to remain faithful to the spirit with which she had sought to imbue them from the start. After all, as one of the earliest Sisters to join the Congregation pointed out, it was not perhaps the qualities of those who visibly led the Society which were of such crucial importance, as those of the little people who had no aspirations to leadership. She herself had learned to value the importance of the smallest brick in the construction of a building. Mother Teresa's successor might not be as obviously charismatic. The eyes of the world might not pursue her in quite the same way but the future did not depend upon such considerations. It depended on the soundness of the "smallest brick". Mother Teresa had formed her Sisters well, Father Van Exem shared her confidence so well that even those who left the Congregation remained Missionaries of Charity in their attitudes and their values, for life.

Public interest remained focused, however, on the question of who the next Superior General of the Missionaries of Charity might be, and when, in September, the electoral college gathered from around the world and, to the amazement of the public at large, on 8 September re-elected Mother Teresa, there was talk that her re-appointment had been necessary to prevent and contain discontent among the electors who could not otherwise agree.

Father Van Exem shed a rather different light on the result of the ballot. Shortly before the Chapter he had received a visit from two very senior Sisters. Their conversation ranged around the question of the title of the new Superior General. Would she be called "Mother"? Manifestly the idea of regarding anyone apart from the woman who had always shown them such maternal care as "Mother" was not one they found easy to accept. What would Mother Teresa then be called? They asked Father Van Exem whether it would still be possible to vote for Mother Teresa, and he advised them that it was a difficult question but that if Mother had received authority to step down that was a matter for her. The Holy Father had not, however, said that the Chapter must vote for someone else. The authority of the Chapter of a Congregation took precedence over that of the Superior General. What the Chapter decided would be final.

The outcome of the 1990 Chapter at which, by a Vatican directive, the Missionary of Charity General Council was reduced from six councillors to four, was once again decisive. Mother Teresa, who had celebrated her eightieth birthday only days beforehand, accepted her re-election as the will of God. The world was surprised but the world's ideas of resignation and re-election did not take into account the sacred nature of the Chapter General, the prayerfulness with which the Sisters approached it and their total submission to the Divine will. Nor could it fully, for the Chapter proceedings were a matter on which the Sisters were required not to speak and they kept its secrets faithfully in the silence of their hearts.

"The Sisters were quite happy and I think the Pope is quite happy also", Father Van Exem would elaborate. "The bishops are happy and the cardinals are happy because when they want a crowd at a service or function they invite Mother Teresa." Certainly her presence anywhere was sufficient to guarantee a good attendance, and for precisely this reason her private dream of withdrawing to some degree from the maelstrom that accompanied her every move was in any case incapable of fulfilment. Had she been transferred to some other Missionary of Charity House in some other capacity the world would not really have left her to her own devices. "I had expected to be free," Mother Teresa would afterwards admit, "but God has his own plans. It is God's will and we have to do what he wants from us. God's work will continue with great love." There were those who saw the great fatigue in her and did not really understand, but she had always insisted upon acceptance and total surrender. "I had to, you know", was all that she would say, when someone who had known her for many years actually ventured to ask why she had resumed her role. Writing of the outcome of the Chapter to a close friend, she referred to how she knew she could count on that friend's continued support through prayers and sacrifices, and of her own "obedience": "Yes, it was the prayers and the loving concern of the Sisters and the Poor, and in obedience to God's will, I accepted to continue."

In other respects the old order had been changing. In 1986 at the Chapter of the Missionary Brothers of Charity, after twenty-one years as their General Servant, Brother Andrew himself had asked to be relieved of his position. After what Brother Andrew himself described as "quite a saga of fears, uncertainty and sadness", Brother Geoff, previously the Brothers' General Secretary, stepped into the role and Brother Andrew had the satisfaction of seeing the young man he had introduced to the life taking over and freeing him from the burden of managing, disciplining and planning. It was a step which he had been pondering for some time. A couple of years previously he had been travelling to one of the Brothers' remote communities on a small island off the Philippines. The journey had involved transferring to a series of ever smaller boats as the waves of the Pacific Ocean grew bigger and bigger. He had noticed then that the local fishermen frequently had even smaller craft with which they could travel far, reach under overhanging rocks where larger boats could not venture, and catch shell fish of many kinds. "In one of these little boats I seemed to hear God suggesting that maybe I should be thinking of moving into a smaller boat."

For Brother Andrew concrete images saved many words. He said that he saw his new life as being that of a "troubadour in a small boat". The image of the troubadour had come to him from a Trappist friend, who for years had been sharing with him the broad perspective of his life of contemplation. He wrote of Brother Andrew's change of roles: "Well, now you've changed from General to Troubadour." The way ahead was uncertain. Brother

Andrew hoped to remain a member of the Missionaries of Charity and to continue to give the Brothers his support but he had never been a sailor and could not sing a note: "So that leaves one factor unchanged – namely, God will have to do it as he has been doing it all along up to now."

Within the year he had left the Missionary Brothers of Charity. Having written regularly to friends around the world about the evolution of the work, in November 1987 Brother Andrew, though reluctant to cause any further pain, felt obliged to share the circumstances of his leaving also. He had been called to America by his superiors for a meeting, the purpose of which he did not know:

On arrival I was presented with a list of occasions over the years when I had drunk too much, behaved foolishly and gave bad example. Arrangements had been made for my own good, to go immediately for treatment to a clinic for alcoholics.

I confess to getting drunk a number of times over the past twelve years, and I deeply regret the damage I have caused. But I could not see myself as an alcoholic in need of treatment. After thirty minutes for prayer I replied that I was not willing to go to the clinic, which meant that I could no longer continue as an MC Brother, and I have requested a dispensation from my vows.

My parting prayer for the Brothers is that they always remain close to Jesus and the poor in great simplicity.

The only comment he wished to make on his decision was that rightly or wrongly he could not accept to go for psychiatric treatment. He felt it would have been a denial of the truth of his being:

In a poor way I understand how Christ was crucified for the truth of his being. He only had to deny that he was the son of God. (The comparison is rash and absurd, for Christ, of course, was someone else.)

The following of Jesus is no game like Trivial Pursuits. It is no abstract ideology or theology. It is life-personal, flesh and blood, human life in the midst of the drama of a terribly real conflict between life and death. And we are all part of that.

Maybe this sad story has value if it witnesses to this basic existential aspect of the life of each and every one of us.

Perhaps this humiliating story of Brother Andrew who was admired, praised and loved by many wonderful people, may in a strange way offer a little comfort to other humiliated, hard-pressed, embarrassed people, struggling with a disgrace, a failure, a fall in their own lives or in their dear ones – a painful break-up of a relationship, abandonment, a lonely pregnancy, a police case, being written off.

Mother Teresa knew nothing of the fears and decision that led to Brother Andrew's leaving the Missionaries of Charity. She was not consulted by them, and Brother Andrew had resigned before she heard what had happened. It was seen by a number of the Brothers themselves as both unfortunate and unneccessary. Others left the Missionary Brothers in his train, although whether this was directly attributable to Brother Andrew's going or to a kind of "mid-life crisis" which would have occurred in any case the Brothers themselves were reluctant to say. One American Brother would point out that those who left were not the younger Brothers but men who had reached an age when they were likely to have questioned what they were doing with their lives, whatever their chosen vocation or profession. At the same time the Brothers recognized a real need to look at their life and see whether adjustments should be made whilst still holding on to the profound inspiration relayed to them by both Mother Teresa and Brother Andrew.

Certainly Brother Andrew was deeply missed. One Brother in India spoke of how he had been a great source of strength, of how, although he had been known as *Brother* Andrew he had been a father to them. He had scolded them. There had been times when he had been angry with them but he had always been available. Brother Andrew had had the special gift of making everyone feel important, no matter how weak and incompetent they were. Caught up as Brother Mariadas was in the desperate needs of the lepers at the Gandhiji Prem Nivas Leprosy Centre, there were times when he and others around him felt that the life did not allow them sufficient time and space for the prayer that was so vital to the work. It was not so much of a problem in the more structured lives of the Brothers in Western countries, but in Titlagarh where the work with lepers could easily consume every waking moment, it was a danger. Brother Mariadas was in frequent contact with Mother

Teresa whose attitude was unequivocal: "Mother says, 'Tell your Brothers, if they don't want to be holy, they can go home'."

For all her sharp dismissiveness, if she detected the lack of inclination to be holy, she knew the fragility of religious vocations which she likened to tiny seeds and she felt it the responsibility of the Congregation to ensure that they blossomed rather than withered and died. The number of professed Sisters leaving the Missionaries of Charity had increased in more recent times. Such an increase, by no means substantial as it was, had to be viewed in relation to the much greater number of Sisters joining the Congregation, but Mother Teresa was also on the alert lest their leaving might be in any way attributable to a lessening of the joy which had been so obvious a part of their life together in earlier days. She stressed ever more vigorously the importance of precisely that joy, of smiling and of loving one another. "Pray that we do not spoil God's work", she would insist. "To know oneself and not to be untrue is the essence of living." Knowing oneself meant recognizing one's shortcomings and surrendering them cheerfully to God: "Self-knowledge puts us on our knees", she would say. Sometimes the little pencil was a broken pencil. Sometimes it needed sharpening just a little more.

There were similar messages for her Co-Workers too: reminders of the need to grow in holiness through love for each other and the poor they served, of the need to forgive endlessly, and to avoid the sharpness of tongue which was so frequently the cause of hurt. "I want my Co-Worker family to be a living example of peace, of love and compassion, to be the living reality of God's love" was the wish she expressed to Co-Workers throughout the world from the Chapter in Paris on 12 May 1988 which brought together Co-Worker representatives from forty-eight countries. At the same Chapter, Ann Blaikie, who had served faithfully since 1954 as one of Mother Teresa's other selves and as international link, had handed over her position to a South African couple, Margaret and David Cullis. A new generation of Co-Workers who had not had the privilege of being hand-tooled by extensive direct personal contact with Mother Teresa was taking over from those who had first been prepared to roll up their sleeves for an unknown nun, association with whom brought no kudos but only labour "without seeking for any reward". Like the new generation of Sisters and Brothers, these Co-Workers would have to discover the spirit of Mother Teresa by other means.

In Antwerp Jacqueline de Decker had yet to find someone to step into her shoes. In addition to the series of operations she had undergone and all the discomforts and frustrations of being confined to a surgical collar and corset, she was now suffering, like Mother Teresa, from angina pectoris. Yet there were sick and suffering links now in fifty-six countries, and if the number of links did not seem to increase very much beyond five thousand, the numbers making up the "glorious company in heaven" were swelling. Sometimes misunderstandings arose. Sick and Suffering Co-Workers did not always fully appreciate that the link with the Missionaries of Charity must remain an essentially spiritual one – personal gifts and donations to Sisters or Brothers were not permitted. Sometimes they were discouraged at the infrequency of replies from Missionaries of Charity who were allowed to write to them only twice a year, and who sometimes did not fulfil even this small quota. For their part, the Sisters and Brothers, caught up in the immediacy of the need surrounding them, did not always appreciate what a few lines could mean to a person in pain. Even Mother Teresa's letters to Jacqueline de Decker opened with increasing frequency with an apology for the long interval since her last correspondence, although she invariably made a point of contacting her "other self" prior to her operations. Somehow, however, Jacqueline de Decker still managed, in addition to co-ordinating the link between the sick and the Sisters and Brothers, also to look after the welfare of some two thousand prostitutes in Antwerp, and somehow she was still "a bit of a clown for God".

Human and imperfect as it was, the Missionary of Charity family was still growing. While other religious congregations suffered increasingly from a lack of vocations there was no such shortage of applicants to join the Missionaries of Charity. By the year 1990 there were 3,068 professed Sisters, 454 novices and 140 candidates. There were novitiates in Calcutta, Manila, Rome, Poland, San Francisco and Tabora, Tanzania and a contemplative novitiate in New York. The Sisters had over four hundred houses in over ninety countries. The Brothers, for their part, had novitiates in Calcutta,

Vijayawada in South India, Manila, Seoul, Los Angeles, Manchester and elsewhere. They had 380 professed in 82 communities in 26 countries. For a while Brother Geoff had felt it better to strengthen existing communities and give more attention to the formation of the Brothers than to open new houses, but the work of the Brothers' small communities was also bearing fruit.

In the spring of 1991 I visited the Brothers in a part of Los Angeles where drugs were sold on the street corners and a substantial proportion of the restless population was made up of teenage immigrants, mostly from Mexico and Central America, who had found their way into the United States in pursuit of a slice of the "American dream". The families of these undocumented immigrants were far away, work invariably proved much more difficult to come by than ever they had imagined, and prostitution was often the only means to a meal. In such a context, the Missionary Brothers provided a home for boys from the streets. Some of these youngsters had fled from broken homes, from step-fathers who physically abused them; some were orphans; one who had been left a substantial estate by his much loved grandfather had been forced to run away from relatives bent upon taking his life. Others, from countries such as El Salvador or Guatemala, were fleeing enforced conscription into the army. They were nurtured with love, educated in nearby schools and given hope of a stable future. In separate accommodation the Brothers cared for the needs of homeless men found on the streets of Skid Row, for those who were mentally ill who had found themselves discharged from hospital with nowhere to go and no one to look after them. They were given shelter and care until they were well enough to work and support themselves. About a mile away, in a sagging row of clapboard houses "Nuestro Hogar" provided accommodation for ten young men under the age of twenty-one, and showers and a meal for any one of Los Angeles's estimated twelve thousand poorest of the poor who cared to drift in. There was a washing machine in which they could wash their clothes, an array of donated garments available for people needing to look tidy for job interviews. There was also a liberal supply of free coffee and a television to watch. The day of my visit happened to be a national holiday and the sitting room was packed to bursting point with young Hispanics, their eyes glued to a Disney cartoon.

Three times a week also the Brothers and the Co-Workers went out into the streets of Los Angeles to distribute sandwiches, clothing and sometimes blankets to the drug addicts, the alcoholics and the destitute of the city. All this very "ordinary" drama was acted out away from the lights and the headlines, and if there were times when the Brothers, like the Sisters, were inclined to feel that what they were achieving was so little in relation to the magnitude of the need, the boys and young men who found a home, companionship, clean clothes, a warm meal or simply a sofa on which to snooze undoubtedly had a different estimate.

Based in Australia, Brother Andrew had found himself admitted in a special way to the company of precisely the small, broken, fragile and rejected souls about which he had spoken and written so much. He still had his priesthood and with it he assumed what he called a "professionally itinerant state", giving talks, conducting retreats, writing and continuing to be an inspiration to many. In 1991 his "itineracy" would take him once more to Calcutta, to Mother Teresa, the Brothers and the Sisters, after which he would write of his "great experience of so much love" and of his continuing amazement at all that was being done.

The community of Missionary Fathers, although still small in number, had been growing. At first they had continued to work in the soup kitchen in the South Bronx until the house there had become too small. A number of applications had begun to come in from priests in the Third World, for whom additional English studies were not necessarily appropriate. At the same time it was recognized that they could not move to Calcutta, for what Father Joseph Langford described as "protocol reasons". The Indian government would not have accepted their presence, so the search had begun for another "Calcutta", a place where they could be rooted in an experience as close to that of Calcutta as possible. Father Joseph Langford believed they might find it in Tijuana, Mexico. The Bishop agreed. Mother Teresa had gone to inspect the proposed location, and in June 1989 the Missionary Fathers moved lock, stock and barrel to Tijuana. Their numbers there swiftly doubled. In April 1989 Mother Teresa reported that the thirty-three seminarians and nine priests were "really doing very well" in Tijuana, and asked for prayers that they would soon have their own seminary. The Missionary Fathers of Charity had a particular role in the passing on of Mother Teresa's message. Mother Teresa had always wanted the work to speak for itself. The Sisters and the Brothers were forbidden in their humility to speak about it to the world, but the Fathers, who as priests and ministers had a duty to "proclaim", could ensure that her message did not die with her. As part of their apostolate the growing number of Missionary Fathers endeavoured to help people to make the link between the life led by Mother Teresa and the life they were leading in the Calcutta which existed in their own neighbourhoods.

By 1990 there were some three million Co-Workers struggling to do small things with great love throughout the world. In 1981 a separate branch had also been formed for young people. "The young", Mother Teresa had told the Youth Co-Workers, "have a great mission. They are being sent to spread the Good News to the Poor." Since 1984 the medical branch of the Co-Workers had developed across all five continents. The year 1989 had brought another movement spiritually affiliated to the Missionaries of Charity. The Lay Missionaries of Charity formed a body for lay people, both married and single, who wished to "quench the infinite thirst of Jesus on the cross for the love of all souls, by means of the annual profession of four private vows." The vows they took were those of "[conjugal] chastity, poverty, obedience and wholehearted and free service to the poorest of the poor, lived according to each one's own state of life." The patron of the Lay Missionaries of Charity, the model of their life and the source of their inspiration, was to be the Holy Family of Nazareth. The sign of their consecration was to be a simple crucifix which they would receive at the beginning of a period of formation, to be worn over the heart or round the neck, and a larger one which would be given at the time of first profession. The Lay Missionaries of Charity were to be open primarily to those Roman Catholic Co-Workers "who wished to give further and deeper expression of their unity with Mother Teresa and the Missionaries of Charity on a spiritual level." It was intended that their spirit of prayer, meditation, contemplation, acts of mercy and compassion would lead to wholehearted simplicity and purity of living and a lifestyle infused with spiritual love. By radiating God's love, they were to be an inspiration to all and especially to the local Co-Worker groups.

Mother Teresa still marvelled at a growth she had not anticipated and a story which she told as if it were not her own:

I did not know that our work would grow so fast or go so far. I never doubted that it would live, but I did not think that it would be like this. Doubt I never had, because I had this conviction that if God blesses it, it will prosper. Humanly speaking, it is impossible, out of the question, because none of us has got the experience. None of us has got the things that the world looks for. This is the miracle of all those little Sisters and people all around the world. God is using them – they are just little instruments in his hands. But they have their conviction. As long as any of us has this conviction, we are all right. The work will prosper.

When the outcome of the Chapter General in September 1990 proved also to be very different from what she had anticipated there were no half-measures in her commitment to continuing God's work. Mother Teresa still identified herself with Teresa of Lisieux, the "Little Flower" who never left the four walls of her convent and died at the age of twenty-four. She wanted to associate herself with the saint who claimed, "Holiness is not a matter of this or that pious practice; it consists of a disposition of the heart which makes us small and humble in the arms of God, aware of our weakness, yet confident, boldly confident in the goodness of our Father." Others saw in her a follower of Saint Teresa of Avila, a dynamic and determined woman who was constantly ready to go out and start new foundations. As the pillars of Communism crumbled in a succession of Eastern bloc countries, the opportunist in her could not resist the challenge to take Jesus to those whom she saw as having been starved of his presence.

The years 1990/1991 proved to be particularly fruitful in terms of the opening of foundations in communist countries. By the Spring of 1990 Mother Teresa had already opened five houses in the Soviet Union – two in Moscow, two in Armenia and one in Georgia – and had actually been asked to establish another four Missionary of Charity foundations there. She had also received permission from Cuban President Fidel Castro to increase from four to seven the number of Missionary of Charity houses in his country. Even in the interval between her resignation and her re-election, the Missionaries of Charity had managed to open the first soup kitchen for more than forty-five years in Budapest. In a prefabricated hut in the city's rundown district of Josefstown they provided lunch for the elderly, the homeless and the disabled.

In his *Urbi et Orbi* address on Christmas Day 1989, Pope John Paul II had prayed for a special blessing on the "noble land of Romania which is celebrating this Christmas in fear and trembling, with sorrow for the many human lives tragically lost and in the joy of having taken once more the path of freedom." He spoke in impassioned words of the suffering of the people of Romania, and for those accustomed to reading the signs it came as no surprise that on 30 April 1990, "retired" or no, Mother Teresa arrived in Bucharest, expressing a particular desire to meet children suffering from AIDS. She met with Prime Minister Roman and Foreign Minister Serak and immediately set about establishing a children's home. Estimates by some relief organizations put the number of orphaned, "forgotten" children, condemned to institutions under the Ceausescu regime, at a hundred thousand. Many were infected with HIV. Others were physically and mentally handicapped. They were malnourished, suffering from scabies and rickets, and had been locked away in "homes" where medical care was virtually non-existent, in conditions of sensory deprivation more desperate than the Sisters arriving from India had ever previously witnessed. A Co-Worker who delivered urgent supplies to the Sisters in Romania would afterwards describe with horror his entry into one orphanage which smelt of urine and excrement. "There was one boy lying on a bed – it had no sheets or blankets, just a blue plastic cover, and he was lying in a pool of vomit and urine, and eating it."

With the full support of the new Romanian regime, the Mission-aries of Charity set up their children's home temporarily in a sports pavilion on the outskirts of Bucharest. In the changing rooms, still decorated with team photographs, the Sisters arranged rows of cots with clean blankets and fresh sheets. They had been told by the Minister of Health that they could take thirty children from the orphanage where an estimated hundred and eighty children had died during the previous winter. In fact they managed to take sixty, and provide them with things so far unknown to them: regular food, new clothes, smiles and love. The arrangement in the sports pavilion was only a temporary one because on a plane journey to Romania from Rome Mother Teresa had found herself chatting to a businessman who asked her why she was visiting Bucharest. By the time she had finished explaining, he had offered to fund the construction of a new, purpose-built home.

As eastern Europe began to open its doors to her, Mother Teresa went on to Czechoslovakia. On 13 May she received a warm welcome in the township of Nita, in central Czechoslovakia, and promptly opened two houses to which people came flocking in busloads just to welcome the arrival of the Sisters in their white "sheets". The shy Sisters found themselves overwhelmed by the older generation of local people who had kept their faith under very difficult circumstances and who greeted them with songs and tears of joy. Leaving behind her a small group of Sisters who would visit families and minister to their spiritual and material needs, in July Mother Teresa returned to Calcutta.

By then she was asking for special prayers for the fulfilment of two longstanding and very particular aspirations of hers. One was the opening of a house in China; the other was a Missionary of Charity foundation in the homeland which still held a special personal attraction for her, Albania. Quite apart from being the country of her roots and the poorest European country, Albania was the last bastion of Communism in eastern Europe, a country which was, as Mother Teresa put it, "legally atheist", where religious practices had for many years carried prison sentences of between three and ten years. Since 1967 over two thousand places of worship had been closed to the purposes for which they had originally been intended. Most were mosques but there were six hundred former Orthodox churches and 327 former Catholic churches being used as sports stadia and other secular purposes. The Orthodox Church had suffered but the Catholic Church had been the primary target for persecution, since resistance to Communism had been strongest in the Gheg-speaking Catholic north.

By 1990 over 100 of 160 Catholic clergy had died in prison or labour camps, many of them in the first decade of Communism. With people unable to travel without government permission, even to a family wedding, and with surviving clergy kept under even stricter surveillance, organizing a structured catacomb church had proved impossible. School children had been encouraged to denounce parents who·prayed, or kept icons, Bibles or crucifixes in their homes. Most parents therefore kept their faith secret; there was no religious instruction; as in Romania, forty years of Communism had undermined basic moral and spiritual values; and God was effectively banished from Albania. Mother Teresa, however, had been quietly conducting a crusade to bring him back. By May 1990 the communist regime in Albania had been forced onto the defensive. The twenty-three year-ban was lifted. No longer were religious practices punishable with imprisonment, although permission was still being withheld for disused places of worship to be reconverted. Mother Teresa was swift to see a long-awaited opportunity.

Even before the lifting of the ban she had made approaches to the Albanian Government under Mr Ramiz Alia, telling him as always that she and her Sisters wanted only to bring tender loving care for the people of Albania. "The President told me that to open a house there I would have to break the law", she would confide with mischievous satisfaction in February 1992. "I told him, 'Then I am ready to break the law'." The idea of being a law-breaker for God was one which obviously amused her. Mother Teresa succeeded in obtaining permission to take her Sisters to Albania. The first date cited for the opening of a Missionary of Charity foundation there was 8 December 1990, but eventually it was not until the spring that Mother Teresa's schedule, at most a programme of guidance rather than something to which she rigidly adhered, brought her to Rome in readiness to go to Albania. On 21 February 1991 jubilant crowds sent toppling a towering statue of Enver Hoxha, a hated symbol of Albania's Stalinist past. Tens of thousands of people gathered in the capital, Tirana, to call for democracy and greater freedom. By the 27th Mother Teresa, having only recently returned from Cambodia, was in Rome. Her planned visit to Albania was to be kept very private. So determined were those around her to keep her whereabouts secret that her name was not even on the Air India passenger list sent specially to the Missionaries of Charity in Rome. A house close to a disused church in Tirana had been made available to the Missionaries of Charity, and by 1

March she had already registered their ownership of it. She had also, to her overwhelming joy, found an Albanian priest to accompany the first four Sisters to Tirana, of whom one was, like Mother Teresa, an Albanian from Yugoslavia. Originally the date for their arrival in Albania had been fixed by the Albanian President for 4 March, but it was he who brought it forward to the 2nd, a fact which Mother Teresa saw as significant because it was the birthday of Pope Pius XII, the first pope to have given his blessing to her Congregation. It was also the birthday of James, Cardinal Knox, the bishop who had given so much encouragement to her and her Sisters in the early years of the Congregation. Before flying to Albania on 2 March Mother Teresa received a blessing from Pope John Paul II and his instructions: "Go and prepare the way."

In the year of the diamond jubilee of her religious vows, Mother Teresa at last brought her Missionaries of Charity to the country of her birth. It was a time when hundreds of other Albanians were desperately trying to leave their homeland. In the southern port of Vlorë people jostled fiercely with each other to board cargo boats with no engines, in a bid to get to the Italian port of Brindisi in search of better economic conditions. Yet the homecoming of one of the country's most famous nationals was not without its impact. Despite the fact that people in Albania had been so effectively cut off from the remainder of the world, they seemed to recognize her wherever she went. The showing on Albanian television of the Petries' film about Mother Teresa had undoubtedly contributed to this fact, but to the Sisters who would afterwards make their way into the mountain villages and find their saris recognized and welcomed, the manner in which they were greeted with cries of "Nonna Teresa" remained something of a miracle.

For Mother Teresa the warmth of the reception she received was particularly moving. In her old age there was some solace in the discovery that the graves of her mother and sister in Tirana had been anonymously tended. Each day crowds gathered outside the first house the Sisters opened in Tirana and, physically weak but delighted, Mother Teresa greeted them and gave them her blessing. "We have come to give tender love and care, as we do throughout the world", she told them. "We will begin slowly and see what is the greatest need." Within three weeks Mother Teresa had collected more Sisters from Rome and returned to Albania to open a second house. She was already envisaging a third, and by the time she left she had in fact opened three: two in Tirana, one of which was a home for destitute sick people, and another in Shkoder which was a home for abandoned crippled and mentally retarded children.

Two of the buildings provided by the State had previously been government residences and were accordingly sizeable properties. The third had been purchased by the Missionaries of Charity themselves when it was disclosed that the original property made available by the State actually belonged to the Franciscan Order. Mother Teresa had been most insistent that it should be returned to the Franciscans, and the small building they purchased in lieu became a centre where the Sisters taught the catechism and gave instruction to those who were, in Mother Teresa's words, "so hungry for God". It was a source of particular satisfaction that she had been instrumental in the opening up of Tirana's Cathedral Church of the Sacred Heart, which for many years had served as a cinema hall. Thousands of people participated in the first Mass to be celebrated there since the ban on religion. The President actually asked her to open six churches previously used for secular purposes. This she did and promptly insisted on reopening a mosque for the Muslims also. After she and her Sisters had helped to sweep and clean it, Muslim-Christian relations in the new Albania were off to a good start. Mother Teresa's return to Albania would subsequently be seen by many as having helped to re-instate the place of religion in the country. In July Pope John Paul II would meet the Albanian prime minister, Ylli Buffi, and ties between Albania and the Vatican broken off in May 1945 would be renewed in September 1991. The Vatican appointed Archbishop Ivan Dias, an Indian born in Bombay, as the new nuncio in Tirana. Albania gave India a daughter, the popular word went round, and now India is giving Albania a son.

Mother Teresa arrived back in Rome on 20 April 1991 suffering from a bad cough but determined that the next stop was to be Romania. The Sisters' three new houses for handicapped and retarded children in Romania were flourishing. With care and stimulation many of the children were developing rapidly, and the appearance of Mother Teresa on Romanian television combined with the Sisters' work was giving rise to numerous vocations. Mother Teresa wanted to bring a group of young Romanian girls back to Rome for their postulancy. "A house has opened in Cambodia," she announced on the 22nd, "and they want us to go to Vietnam, but I have to go to Romania to see about sixteen passports." She also wanted to go to Washington where thirty Sisters were due to make their final vows, but the most important piece of news was one about which she could not conceal her excitement: "And we've been invited to China!" In a birthday letter she wrote to a friend that month she referred to the shortness of available time. Nothing could now happen fast enough for her.

Mother Teresa brought the sixteen senior postulants from Bucharest to Rome and then, in June, she accepted an invitation from Saddam Hussein to go to Baghdad. It remained unclear whether he had actually received the letter she had written to him before the Gulf War appealing for peace, but she persevered with her approaches. In October 1990 she had actually sent an unofficial ambassador, Father Kevin Doheny, to Baghdad to attempt to secure the release of the British businessman, Ian Richter, who had been held a prisoner there since his arrest in June 1986 on charges of corruption. Ian Richter was not in fact released until 1991, but he was a Catholic. Mother Teresa's dispatching to him of a prayer card and a medallion of St Francis, her awareness of his predicament and the attempted interventions of her personal envoy brought "a little added hope". Early in 1992 the word came through to her from Baghdad that she would be welcome to bring hope to others in Iraq. There were many contradictory opinions about the invitation to open a house there but Mother Teresa could not say "No". During the Desert Storm operation thousands of people had been killed, many others had been left homeless, wounded or hungry. Mother Teresa had eyes only for such suffering and, as Brother Luke in Los Angeles would point out. "While we in America were busy getting ready for our parades and festivities, Mother headed in the opposite direction. She had managed to get herself and the Sisters into Baghdad, setting up facilities for the malnourished and crippled children, and mobile clinics for the sick and wounded." On 11 June she arrived from Switzerland with two

Sisters in an aircraft chartered by the United Nations. The welcome reception from bishops, nuns, the Minister of Health, the Minister of Social Welfare, the Home Office Minister and many others was a warm one, but the scenes that awaited them were of total devastation. One of the Sisters likened it afterwards to a desert. For Mother Teresa war was still incomprehensible in its horror: "The fruit of war is so terrible, one cannot understand how any human being can do that to another – and for what?" Mother Teresa had a meeting with the Minister of Health, Mohammed Sai, from whom she was able to glean information about the medical and humanitarian needs of Iraq. There was an acute shortage of food and medicine, and it would be a long time before the many homes destroyed in the war could be rebuilt.

While plans were made for the opening of a house in Baghdad, she was shown a large imposing building made available for her use as a children's home. It was a huge impersonal place and she did not want to take it. She consistently disliked large, elegant or soulless houses. Sometimes she was obliged to accept them but she invariably made her feelings on the subject clear. On this occasion she asked to be shown somewhere else, and chanced upon a house in the very heart of Baghdad, built in the grounds of the convent of the Dominican Presentation. Mother Teresa was instantly drawn to it and staked her claim in her usual fashion by putting a miraculous medal in the place. With the help of the Dominicans and what Mother Teresa herself would refer to as "many big people" it was swiftly cleaned and ready to be filled with children who were crippled and suffering from malnutrition. The Government also provided her with a vehicle to start up a mobile clinic for the poor who could not walk long distances to have their needs met.

As word of Mother Teresa's presence spread, so many people wanted to come and see her that the nuns had to protect their convent from the tide of visitors. Catholics and non-Catholics alike wanted to bring their children for a blessing: the deaf, the dumb, the blind and the mentally handicapped all found their way to her door. She prayed with them and gave them miraculous medals until her apparently unlimited supply ran out. She wanted to bring in a handful of Sisters as soon as possible, and after three or four days managed to find a way for five of them to be brought in via Amman in Jordan. From Amman the Regional Superior for the Middle East brought them by bus and car to Baghdad.

Mother Teresa was not usually given to sight-seeing. Her concern was for people rather than for buildings or places, but in Iraq she did express the desire to see Babylon. The Sisters took her but it was so hot that she had to be made to sit under a tree. She had been perspiring too much and was desperately overtired, but in the recollection of one of the Sisters accompanying her it was as if she were carried along by the faith of the Iraqi people which remained extraordinary in extreme adversity. "Who ever thought MC will come to these places to proclaim the word of God through works of love?" Mother Teresa wrote on 23 June. "I never thought that our presence would give so much joy to thousands of people. So much suffering everywhere. Among our Sisters a few know Arabic so it will not be so difficult." Muslims and Christians, people of all creeds and backgrounds, came to Mother Teresa with their bottles of water to be purified by her blessing alone. One couple made an impossible journey bearing some bread for her to bless. They told her of their conviction that her blessing on their bread and their drinking water would be enough to preserve them.

On 30 June the United Nations plane took her out of Iraq. By then the Iraqi Government had asked her to open two more houses. She also wanted to open a house not far from Mecca, but for the moment the political situation would not allow it. The dreadful consequences of war led her to share her reflections with her "dearest children all over the world":

Looking at the terrible suffering and fruit of war – same thing, I was thinking can happen through uncharitable words and actions – we do not destroy buildings – but we destroy the very heart of love, peace and unity – and so break the beautiful building our society – which was built with so much love by Our Lady. I know you all love Mother and that you would do anything to show your love and gratitude. I ask of you but one thing. Be a true Missionary of Charity and so satiate the thirst of Jesus for love for souls by working at the salvation and sanctification of your community, your family, and the poor you serve. Let us pray.

The letters she now wrote reflected something of her age and fatigue. How often had she told those who worked with her that they must be empty in order that God might fill them with himself and his love. To be empty, to be poor in spirit had its price. "Often," one of the Brothers acknowledged, "I have wondered what has been the cost to Mother Teresa for God to make within her heart, room for us all." The answer may be surmised from what she often said about acceptance, surrender and the freedom that stemmed from it. Total surrender to her meant not seeking to be put out on the street but accepting the loss of all possessions and being put out on the street if that was the will of God. Equally, it meant not choosing to live in a palace but accepting to live there if that was what God wanted. "Total surrender is to accept whatever he gives and give whatever it takes with a big smile. It is to accept to be cut to pieces and yet every piece to belong only to him. We must accept emptiness, accept being broken to pieces, accept success and failure. To give whatever it takes – if it takes your good name or your health – that is surrender and then you are free."

CHAPTER ELEVEN

Judged on Love

A United States Senator is reported once to have asked Mother Teresa: "Don't you get discouraged when you can see the magnitude of the poverty and realize how little you can really do?" "God has not called me to be successful," she replied. "God has called me to be faithful." In fact there were times when Mother Teresa would look sad, overcome for a while by the feeling that despite all the praise the Missionaries of Charity received for their actions, their "achievements" had little impact on the vast ocean of need. This was not, however, the face she showed in public and there were those who were unsatisfied by her mathematics of love, by her protestations that she never thought in terms of a crowd, only of one person. They were unimpressed by her statements that if the Sisters had helped only one human being it would have been enough, that Jesus would have died for just one person. Her apparent serenity became a source of irritation for some social activists, who saw her work as little more than an expanded soup kitchen which did not address itself, as they felt it should, to matters of social justice and institutionalized oppression. When Mother Teresa won the Nobel Peace Prize she was described as being beyond criticism. This did not in fact prove to be the case. If she was the focal point of universal acclaim she was also the target for some disapprobation, not least for her failure to tackle the root causes of need. Indeed, there were some who maintained that by salving the consciences of those who might otherwise be compelled to bring about change on a wider scale, by removing some of the causes of public embarrassment, she was not in fact serving the best interests of the poor but helping to preserve the status quo. For Mother Teresa, however, what came first was not the problem to be solved but the person affected. Charged with the reproach that she should not be giving the poor fish but fishing rods with which to catch their own food, she sighed the deepest of sighs, "Ah, my God, you should see these people. They have not even the strength to lift a fishing rod, let alone use it to fish. Giving them fish, I help them to recover the strength for the fishing of tomorrow."

Anyone who has touched a person dying in degradation knows this to be true. People with skin hanging in loose folds from their bones, children with stomachs distended with worms, and hollow eyes turning blind for lack of vitamins, lepers with leonine features and open, infected wounds – these are visions that burn the soul and often obscure the political points to be made about the status quo. Inevitably perhaps they change the sense of what is or is not important. Anyone who has nurtured the last residue of human life in a body wasted away by hunger, disease and neglect knows that the mere touch of a warm hand is indeed of immeasurable value. The very poorest of the poor are people who have been deprived even of their humanity. They are often enslaved to the biological needs of hunger and thirst. Their horizons have shrunk to the size of the bowl of rice or crust of bread they so desperately crave. When the concern of another human being, albeit expressed in the smallest and most apparently insignificant way, leads to the request for a clean shirt, for toe nails to be cut, faces to be shaved, there is no denigrating the miracle of the restoration of humanity, the rediscovery of the sense of what is beautiful and right. A place like Calcutta, precisely because it quickly teaches that its problems are going to endure beyond one's own years, also shows the value of sharing a cup of water, spending time with a handicapped child, visiting a pensioner. It was the experience of those who actually worked with Mother Teresa that the closer they drew to oppressed persons, the more unreal many activist concerns appeared. To know the problem of poverty intellectually, she herself maintained, was not really to comprehend it: "It is not by reading, taking a walk in the slums, admiring and regretting the misery that we get to understand it and to discover what it has of bad and good. We have to dive into it, to live it, share it." Once in Ethiopia Mother Teresa asked one of the governors to give her a piece of land on which to build a hospital. "Mother," he replied, "don't you know that we have had a revolution here and it takes care of these things?" "Yes,

I know," she said, "I am also a revolutionary but my revolution comes from God and is made by love."

The Missionaries of Charity came to birth in India. It is doubtful whether they could have been born in complex, highly professional Western society. The materially poor, in their pressing need, call forth a free immediate response that is a liberation also for the carer. It is a liberation from the anger, the long-term studies and ideologies which can bog down so many in the West who worry about the suffering of the Third World and the marginalized. Mother Teresa did not deny that India, like many other countries, needed scientists, technicians, economists and a working plan, but for her the wait for such a working plan to take effect was too long. In the meantime was she to allow the poor on her doorstep to die without solace? "We all have a duty to serve God where we feel called", she maintained. "I feel called to help individuals, not to interest myself in structures or institutions. I do not feel like judging or condemning." Nor did she judge. She did not want to set people against each other but to be a bridge between them. She wanted the rich to save the poor and the poor to save the rich. The only thing that made her angry was waste. It was hard when she had lived so many years in a city where the recycling of rubbish was a spontaneous and perfected art vital to the survival of so many, to see the untouched contents of airline meals discarded with their hygienically sealed cellophane wrappings still intact. In Calcutta nothing was wasted. Thousands of people made their living by searching systematically through the stinking refuse heaps in search of peelings to eat, paper which they could resell for a few paisa, jam jars, string, cardboard, rags. Children scoured the railway tracks for half-burnt pieces of coal, the sale of which would save them from starvation for just one more day. Mother Teresa sent her Missionaries of Charity to the airports to collect the airlines' uneaten food and redistribute it amongst those who had never known what it was to have too much to eat.

From the very begining she had made a deliberate choice to serve the poorest of the poor, not simply the poor but the very poorest among them. Similarly, by her own deliberate choice the Missionaries of Charity used only the most humble means in their work. By doing so, Mother Teresa insisted, they would remain accessible to the weakest and they would understand them. Just as she refused washing machines and even fans offered to her Sisters, so she refused sophisticated equipment in her homes for the dying. She was not always understood, but in her eyes the acquisition of advanced medical equipment would be the first step towards becoming an institution, and it was in the nature of institutions to give priority and the best treatment to those with the best chances of recovery. Given the limited number of beds available, inevitably only those with hope of recovery would eventually be admitted. The dying would ultimately be rejected by the very institutions originally intended for them. Such establishments might serve the poor but not the poorest. Instead the Missionaries of Charity must always keep their doors open to the smallest, those who had no hope of recovery or those who, having been patiently restored to health, would return a few weeks later in a state even worse than before. The Sisters and Brothers would always receive them, but to conventional Western ideas of efficiency it did not make sense. Mother Teresa's vocation to remain "small" also meant that incompetence was not at all excluded, mistakes were made. People were sometimes shocked and critical of the rudimentary levels of treatment available but she believed it was the only way in which to remain genuinely at the service of the poorest of the poor.

Intellectuals were not impressed by her. She was not after all on the cutting edge of the new thinking in psychology, social work, economics or theology. Asked once by a professor of sociology about the reasons she cared for people in the way that she did, she asked him whether he had a flower garden. When he replied that he did, she asked him whether he took care of the flowers in it. He answered that of course he did. "Don't you think", she next enquired, "that a human being is so much more than a flower?" The simplicity of her vision and her utterance did not engage everyone's hearts. Feminists were frequently angered by her consistent exhortation of women to be home-makers and to leave men to do "what they do best". She did not appear to comprehend those members of her sex who wished to be ordained as priests. In January 1979 Mother Teresa addressed an assembly of Delegates of the World Union of Catholic Women's Organizations at Bangalore: "Today many women are anxious to become priests", she told them. "Who could have been a better priest than Our Lady? And she remained in her place, so beautiful, so pure, so humble. So let us be like her and let us become the hands of the Lord and be a sign of joy, of peace, of love." It was the answer she invariably gave to people who questioned her about her views on the ordination of women: "Our Lady would have made the best priest but she remained in her place." In 1984, however, a report went round the world under the heading "Mother Teresa approves of Women Priests". Those who were familiar with her attitudes were mystified. It later transpired that the Indian Hindu journalist who had interviewed her had misunderstood her statement that if anyone had the right to the priesthood it was Our Lady. He had thought she had said "our ladies". In subsequently setting the record straight, Mother Teresa said firmly, "I stand by what the Holy Father has said."

Her fidelity to the traditional authority and teachings of the Roman Catholic Church was another point which provoked controversy. At a time when some theologians, priests and lay people within the Catholic Church had been challenging dogma such as the real presence of Christ in the Eucharist and the infallibility of the Vicar of Christ, her firm traditional allegiances were a source of comfort to other traditionalists. In a private audience in November 1976 Pope Paul VI actually declared that she was his "greatest consolation in the Church". Others felt that she could have used the position of influence she occupied to further the position of women in the Church. Speaking to members of Dutch religious orders on 24 October 1983, Mother Teresa made her views on "upheavals" in the Church quite clear:

There is a great upheaval in the religious life today. Believe me, Sisters, all will be well if we surrender ourselves and we obey. Obey the Church, obey the Holy Father because he loves us tenderly and he wants us really to be the spouses of Jesus crucified. We are surrounded with many temptations against our vocation, against us, changing everything, bringing all kinds of things; that is not what is meant for us. Our young people want holiness, that complete surrender to God.

In the United States in July 1981 nuns with more "progressive" views, whilst acknowledging her to be holy and compassionate, accused her simultaneously of personifying a pre-Vatican II view of faith which could be held up as a model to other women to be docile and "do their womanly caring thing". A storm of correspondence resulted. In October 1983 a study was to be made of American nuns by a Commission on Religious Life headed, at the Holy See's request, by the Archbishop of San Francisco, John Quinn. Hearing of the Commission, Mother Teresa wrote a letter on the vocation of Sisters which found its way into the press:

Though most unworthy to write to you, still I feel I need to turn to you, to beg you to help our religious Sisters in USA to turn to our Holy Father with childlike confidence and love. . . . We, who have consecrated our lives to God – we all know that this consecration
– binds us in a special way to the Church and
– to his Vicar on Earth
and through him to the clear will of God which is beautifully expressed through
– the teaching of the Holy Father
– the written will of God, our constitutions – approved by the Church as our way of life.

Her statement that there had been much disturbance in the religious life of Sisters, "all due to misguided advice and zeal", and her exhortations to demonstrate more complete obedience to their bishops did little to endear her to those who believed her to be authoritarian and patriarchal. She continued, none the less, to stand by the advice she gave to her own Missionaries of Charity:

The suffering of the Church is caused by liberty and renovation badly understood. We cannot be free except by being able to renounce our will in favour of its. We cannot renew ourselves without having the humility to recognize what must be renewed in ourselves. Do not trust those who come to your presence with dazzling words about liberty and renovation – they do nothing more than deceive.

It should be said that there were some United States nuns who welcomed Mother Teresa's stance. In October 1988 five cloistered Discalced Carmelite nuns locked themselves in an infirmary kitchen wing of their monastery following a protracted dispute with a prioress they found too liberal. They considered her introduction of television, music, newspapers and sweets into the monastery a threat to the discipline and austerity of their life. They turned to Mother Teresa to ask her to intervene with the Pope and were delighted when they were asked to send documentation and information about the case to India. They were not the only ones to express their gratitude to her.

In the secular world, Mother Teresa upturned many people's attitudes concerning the innate superiority of the West and the aid it offered to "underdeveloped" countries, by all that she had to say about the poverty of the rich. When first Mother Teresa approached the Indian Government in 1965 for exit visas for Venezuela, the officials were delighted to give permits for Indian missionaries to go overseas. It was not often that they were the recipients of such requests. The idea of a Congregation rooted in India bearing a spiritual message from the slums to supposedly more advanced societies reversed conventional ideas of "missionary" activity, and was not always well received by Europe and North America, however. Nor was the suggestion that physical hunger was relatively easy to resolve with a loaf of bread and a vitamin tablet, while the spiritual poverty of the West was a far more complex problem. Some thought that Mother Teresa was idealizing poverty and so, once again, encouraging its continuation, but it was not poverty itself which she admired:

The beauty is not in poverty but in the courage that the poor still smile and have hope, in spite of everything. I do not admire hunger, damp or cold, but the disposition to face them, to smile and live on. I admire their love of life, the capacity to discover richness in the smaller things – like a piece of bread that I gave to a boy which he ate crumb by crumb, thinking it was better so. While the poorest of the poor are free, we are excessively worried about the house, money. The poor represent the greatest human richness this world possesses and yet we despise them, behave as if they were garbage.

The poor of India had shown Mother Teresa the joy and freedom of leading an uncluttered life, of being able to live and work in simple, direct ways, of enjoying life and beauty without having to possess it or dominate it by mastering it intellectually. Her message to those who had the luxury of choice about so many things, that they should use their choices to better ends, that the breakdown of family life was at the root of many evils, and that people caught up in the pursuit of material goals had no time to be together, to be concerned about each other, was an uncomfortable one for many. She told the story of a child she had picked up from the streets and taken to Shishu Bhavan. The Sisters bathed him, gave him clean clothes, fed him and looked after his every need but he ran away. Next day he was brought to the home by someone else but again he ran away. When the boy was brought back a third time, Mother Teresa directed one of her Sisters to follow where he went:

A third time the child ran away and there under a tree was the mother. She had put two stones under a small earthenware vessel. She was cooking something that she had picked out of the dustbins. The Sister asked the child: "Why did you run away from home?" And the child said: "But this is home because this is where my mother is." Mother was there. That was home. That the food had been taken from the dustbins was all right because it was mother who cooked it. It was mother who hugged the child, mother who wanted the child. The child had its mother. Between the wife and the husband it is the same. He is the hands. He has to work. Are we there to receive him with joy, with gratitude, with love?

Even those who could not share her vision were frequently made to feel uneasy. In particular it was Mother Teresa's absolute opposition to abortion and artificial contraception which occasioned the most controversy:

The other day, she would tell assembled crowds, *I picked up a bundle from the street. It looked like a bundle of clothes that somebody had left there, but it was a child. Then I looked: legs, hands, everything was crippled. No wonder someone had left it like that. But how can a mother who did that face God? But one thing I can tell you; the mother – a poor woman – left the child like that, but she did not kill the child, and this is something that we have to learn from our women, the love for the child.*

In Canada she announced: "When a nation destroys its children which are not yet born because there is a fear of not being able to feed them and educate them in wealth, this is the greatest of poverties." It was a message which she delivered in the same forthright manner to most Western countries, and it was not surprising that in relation to what is arguably one of the most vexing moral problems of our time, some people found her words incendiary. Germaine Greer, who saw Mother Teresa as a religious imperialist, was one of them. In an article published in the *Independent Magazine* on 22 September 1990 she wrote of Mother Teresa's treatment of the rape victims when she was invited to Dacca after its liberation from the Pakistanis in 1972:

Three thousand naked women had been found in the army bunkers. Their saris had been taken away so that they would not hang themselves. The pregnant ones needed abortions; Mother Teresa offered them no option but to bear the offspring of hate. There is no room in Mother Teresa's universe for the moral priorities of others. There is no question of offering suffering women a choice.

Secular aid workers told me at the time that women with complications of late pregnancy, caused by physical abuse and malnutrition, as well as women miscarrying, were turning up at clinics claiming to have been accused of attempted abortion and turned away by Mother Teresa's nuns.

What could not be taken away from Mother Teresa, was the fact that she was morally and logically consistent in her belief in the sanctity of human life and her abhorrence of death brought on in whatever way for whatever reason. Her expressed belief was that "no human hand should be raised to end life" and she lived that belief. The issue of the extent to which she proselytized was more complex. To many Bengalis she became known as "the preacher of love who does not preach", but the allegations of "rice Christianity" were never totally dispelled. There continued to be those who felt that she believed that Hinduism and Islam were wrong and Catholicism was right, and who questioned the validity of the fact that she was ministering to the poor of Calcutta and the world not for their own sake but for the sake of her Catholic God. Her assertion, "We never try to make those who receive become converted to

Christianity" was invariably qualified, "However, together with our work, we bear witness of the love of God's presence." Offset against the claim that "If Catholics, Protestants, Buddhists or agnostics become for this better men, simply better, we will be satisfied", there was always the avowed objective of the Society, to satiate the thirst of Christ for love of souls.

The more cynical wondered whether her failure to proselytize more overtly was not in fact determined by the diplomatic tightrope she walked with the Indian Government. Part of the reasoning behind her refusal to accept government grants, endowments, fixed incomes or security funds for the work of the Missionaries of Charity had been the maintenance of the dependence on Divine Providence; part of it had been to avoid all the complexities of bookkeeping and the "strings" which such financing could entail. Nevertheless she did receive co-operation from the Indian Government in a way that few other Christian societies did. From the earliest days she had been shrewd enough to make a point of not making enemies among Indian officialdom. When Dr B. C. Roy, chief minister of Bengal and a powerful ally of Mother Teresa, asked her to take charge of four government-run vagrancy homes in Calcutta, adding that he would not cause her financial problems by asking her for accounts, she declined on the grounds that she could not spare the Sisters. At the time it was true, but those close to her suspected that she was also avoiding inviting hostility by taking over other people's work. Too open an attempt at conversion would undoubtedly have similarly jeopardized the concessions made to her in connection with customs regulations and other aspects of India's labyrinthine bureaucracy. One Indian government official once said to her, "Tell the truth, you would like me to become a Christian, you are praying for that?" and she answered him: "When you possess something really good, you wish your friends to share it with you. I think that Christ is the best thing in the world and I would like all to know him and love him as I do. But faith in Christ is a gift of God who gives it to whom he likes." The official was apparently satisfied.

There was certainly no disguising Mother Teresa's joy when in his eightieth year Malcolm Muggeridge, together with his wife Kitty, was received into the Roman Catholic Church. Mother

Teresa had coaxed a man in the twilight of his life, troubled by intellectual doubts relating to the Church and the Eucharist, to become like a little child:

I am sure you will understand beautifully everything – if only you would become a little child in God's hands. Your longing for God is so deep, and yet he keeps himself away from you. He must be forcing himself to do so, because he loves you so much as to give Jesus to die for you and for me. Christ is longing to be your Food. Surrounded with fullness of living Food, you allow yourself to starve.

The personal love Christ has for you is infinite – the small difficulty you have regarding the Church is finite. Overcome the finite with the infinite. Christ has created you because he wanted you.

Of the woman who wrote him this "beautiful" letter, Malcolm Muggeridge said: "Words cannot convey how beholden I am to her. She has given me a whole new vision of what being a Christian means; of the amazing power of love, and how in one dedicated soul it can burgeon to cover the whole world. Mother Teresa had told me, in Calcutta, how the Eucharist each morning kept her going; without this she would falter and lose her way. How then could I turn aside from such spiritual nourishment?" One year before he died, Mother Teresa made one of her very "off the record" visits to the Muggeridges' cottage in England. News of his death in November 1990 took her by suprise, but she had always maintained that if a book brought only one soul closer to God then it was worth the effort of the writing. For her there was great joy to be derived from the knowledge that the writing of *Something Beautiful for God* had won the soul of its author. The man who had called himself a "vendor of words" was "now with God".

The fact that authors, film-makers, journalists and photographers chose to make Mother Teresa the focus of so much attention inevitably occasioned resentments and jealousies. Calcutta in its need was full of remarkable people who rose to meet it: unknown saints who remained unsung and therefore deprived of the support and the protection that media attention, for all its drawbacks, could afford. Mother Teresa was well aware of the equally commendable work of countless others in India and elsewhere: "Why all this fuss about us?" she would protest. "Others do the same work as we do. Do it perhaps better. Why single us out?" All her private protestations to the effect that she would rather wash a leper than confront a press conference, could not, however, alter the fact that, as that early BBC interview with Malcolm Muggeridge had revealed, she was quite naturally a "media person". She learned not just to tolerate the media interest, but even to use it to combat misunderstandings about the work.

In Benares, or Varanasi, the "eternal" city, and one of the most important sites of Hindu pilgrimage in all India, opposition to the presence of the Missionaries of Charity was at one stage considerable. Devout Hindus flocked to the "city of Shiva" to spend their last days on the banks of the sacred River Ganges because it was considered especially auspicious to die there, ensuring instant liberation from the series of births and deaths that *Karma* might otherwise ordain to be necessary before salvation was achieved. It was small wonder that the home for the sick and dying destitutes which the Sisters opened there was kept particularly busy and the number of people dying in the home was exceptionally high. It was rumoured that the Sisters were killing the occupants of the home. The police were called in to investigate conditions there and established that the Sisters were in no way responsible for the high mortality rate. It was a publicity exercise, however, which ultimately helped to redeem the reputation of the Sisters. When ten Missionaries of Charity made their final professions in an open-air ceremony in Varanasi, journalists and photographers were actually invited to attend. A commentator explained carefully to the largely non-Christian audience the meaning of the vows. Many local fears were allayed in this way.

She was not always quite so successful. Despite her deep and abiding love for the people of India and her appreciation of the city which was very much "home" for her, she never quite managed to allay the criticisms of certain Calcutta intellectuals that she was advertising the city's poverty in a way that did not take into account the very considerable richness of the Bengali culture. She knew what it was to have her efforts prove abortive. Believing that Pope Paul VI had suffered on account of Archbishop Lefebvre's separation from Rome, she wrote to the Archbishop on numerous occasions urging him to come back, but without receiving an answer. Her approaches to the Reverend Ian Paisley were likewise abortive. Indian Prime Minister Morarji Desai remained unconvinced by her arguments in favour of religion as a matter of individual conscience. Moreover, even her "successes" were sometimes not without a trace of personal irony. In 1992 the President of Albania, Mr Ramiz Alia, awarded the citizenship of Albania to the woman who had once been compelled to make a choice between visiting her dying mother in her homeland and serving the poor of the world. The presidential decree in 1992 would mean that from then on she would be entitled to travel on an Albanian diplomatic passport. Mr Alia also created a "Mother Teresa Prize" to be awarded to those who distinguished themselves in the field of humanitarian and charitable works.

For those who thought in terms of bringing about collective change and of "conscientization", the high profile and the influence which some begrudged her was her redeeming feature, for if public opinion is one of the most powerful factors for changing social structures, it could certainly be claimed that few people had mobilized public opinion as strongly as Mother Teresa. Over a hundred thousand schoolchildren in Denmark going without a glass of milk every day in order that others might eat; eight hundred thousand capsules of Lampren sent annually from Switzerland to the lepers in West Bengal; five thousand tonnes of high-quality processed food dispatched at a week's notice for the famine-stricken people of Ethiopia and Tanzania – these were some measure of Mother Teresa's impact. Thanks to her and to the publicity she received, albeit against her own wishes, the poor were more known, more loved and better defended, even if sometimes the publicity was out of all proportion to what she actually did. The Sisters' foundations were often tiny; their daily work of visiting the lonely, tending the sick, teaching children the catechism was often unspectacular. Yet thanks to the combined efforts of small people prepared at her inspiration to give their all, thousands of lives had been saved, and thousands more had been given a new awareness of poverty, *Ek, Ek, Ek* as Mother Teresa would say in Bengali, "One by one by one." It was not those whose lives were saved who worried about whether the relief of human distress should be undertaken for its own sake or because she believed she was tending to the suffering Christ in them.

In 1991 the Chief Minister of West Bengal, Jyoti Basu, a life-time Communist, telephoned Mother Teresa. They had known and respected each other for many years. Because of the limited social welfare resources of his government, a substantial number of women who had been kidnapped or trapped into prostitution were being kept in prison because there was no other option. The Chief Minister did not believe they should be there. Mother Teresa took forty of the women. He made state land available and she built a home for them. The women freed from the Calcutta gaol through the ready co-operation of a Christian nun and a committed Communist were not among Mother Teresa's potential critics.

Perhaps it is true that the way in which we respond to Mother Teresa as someone who preached and lived sacrificial love reveals more about us than about her. As Brother Andrew once wrote of her enormous fruitfulness, beauty and lifegiving abilities: "Unless my life comes anywhere near hers in its effective concern for the poor and suffering, then I can only look very stupid in making my relatively petty negative points." She herself believed that when the hour finally came for her to "go home to God" she would be judged by her actions and the love that had been put into them:

Today, the Poor are hungry for bread and rice – and for love and the living word of God; the Poor are thirsty – for water and for peace, truth and justice; the Poor are naked – for clothes, for human dignity and compassion for the naked sinner,

The Poor are homeless – for a shelter made of bricks, and for a joyful heart that understands, covers, loves. They are sick – for medical care – and for that gentle touch and a warm smile.

The "shut-in", the unwanted, the unloved, the alcoholics, the dying destitutes, the abandoned and the lonely, the outcasts and the untouchables, the leprosy sufferers – all those who are a burden to human society – who have lost all hope and faith in life – who have forgotten how to smile –who have lost the sensibility of the warm hand touch of love and friendship – they look to us for comfort – if we turn our back on them, we turn it on Christ, and at the hour of our death we will be judged if we have

recognized Christ in them, and on what we have done for and to them.
There will be only two ways: "come" or "go".

"Ye shall know them by their fruits" was a biblical text she regularly
quoted and one on which she rested her case.

CHAPTER TWELVE

Going Home to God

"Why did they do it?" Mother Teresa's question was in response to a bout of criticism which found its most vehement expression in a programme broadcast on British television in November 1994 and in a subsequent book entitled *The Missionary Position: Mother Teresa in theory and practice*. The attacks gave rise to an even more vociferous rally to her defence but there were also those who came out, if not entirely in support of the view that Mother Teresa was a "demagogue, an obscurantist and a servant of earthly powers", then at least of the opinion that her service to humanity was not without avoidable flaws. Discussion as to the accuracy or otherwise of such allegations filtered its way round the world. In the twilight of her life, it seemed, far from being allowed to retire to peace and obscurity in the home for the dying in Calcutta, Mother Teresa was to know what it was to be a very public sign of contradiction. She was, furthermore, to do so from a vantage point of growing physical weakness and vulnerability.

Her health had become an increasing problem. In December 1991 she had visited Washington to attend a ceremony at which twenty-seven Missionary of Charity Sisters made their final vows. She also took the opportunity to visit President Bush in the Oval Office and speak to him of the work the order was undertaking in Albania and of some of her future plans. She had gone on next to visit the Missionary of Charity foundation in Tijuana, Mexico. To those close to her there seemed an extreme frailty about her but also an even greater sense of urgency. Never before had she programmed herself quite so tightly. There were those amongst the Missionary Fathers and the Sisters she visited who believed they saw in her arrangement for the Sisters' professions to be brought forward and her urging of those due to be ordained in a few months' time to make the commitment now, a premonition on her part that this might be her last journey so far from India. As it was, she interrupted her stay in Tijuana to open a new house in Los Angeles. The Missionaries of Charity with whom she stayed there were suffering from an extremely virulent form of 'flu which their Mother General also caught before returning to Tijuana. On 26 December 1991 she was found to be suffering from bacterial pneumonia. The cardiologist called in to check how her heart was coping could not believe that, despite the fact that it had been known for so long that the world-renowned Mother Teresa had a heart disease, she had been travelling without any medical records. The unlabelled medication she had been taking had to be put under a microscope in San Diego in order to establish what it was. Resistant at first to the doctor's insistence that she must be hospitalized, she succumbed to the united persuasion of the Sisters accompanying her, Father Joseph Langford and the local Roman Catholic bishop. She was still protesting, however, as she was taken across the border into the United States. The local hospital in Tijuana would have been her personal choice. Instead, she found herself in the Scripps Clinic and Research Foundation in La Jolla, San Diego, California. There she underwent an angioplasty procedure to clear clogged coronary arteries, after suffering heart failure brought on by the pneumonia. Despite widespread fears for her life, however, her condition gradually improved. When a call came through to her from the Pope, doctors found themselves struggling to keep her off the telephone and still hooked up to her oxygen mask. She even took advantage of her spell in hospital to appeal for much needed blood donors and in response, despite a torrential rainstorm, the amount of blood donated in San Diego next day doubled.

Some three weeks later she was almost back to her feisty self. Before leaving the Scripps Clinic, as a mark of her gratitude, she organized a Mass for the three doctors who had cared for her. Two of them were Jewish. "What are we supposed to do?" the Jews sought advice of one eminent Catholic church leader. "Do whatever she tells you," was the response. "That is what we all have to do."

At the beginning of February 1992 Mother Teresa arrived in Rome. It was bitterly cold and the rooms of the Missionary of Charity house in San Gregorio were scarcely the ideal accommodation for an elderly woman convalescing after an illness that had brought her close to death. The Sisters were permitted to tear up cardboard boxes to place as insulation on the otherwise bare stone floor of her room but that was virtually the only concession to her physical weakness she would allow. I was there to accompany her friend and "other self" of many years, Ann Blaikie, who was by this time herself suffering from the early stages of Alzheimer's disease and who had wanted to see Mother Teresa, as she thought then, for the last time. The fact that Mother Teresa was so desperately frail was not preventing her from spending time in the Vatican. She was busy trying to arrange for the opening of a house for the Missionary of Charity Fathers in Rome. Nor were the queues to see her any shorter. When finally she entered the "parlour" where we had waited for some hours, the meeting was an uncharacteristically emotional one. Mother Teresa had rigorously avoided all physical demonstrations of affection in her younger years. Now such inhibitions were apparently cast aside. "My suffering", she told Ann Blaikie not for the first time and not without a certain satisfaction, "has brought the world to prayer." Then, pointing to some mozzarella cheese, set out on the table before us, she urged: "Eat some of that. It's very good!" She herself was going to rest but only briefly. At Mass a little later she could scarcely rise from her knees, but that did not prevent her from speaking afterwards to a group of Italian Co-Workers and updating them on her foundation statistics. Her parting shot to me when we left Rome next day was: "You're going back to London aren't you? Would you please tell Princess Diana that I do not think I shall be in Calcutta when she is due to see me there but she is welcome to come and see me here."

The message, in fact, was relayed by somewhat more official means. When on 15 February the Princess of Wales visited the mother house of the Missionaries of Charity in Calcutta, Mother Teresa was still too ill to leave Rome, having been admitted once more to hospital. The Princess was welcomed instead by Sister Frederick and a group of novices who sang and danced and showered their royal guest with flower petals in traditional Indian style. In the chapel she took off her shoes to pray with the Sisters. There were tears in her eyes as they sang a hymn of love for the poor. Princess Diana's period in Calcutta also included a visit to the home for the dying. She was not afraid to touch the suffering bodies of India's most rejected and they, not knowing that they were meeting a Princess, simply smiled in return. She was manifestly deeply moved. She was moved too by the hand-written message Mother Teresa had sent from Rome to greet her. Within the week she flew to Italy to meet for the first time in the flesh the woman whom she had long admired.

By the following June, with the newspaper serialization of Andrew Morton's book *Diana: Her True Story*, the Prince and Princess's marriage problems were becoming public knowledge. Mother Teresa's reaction was a characteristic emphasis on her belief in family unity. "I am praying so much for her happiness", she said when invited to comment on Princess Diana's difficulties, "I am praying that her family may remain together, which is very important." She added: "She and her husband should pray too. Prayer can help them through their troubles."

On 9 September 1992 she met Princess Diana again, this time at the Missionary of Charity home in Kilburn, London and this time at the older woman's request and "in secret". The world could only speculate as to the advice Mother Teresa offered the Princess who had obviously won her particular sympathy. By this time, however, despite her apparently undiminished capacity to attend meetings with people of influence, even those in whom others were unable to see the potential for goodness with which she credited every human being, and despite her determination whenever possible to attend the professions of her Missionaries of Charity and the opening of new houses, Mother Teresa herself was becoming increasingly vulnerable and dependent on the advice and support of the Sisters and others closest to her. She also appeared to be experiencing the desire to set certain aspects of her own "house" in order.

On the weekend of 7-9 May 1993 a gathering of Co-Workers took place in Belgium, the object of which was primarily to celebrate the eightieth birthday of Jacqueline de Decker. Early Co-Workers and friends of many years travelled to Antwerp, some of them from as far afield as the United States, for what was to be a joyous reunion. Because, however, so many members of the Co-Worker governing body were to be there, it was decided to take the opportunity simultaneously to hold a meeting of the governing body to discuss the Co-Worker Chapter due to be held in San Diego in the following year. Since Mother Teresa was already in Europe at the time it would also be an opportunity for her to address the governing body about certain causes for concern that had been brought to her attention in the Calcutta mother house, concerns which some months previously had induced her to try and persuade some of the leading Co-Workers actually to come to Calcutta. This had not been possible but the Antwerp gathering presented her with an ideal occasion for a meeting. Mother Teresa was due to take part in the celebrations on the 8th. On the evening of the 7th, however, Brother Geoff, General Servant of the Missionary Brothers, announced to a stunned assembly that allegations had been made regarding the misuse of money which should have been given to the poor to finance, for example, Co-Workers' travel around the world, the newsletters and postage. He also informed them that it was Mother Teresa's intention next day to dissolve the Co-Workers as an official organization and to cancel their San Diego Chapter.

The announcement was a shock and a source of hurt to many. Some who had known Mother Teresa in the early days in Calcutta recognized that such a move was not altogether out of character. It had not always been easy to rise to the demands of a woman who at one moment required funds to meet the needs of the poor and at the next gave directions that they were not to make the Christmas cards needed to raise the necessary money. Mother Teresa had long been afraid of the possibility of money becoming too central a preoccupation. Nor was her concern that the association might become too organized, that it had too many office-bearers and was in some way losing its simplicity, new. Indeed, it was not the first time that Mother Teresa had expressed the wish that the international association of Co-Workers should be disbanded as an "organization". Some years previously she had written a letter to Ann Blaikie to that effect. The then international link had succeeded in allaying her fears and the letter had been kept in confidence, but Ann Blaikie, although present at the Antwerp gathering, was no longer equipped to argue the case. Next day, with the support of Brother Geoff, Margaret Cullis and the Co-Workers strongly refuted any allegations of misuse of funds. Mother Teresa's adamance that every penny donated for the poor should actually reach the poor was well known and shared whole-heartedly by those who worked with her. The money spent on travelling to Co-Worker chapters and other similar events came strictly out of their own pockets, as did the financing of the newsletter and the postage for it. Nor was it money that would otherwise have gone to the poor. In order to ensure the kind of family spirit which made the work throughout the world possible, correspondence and the occasional meeting was, they reasoned, important, and Mother Teresa seemed convinced. What appeared to concern her most was that the Co-Workers should maintain the simplicity and joy that had characterized their role when first they had begun "sharing, serving and loving" in the home for the dying. At the same time she seemed to want the Missionary of Charity Order to be one body with no semi-independent sub-structures. She wanted the Co-Workers to work wherever possible in closer conjunction with the Missionaries of Charity. Many of her fears were laid to rest. On the strength of what was revealed at the meeting she said that it did not now seem necessary to dissolve the structure of the Co-Workers. As a token of gratitude for twenty-five years of Co-Worker service and to mark the fortieth anniversary of the Association, the planned Chapter in San Diego could go ahead. The celebration of Jacqueline de Decker's eightieth birthday proceeded as planned. Almost immediately after leaving the Antwerp meeting, however, Mother Teresa wrote a letter contradicting much of what she had said. The Chapter in San Diego was not to be.

Shortly afterwards she fell on a wet floor in the bathroom in Rome, and injured three ribs. Increasingly now she was attended by Sister Gertrude, the second of her former Loreto pupils to join the Missionaries of Charity, who had struggled under almost impossible conditions to train as a doctor so many years previously. It was during one of Sister Gertrude's brief absences that the accident occurred. "You see what happens when you leave me?" Mother Teresa reproached her playfully on her return. Her injuries had not succeeded in crushing her spirit. Nor did they prevent her from meeting her commitment to a heavy schedule, first in Poland and then in Ireland and the United Kingdom. Among other things, she wanted very much to sort out another house in London before the cold of winter set in. She arrived in Dublin on 31 May. On 1 June she presented Mary Robinson with a statue of the Virgin Mary and met with Pro-Life campaigners. The views she expressed in Ireland on abortion and divorce were as uncompromising as ever: "Let us make one strong resolution that in this beautiful country of Ireland no child may be unwanted... Let us promise Our Lady who loves Ireland so much that we will never have in this country one single abortion ... Let us promise that there will be no more divorce." On 2 June she received the Freedom of the City of Dublin and then, despite rumours that because of her fatigue and pain she might cancel the next stage of her journey, went on to Belfast. Her next stop was Edinburgh and then on 6 June she arrived in London.

On 7 June she finally opened a thirty-five room hostel for the homeless in St George's Road, Southwark. An appeal launched by the *Daily* and the *Sunday Mirror* in 1988 had raised nearly £300,000 for the lonely and the homeless of London. The delay in converting the money into something more concrete had given rise to speculation about the misappropriation of the funds on the part of Robert Maxwell but was in fact attributable to Mother Teresa's inability to find a suitable building for her Order's purposes. Her vision of a refuge was, as always, very modest, so modest that in June 1993 her plans to convert a disused magistrates' court in Kennington, South London to house up to 33 homeless people had been turned down by Lambeth Council on the grounds that it would cause "a loss of amenity to nearby residents". The five-storey building for which, on 7 June, she signed the deeds in Southwark, would not only provide a place "for the people sleeping on the streets to have supper and lay their heads for a night", it would also provide accommodation for a number of Sisters. Mother Teresa was manifestly satisfied at last: "We have been praying and praying for this home". Having also squeezed in a brief visit to Princess Diana at Kensington Palace and Mass at St George's Cathedral in South London, next day she left for Oxford where she addressed the Oxford Union. Even those who strongly disagreed with her on issues such as contraception and abortion were, it seemed, deeply affected by her presence. For forty-five minutes she spoke to an attentive audience of students, but she was obviously exhausted. Asked during question time afterwards what she thought of liberation theology, she responded in a manner which was not entirely clear: "I don't know. It has not come to England yet."

"She lives from day to day," I was told, as I watched her make her way gingerly down the stairs of the Missionary of Charity home in Bravington Road, London in the early hours of the morning two days later. Mother Teresa was at her best first thing in the morning but that morning she was so weak that Sister Gertrude had not managed to find a pulse at all. Her cautious movements betrayed the fact that she was in considerable pain. Yet outside the house, as she left for Mass at Kilburn Roman Catholic Church, people still pressed to see her. Among them were those who knew her suffering and yet could not resist reaching out to touch her, and instinctively she reached out in response, still handing out the prayer cards which she referred to as her "business cards". On them were printed the words:

> The fruit of silence is prayer
> The fruit of prayer is faith
> The fruit of faith is love
> The fruit of love is service
> The fruit of service is peace.

"This is good business," she liked to tell people as she dispensed them and in their eagerness to receive her blessing the recipients had a tendency to forget the fragility of the elderly woman in their midst. It was not perhaps surprising that those who were close to her on a daily basis saw fit increasingly to protect her from the demands of those they felt should know better than to be an additional drain upon her limited reserves of energy.

In August 1993 Mother Teresa was yet again admitted to hospital. At the time she was in Delhi to receive an Indian Government award for "promoting peace and communal harmony" but was taken ill hours before the ceremony and was driven first to the All India Medical Institute of Science, suffering from a fever and vomiting. Congestion of the lungs and breathlessness set in after this malaria attack and once more her heart gave serious cause for concern. She was duly transferred to a coronary care unit and once again came close to death when doctors operated on a closed heart vessel. Her eighty-third birthday was spent in hospital as countless destitute people flocked to the Missionary of Charity houses to hold a vigil for "Mother". Next day she was discharged and boarded a special plane provided by the Indian Prime Minister to return to Calcutta.

There were those amongst the Co-Workers who were still unclear about what her precise wishes for the Association were. Mother Teresa was subject to the same occasional spells of memory loss, confusion and dependency on others around her that beset many others of her years. She was no longer as accessible as she had been, even to friends of the earliest years, and there was speculation as to whether, in her vulnerability, she had lost sight of the hundreds of thousands of "ordinary" people throughout the world who were faithfully following the Co-Workers' way of life and doing precisely "the small things with great love" which Mother Teresa urged them to do. At the same time, if such allegations as the misuse of funds were clearly without factual foundation and if occasionally Mother Teresa appeared to be acting inconsistently, there were still those who perceived in the call for a return to greater simplicity the spiritual fruit of deep prayer which should not be ignored. It was true that in more recent years there had been a certain kudos attached to involvement in the work of the world-famous Mother Teresa. As Brother Andrew would afterwards reflect:

The basic reality is that there is power involved in something as wonderful and successful as the Missionaries of Charity. And there are people who know that – consciously or unconsciously. And being human they go for it. This is bound to be. It happened with St Francis of Assisi. It has happened through the ages with the Church. So it's par for the course in the Church to say nothing of politics, revolutions, media personalities and financial takeovers. But the Holy Spirit is not put out of business through the operators and manipulators. In fact he uses them. I believe Mother Teresa, beneath or through, whatever advice or pressures she has on her, is truly sensitive to the values of simplicity as a key mark of Jesus and His Gospel.

On 30 August 1993 Mother Teresa sent a letter to Co-Workers throughout the world, thanking them first for their concern for her health. It was a letter in her own writing in which only the occasional missing word or punctuation mark betrayed her personal frailty:

I had wanted to bring all of you to Calcutta for a chapter to tell you what is in my heart regarding the Co-Workers. Now is not possible. May God's blessing be with you all and help you to accept my decision which I have made after much prayer and penance and suffering.

I am very grateful for all the wonderful work each one of you has done right from the beginning. These twenty-five years have been something beautiful for God. I want to thank you especially those who were with me from the beginning specially Mrs Ann Blaikie. Jesus said – "You did it to me. Your reward will be great in Heaven."

Dear Co-Workers, to keep up your spirit as Co-Workers, you need only remain in close touch with the Missionaries of Charity and among yourselves wherever you are. I want you to work with Sisters, Brothers and Fathers directly – the humble work, beginning in your own homes, neighbourhood, your parish, your city; and where there are no Missionaries of Charity, to work in that same spirit wherever you may be. It is this that will transform the world. If you pray, God will give a clean heart and a clean heart can see the Face of God in the Poor you serve.

Now that times have changed and Sisters are in 105 countries of the world, we do not need the Co-Workers to function as an "organization" with Governing Board, Officers, links and bank accounts. I do not want money to be spent for newsletters, or for travel as Co-Workers. If you see anyone raising money in my name please stop them. And any money offered to you for Mother Teresa or the Missionaries of Charity must be directed immediately and entirely to the Missionaries of Charity. As long as you observe these points, you belong to the family of the Missionaries of Charity and can be Co-Workers of Mother Teresa. However, I do not want the Co-Workers as an "organization" to continue. I have written to all the Bishops around the world that I have made this decision.

Let us all remain united in the Heart of Jesus through Mary as one spiritual family. My gift to you is to allow you to share with us in God's work, to be carriers of God's love in a spirit of prayer and sacrifice.

I appeal to you once more – be what Mother is asking you to be in each city and town – simple Co-Workers, helping the Sisters to bring Jesus to

the Poor. I send my special blessing and deep gratitude for doing as I ask
you. Let us all be one heart full of love in the Heart of Jesus full of love for
Mary and through the Immaculate Heart of Mary, the cause of our joy.
    Let us often say – Mary Mother of Jesus be Mother to us now.
    Each one of you are in my daily. Let us be one heart full of love. Let
us pray.

By 17 September Mother Teresa was once more fighting for her
life as surgeons struggled to clear a blocked heart vessel. Pope John
Paul II sent her a message saying, "The whole world needs you."
Her consultant could only marvel at her will power. As for Mother
Teresa, she was still conscious of the work that was almost, but not
quite done. Three days later Father Celeste Van Exem, her spiritual director and wise councillor of so many years, died in St
Xavier's College, Calcutta. She had remained close to him to the
last. On Easter Sunday that year she had taken a group of the first
Sisters to join the Missionaries of Charity even before they had
officially become a congregation, to visit him. On 12 April that first
group had completed forty years as professed Sisters and a visit to
the bedside of Father Van Exem had seemed an appropriate way in
which to mark the occasion. "He has gone straight home to God,"
Mother Teresa commented on his death. "He was very holy." She
was too ill herself to attend the funeral on 22 September but,
together with Sister Nirmala, she stood at the window of the
Mother House to watch as his coffin was born down Lower
Circular Road to be buried at St John's Cemetery. Shortly before
his death and while she was in intensive care, on the 16th, he had
written her a letter:

> *Dear Mother,*
> *Tomorrow morning I shall say Holy Mass for the following intercessions:*
> *1. That you may have no operation*
> *2. That you may be in China by the 7 October 1993*
> *3. That the Lord may take me and not you if that is His will.*
> *His will, not mine.*
> *I am with you and the Sisters, all of them. There is a Calvary for every*
> *Christian. For you the way to Calvary is long. But Mary has met you in*
> *the road. You did not go up the hill; this is for later.*

I adore the Blessed Sacrament which, I am sure, you have in your room.
Pray for me and all my companions, especially the companions of Jesus
with whom I am.
Yours sincerely in O.L.
C. Van Exem, SJ

Father Van Exem had told her that he was offering his life that she
might go to China because he knew that the objective of taking her
Sisters into China was still a priority. So too did many others. At the
gathering in Antwerp in May 1993 Mother Teresa had reported
with obvious satisfaction that progress was being made with regard
to the invitation to go to Shanghai and that she had received
permission to take a priest for her Sisters. She had spoken with
amusement of how she had been asked whether the Sisters would
wear Chinese dress but explained their retention of the sari in terms
of it being the cheapest attire available to them. "Especially I want
you to pray for China," she had urged seminarians at Menouth
College in Ireland in June 1993. "I'm giving you China, all right? If
we don't succeed, I will blame you." At the time of Father Van
Exem's death her plans were to go via Hong Kong to China in time
to open the first foundation there on the anniversary of the congregation's erection on 7 October 1950. "Millions of hearts are waiting
for you" – she had been promised a welcome both from the government and from the Church, but the visit had once more to be postponed. It was only at the end of October 1993 that she finally
arrived in China from Singapore. Mother Teresa emerged from
Shanghai airport, pushing her own baggage trolley, piled high with
the usual assortment of brown cardboard boxes, announcing simply
that the reason for her visit was "to help the poor". Asked, however,
whether her visit, following that of the Vatican envoy Cardinal
Roger Etchegaray in September, represented a further opening of
China to the Church, she replied, "yes". In fact she had set her
heart on opening a home for handicapped children in Shanghai
where she stayed for two days before travelling on to Beijing at the
invitation of Deng Pufang. Nevertheless December 1993 saw her
once again in Rome for the professions held on the 8th and 9th,
after which she visited Poland, before returning to India. China, it
seemed, needed "more time and prayer".

On 3 February 1994 Mother Teresa attended a "National Prayer Breakfast" in Washington. She went reluctantly at the invitation of President Clinton. When she had finished giving a very long speech, much of it against abortion, no one at the top-table where the President was sitting applauded. President Clinton did, however, afterwards apologize to her. What is more, the breakfast also brought Mother Teresa into conversation with Hillary Rodham Clinton. The two women found common ground at least in their attitude to adoption. A year later Hillary Clinton and her daughter visited one of the Missionary of Charity homes in New Delhi and on 19 June 1995 a shelter for children was opened in Washington DC. It was, in the words of Mrs Clinton "one of those moments when the afflicted and the comfortable come together."

In March 1994 Mother Teresa once more set out for China, this time very quietly. She did not want publicity to jeopardize a highly sensitive situation. She had set her sights on opening the house for handicapped children on the Feast of St Joseph. She met first with the Archbishop of Shanghai and then went on to Beijing to meet Deng Pufang, head of the organization for the care of the handicapped who was himself confined to a wheelchair. Deng Pufang, she afterwards reported, told her that he looked forward to the day when China "could have the Missionaries of Charity reaching out tender love and care to the poor". Mother Teresa also visited the Cathedral of Our Lady of Sheshan, patroness of China, but for a third time her mission proved abortive. With the failure of its bid to host the Olympic games, China was becoming less open. By May Mother Teresa had opened two new houses in Vietnam but the goal that was closest to her heart was denied her. She had been expected in Rome in May for the beatification of Brother Damien. As it transpired the ceremony was postponed due to the fact that the Pope was taken ill, but, in any case, one of her Sisters let it be known, for her China was still *the* primary objective. It was vital that she created that opening: "She still has that charism – that of opening doors which others cannot."

She was still also calling for holiness. Always exigent in her spiritual requirements and never perhaps totally conversant with the daily demands and pressures of what many would regard as "ordinary" living, it was as if Mother Teresa, in her desire to ensure that the legacy she left was as pure as possible, was now prepared to make even fewer concessions to the humanity of "ordinary" people. The response of Co-Workers to Mother Teresa's letter of 30 August 1993 was confused. Some felt it questionable whether constitutionally Mother Teresa even had the right to disband an association of which she was just one member. Yet the reaction to somehow continuing the Co-Workers at grass roots level whilst removing the "hierarchy" was on the whole positive. Many were able to see in it the call to a spiritual maturity no longer so focused on the person of Mother Teresa and a preparation for the time when she would no longer be with them. As Father Paul Chetcuti, international spiritual advisor to the Co-Workers wrote:

We have said so often in the past that we are all Co-Workers of Jesus. Mother is just a small pencil in the hands of the Lord. With this small pencil Jesus has called us to serve and love him. With this same pencil he is calling us to concentrate more on him. Perhaps we have forgotten the hand that has been writing all these years and concentrated too much on the pencil. So the difficult and hard words that the pencil has just written may be an invitation to look a bit higher up and see the Author of Life calling us closer to Him, for his own sake and nothing else ... Let us continue to be Co-Workers of Jesus. No single act of love and of service to the needy must be stopped ...

The burning question remained, however, that of how that service was to be continued in practice, and of how contact was to be maintained between those who shared a commitment to the Co-Workers' recently simplified guidelines. Such contact was for many a deeply felt human need if the spiritual dedication Mother Teresa called for was to be sustained in an increasingly atheistic world. Furthermore, how were the poor to be served in the innumerable places where there were still no Sisters or Brothers but plenty of Co-Workers who were in some cases better equipped to meet local needs? In Antwerp, for example, there were no Missionaries of Charity but a multitude of poor people with moral, social and psychological troubles. As Jacqueline de Decker once remarked of the city's prostitutes, her "girls", "They need a comprehensive heart to help them in their own language, not just a soup kitchen!"

And how did Mother Teresa imagine that, for example, the "Link for supplies" who co-ordinated the transportation of container loads of vital provisions to the Missionaries of Charity in various parts of the world could be replaced by a Sister whose vocation scarcely qualified her to deal with shipping and export formalities? The response from Mother Teresa to this latter query was pragmatic: the "Link for supplies" should continue.

In an attempt to dispel any confusion, on 10 October 1993 Mother Teresa wrote another letter to "Margaret Cullis and all Co-Workers", underlining the fact that the decision she had made on 20 August still stood:

I must repeat: I do not want office-bearers on any level. Each group of Co-Workers, work with your local group of Sisters or Brothers. Where there are none, contact the regional superior and keep in touch with her about working as Co-Workers beginning in your own neighbourhood ...

Later in the same letter she stressed the fact that she wanted the spiritual and the simple work of the Co-Workers to continue:

I also want all the Co-Worker groups coming together for prayer, work and sharing to continue. Co-Workers serving the Poor by putting together shipments of used clothing, blankets and bandages, please continue this humble and beautiful work.

The Link for the Sick and Suffering was to continue also:

The beautiful work started and kept up by Jacqueline de Decker of linking the sick and suffering with MC Sisters will continue and since Jacqueline has written several times of her health condition, requesting for help, I will be sending an MC Sister to learn the work from her.

On 26 May 1994, however, Mother Teresa wrote to the Missionary of Charity regional superiors telling them that no more correspondence was to pass between the Sisters and the Sick and Suffering Co-Workers: "In this spiritual way, we hope to encourage more people who would like to have this spiritual link of prayer and sacrifice but for some reason are unable to write." "You my dear

Sick and Suffering Co-Workers", she added, "are in my daily prayer and in the prayers of all the Sisters and I will keep in touch with you through these letters." The spiritual emphasis of Mother Teresa was fully appreciated but in human terms this direction was a bitter tablet to swallow for those for whom the briefest of notes from their adopted Sister meant so much and who derived great joy from writing or dictating the occasional letter themselves.

For the Co-Workers it was a time in which to come to terms with their own "poverty", a time to accept rather than to understand, as Mother Teresa herself was being called upon to accept things which she too manifestly had difficulty in understanding but to which she responded without acrimony. Her reaction to the man who called her "Hell's Angel" in the programme shown on British television in November 1994 was to give instructions that she did not want her friends and followers to speak out in her defence but rather simply to pray: "May God forgive him, he doesn't know what he is doing." She added: "Pray that that man realizes what he has done because Jesus said whatever you do to the least you do to him." Her accuser was derisorily dismissive of such prayers. Instead, in the Autumn of 1995, he published a book underlining the criticisms first voiced in the programme. The book appeared in the shops at the same time as *A Simple Path*, a volume faithfully recording Mother Teresa's spirituality in a similar vein to many others that had preceded it but one which was initially marketed as an "autobiography". Those who knew her could not fail to be aware that this was not the kind of publicity that occasioned her much joy.

The awards and the acclaim were still there for her. In August 1992, in New York, she had received the Knights of St Columbus' Gaudium et Spes Award from Cardinal John O'Connor. In the same month she had been made an Honorary Fellow of the Royal College of Surgeons in Ireland. In December 1992 in Calcutta, she received the United Nations cultural agency's peace education award to "crown a life consecrated to the service of the poor, to the promotion of peace and to combating injustice". The $50,000 cheque presented to her by the UNESCO director general was used to set up a home for the handicapped near Calcutta. In January 1993 she was recommended for the papal award, Pro

Ecclesia et Pontifice. October 1994 brought her the U Thant
Peace Award for her "sleepless service to humanity". Most of these
honours now were bestowed upon her in a location of her choice
for her travelling was becoming more and more restricted. Yet she
was determined still to go where she felt God was calling her, in the
knowledge that it was still her personal presence that produced
results.

In May 1993 Mother Teresa had attended a meeting of Mother
Generals in Rome at which the heads of religious orders were
blatantly posing next to her while others took their photographs.
Asked how she put up with it, Mother Teresa's answer was
predictably: "For Jesus". So it was that she still appeared in pictures
with England's batsmen before the First Test against India or with
Miss Universe, Sushmite Sen of India. "I only have to cough and
the world knows about it", she remarked in May 1994 when,
having been bitten by a dog kept by the Sisters in one of the Delhi
houses, she was subjected to two stitches and a course of anti-rabies
injections, and the media once more homed in on her. Yet for the
Jesus who, she believed, had specifically identified himself with
suffering humanity, she was still prepared to be actively involved,
especially in the creation of further homes for AIDS sufferers, be it
in Baltimore or India. Similarly she was still prepared to plead with
the Governor of California for the life of an American killer on
death-row, to rally her Sisters to the aid of the victims of an earthquake which devastated the central Maharashtra region of central
India in 1993 or of the blood bath in Rwanda in 1994, to stand up
for holiness, especially in priests and religious, and to take every
opportunity to speak out in defence of the unborn child, no matter
how controversial her views might be.

As, in 1995, the Missionaries of Charity began to prepare themselves spiritually for the 1996 Chapter, speculation as to Mother
Teresa's successor and the future of the Order was revived. The
question of continuation, however, was one that always worried
others more than it did Mother Teresa herself, who accepted quite
simply that the congregation and the work would endure if it was
God's will for it to do so. There was, all the same, a strong sense of
transition. The first Co-Workers, those who had been prepared
to befriend and support a "little unknown nun" in the slums of

Calcutta, were nearing the end of their lives. On 14 January 1996, at the age of seventy-nine, Ann Blaikie died peacefully, of a pulmonary embolism. Her funeral Mass, held in Bramley, Surrey at the church in which she had been active for many years, was attended by Co-Workers from far and wide. Alzheimer's disease had spared her from really understanding the decisions Mother Teresa had made with regard to the Association of Co-Workers to which she had given her life. In a letter dated 15 January 1996, addressed to the family and read out at the funeral, Mother Teresa wrote:

This morning, I remembered your dear mother, Ann, at Holy Mass in a very special way. I was sorry to hear that she has left us – but I am sure that Jesus welcomed her into heaven by saying, "My dear child Ann, remember all the times you gave Me to eat and to drink, all the times you clothed Me, housed Me, visited Me and comforted Me. Whatever you did to the poorest of the poor in Calcutta and around the world, you did it to Me."

You know that I always think of Ann with much love and gratitude. She shared so much with me in the early days of the Society. What she started to do then is now still being carried on by Co-Workers around the world ...

Elsewhere too, Mother Teresa had made it clear that she wanted the Co-Workers to continue but in reality, in some parts of the world, in the absence of the newsletters that had kept them in touch with the remainder of the Association and without overt leadership, the Co-Workers were declining in number. Mother Teresa herself was still writing to her Co-Workers, urging them, above all else, to pray and to join the Missionaries of Charity in their times of prayer. She also tried to pass on to them the news some were missing now that the Co-Worker newsletter was no more. She had written to them at Christmas 1995, of how British Airways had provided the occupants of the Missionary of Charity children's homes in Calcutta with an early Christmas treat by giving them a free one-hour plane trip. She wrote of how that year the Missionaries of Charity had opened a further fourteen foundations "all over the world where Jesus waits in His distressing disguise for a kind word, a smile, a little bit of food or medicine".

She was still travelling whenever possible to attend the professions of her Sisters in different parts of the world (around the world that Christmas 52 were making their first vows and 76 their final commitment) and to be present at the opening of new houses but, she was finally obliged to acknowledge that, "since we are spreading out in so many countries, it is getting harder for me to be present for the blessing of these new Tabernacles."

During the night of 31 March/1 April 1996, Mother Teresa fell out of bed at the mother house in Calcutta and broke her collar bone. She was driven through the chaos of Calcutta's traffic to the Woodland's Nursing Home and next day was said to be in a "stable" condition, but she had been obliged to cancel a visit to witness the arrival of a large shipment of pharmaceuticals. Nevertheless, June of that year saw Mother Teresa travelling once more, to the United States, Rome and then Ireland. In the convent in Dublin she missed a step, spraining her ankle badly. She succumbed for a while to using a wheelchair but injury was not to prevent her from attending the opening of a house in Armagh on 14 June, an event all the more prized because of the necessity some years previously to close the Missionary of Charity foundation in Belfast. In Cork, Sligo and Liverpool she was joined by well-wishers wherever she went. Co-Workers and Missionaries of Charity alike were able to be with her for Mass and for Holy Hours in various locations. Four days later she opened the 565th convent of her Order, in Swansea, before passing through London on her way back to Rome. Her voice and her hands were strong and in London she declined to use the wheelchair brought to her, but there were times when she could not remember from one day to the next whom she had seen or what had been said. It was Sister Nirmala who accompanied Mother Teresa during this visit to Britain and Northern Ireland and who journeyed with her as far as Rome.

Scarcely had Mother Teresa arrived back in India, however, than tragic news reached her from the USA. On Saturday 6 July both the Superior and the Regional Superior for New York had been killed in a car crash. Both Sisters had been due to represent the United States at the Missionary of Charity Chapter planned for October. Mother Teresa, unable to embark so swiftly on another long journey, sent word to Sister Nirmala in Rome to go the States as her representative.

During the third week of August Mother Teresa was once more admitted to the Woodland's Nursing Home in Calcutta and by the 23rd her condition was giving serious cause for alarm. She could breathe only with the assistance of a respirator. The senior Sisters gathered at the hospital to pray and Sister Nirmala flew back from Brooklyn where she had been preparing the Missionaries of Charity for the forthcoming Chapter, to arrive in Calcutta on Saturday the 24th. Once again the Pope and Princess Diana were among those who sent goodwill messages for Mother Teresa's recovery. People throughout the world prayed for what many were beginning to believe was impossible, and sure enough, by Sunday 25 August Mother Teresa had regained consciousness. Her fever had dropped. That evening she received the Sisters who had gathered at the hospital and on the eve of her eighty-sixth birthday, to the amazement of her doctors, she breathed without the respirator and set about writing notes in response to those who had expressed their concern about her precarious condition.

Two days later in her flat in Antwerp, Jacqueline de Decker rose awkwardly from the desk at which she had been working, and fell. Next day it was discovered that she had broken her knee and she was swiftly admitted to hospital. Her role as international Link for the Sick and Suffering was being assumed by a Missionary of Charity Sister. She continued to offer her suffering for Mother Teresa but the lack of any direct personal contact with the woman to whom she had given her life had added an unprecedented dimension of spiritual anguish to her physical pain.

On Friday 6 September, after repeated protestations from Mother Teresa that she was fit to be discharged, against their better judgement her doctors were induced to let her leave hospital. She did so at 5 a.m., announcing that her health and her life were in God's hands. Tuesday 10 September was the fiftieth anniversary of the Inspiration Day which had sown the seeds for the congregation of the Missionaries of Charity. Sisters Agnes and Gertrude were amongst those who gathered at Mother Teresa's bedside but she had let it be known that she wanted the day to be one of quiet reflection. She was manifestly still not out of danger and on 16 September, borne down the stairs of the mother house on a stretcher, she was readmitted to hospital after falling and saying that she felt dizzy. A brain scan revealed a shadow on the brain, but on the 25th, alert and cheerful, she was once again discharged.

At the beginning of September the Missionaries of Charity went into retreat to prepare for the election of a new superior general, set for 7 October; and once again the world began to speculate about who might appropriately step into her shoes, but the Chapter was postponed. That same month Mother Teresa became only the third person to be given honorary US citizenship for the way she had "nursed the sick, cared for the poor, and shown us, through concrete actions, how we can make real our dreams for a just and good society". By Friday 22 November, however, she was once more suffering from chest pains. The following night and again on Sunday morning she suffered heart failure. In the specialist heart centre to which she was transferred from the Woodland's Nursing Home surgeons felt obliged to postpone a proposed angiography because her condition was too critical for intrusive medical procedures. One week later she underwent life-saving surgery to remove artery blockages, but her condition was still critical. Long-standing lung and renal problems made drug treatment to correct her irregular heartbeat difficult.

Every time rumours spread of her death, traffic in the area of the hospital in Calcutta came to a standstill as people sought news. The hospital switchboard was jammed and the Sisters were joined in their continuing prayers for her recovery by Buddhists, Sikhs, Hindus and Muslims. There were reports that she had lost interest in regaining even the strength necessary to continue the work and that she had finally set her tired, weak heart on heaven. She had helped so many people to die that she could doubtless accept mortality much better than her doctors. Yet by 4 December she claimed that she felt better and that she wanted to go home to be with her Sisters in A.J.C. Bose Road. The laughter and joy of the Missionaries of Charity had always been a source of strength and comfort to her. What was more, it had been pointed out to her that she had a duty to work hard to get well and she was not one to fail in a duty. On Thursday 19 December 1996 she walked out of hospital to return to the mother house by car. Much of her time, however, was now spent confined to bed with severe back pain.

In January 1997 Archbishop Henry D'Souza of Calcutta announced that Mother Teresa had made it clear that she wished to resign as general superior of her Order and that there was to be no repeat of 1990 when she had resumed the position, despite her desire to step down. Her health would simply not permit her to continue. Contrary to expectations, the election of her successor was not held on 2 February 1997. The Pope, in a letter to the Chapter Members of the Missionaries of Charity, exhorted them to seek the will of God in their decisions. Consequently, it was announced, the one hundred and twenty-three delegates who had gathered in Calcutta would cast their votes as and when they were really ready to elect Mother Teresa's successor. The transition from charismatic founder to successor in religious congregations was invariably problematic. Manifestly the choice was proving a difficult one. The announcement finally came on Thursday 13 March. Sister Nirmala, former head of the Contemplative Sisters, was to be overall Superior General. Sister Nirmala was a Hindu convert, from a Nepali family, and a profoundly spiritual, well-educated and wise woman. The choice was clearly one of which Mother Teresa herself approved. Asked whether she considered herself the right person to assume the foundress's awesome mantle, the newly appointed Superior General replied: "The Lord will make me fit for the job, if you pray for me."

Sister Nirmala's first journey outside India in her new capacity was not, as Mother Teresa might have wished, to China but to Africa. At the entrance to a new Missionary of Charity convent in Nairobi, a Jesuit priest stepped forward to welcome her: "Mother Nirmala, welcome to Nairobi and Africa." Immediately, she corrected him: "Father, please call me Sister because we have only one mother, Mother Teresa." For the duration of the foundress's life time at least, the very idea of another "Mother" remained inconceivable.

"Mother" appeared more relaxed with the resolution of the question of her successor. There were, however, still moments of profound sadness in store for her. In the mother house Sister Agnes, the first Sister to have joined Mother Teresa so courageously in the slums, was suffering dreadfully, if with extraordinary acceptance, from cancer. She died at last on 9 April 1997, while

Mass was being said at her bedside. Mother Teresa had lost another precious companion of many years.

There were also issues as yet unresolved. At Easter 1997 a letter went out to Co-Workers throughout the world asking them whether they in fact felt the need for an international link, for newsletters, national links and national meetings. They were invited to reply to Mother Teresa and Sister Nirmala by the end of May. The events of the ensuing months, however, were to prevent both Mother Teresa and Sister Nirmala from having the time to act upon the Co-Workers' response.

On 16 May Mother Teresa arrived in Rome. She wanted to be present at the profession of a number of new Sisters. She also wanted to outline to the Pope a plan for "rehabilitating" the thousands of prostitutes in the rundown areas of Rome; and to introduce her successor to him. There were times now when she was having to be given oxygen three times a day and she was unable to go to Poland as she had originally intended. She did, however, manage to journey to the United States, again for the profession of some of her Sisters, but also to receive a Congressional Gold Medal in recognition of her "outstanding and enduring contributions to humanitarian and charitable activities". Reports that she was at death's door were belied as, frail but smiling, she was seen walking hand in hand with Princess Diana in the Bronx.

She longed to return to Calcutta. India, even in the monsoon, suited her and on her eighty-seventh birthday celebrated in the mother house, she made an appearance, still smiling for the world. "I have no problem with Dominique Lapierre", she was heard to say. "Bless him and his film." Controversy, fanned by the press, had once more arisen in connection with the venture, as the news was announced that a film of Dominique Lapierre's script *In the name of God's Poor* was to appear on American television with Geraldine Chaplin playing the role of Mother Teresa. Mother Teresa's birthday comment was in apparent contradiction of reports that she was distressed at the treatment of her life. Dominique Lapierre, for his part, held on to the words of the director of the Holy See Press Office written after he read the script in 1991: "We can see the tremendous formal beauty of this film. But it is mostly as a Catholic that I remain impressed. This film shows with enormous catechetical efficacy the ethical contents of love for the 'poorest of the poor' and I believe that it should cause a great impact on the many people who will see it, both Catholic and agnostic."

Dominique Lapierre's great regret was that Mother Teresa would never see the film.

The untimely death of Diana, Princess of Wales, in a car crash in Paris brought Mother Teresa once more before the cameras. She spoke of the Princess's love for the poor and promised that she would offer special prayers for her. It was to be her last public statement. On Friday 5 September 1997, on the eve of the funeral of Diana, Princess of Wales, Mother Teresa's exhausted heart finally beat its last. Her body was laid to rest first in the chapel of the mother house where only invited guests were able to see it, but then transferred in a Missionary of Charity ambulance with the single word "Mother" written across the windscreen, to St Thomas' Church in Middleton Row, Calcutta. It was a church used by the Loreto Sisters who had a school nearby but what had determined the choice of the building was its accessibility to the crowds of mourners, especially India's poor, who thronged to pay their last respects to their "Ma". Mother Teresa had once advised Princess Diana that when she was suffering or in distress she should reach out to others who were suffering, and she would find that they in turn reached out to her. The immense outpouring of affection that marked the funeral of Princess Diana was to provide very tangible evidence of the truth of those words. Just one week later the state funeral India afforded one of its most celebrated nationals underlined that truth. The Missionaries of Charity had accepted the pomp and circumstance of what might otherwise have seemed a somewhat incongruous honour because it was bestowed upon their foundress as a mark of the love of the Indian people. On 13 September Mother Teresa's body was borne through the streets of Calcutta on the same gun carriage that had carried the bodies of Mahatma Gandhi and Jawaharlal Nehru, as tens of thousands of people lined the route to catch a final glimpse of the woman who, in celebration of the fiftieth anniversary of India's independence, had written:

When I look around our country, the land God has given to each one of us to call our home, I see so much of His blessings and goodness: in the smallest flower, the tallest trees, the rivers, plains and mountains. But where do we find most the beauty of our country? We find it in each man, woman and child.

A state funeral mass attended by numerous dignitaries from all over the world, among them the Duchess of Kent representing the Queen, Hillary Clinton, Bernadette Chirac and the Queens of Spain, Belgium and Jordan, was held in Netaji covered sports stadium. Cardinal Angelo Sodano, the Vatican Secretary of State, and Archbishop Henry D'Souza were among the many church leaders officiating at the service. The liturgy reflected Mother Teresa's capacity to transcend all differences of nationality and creed, and her work amongst the orphaned, the leprous and so many of the world's suffering found symbolic representation in it. Afterwards in a private ceremony, as soldiers outside fired a last salute, she was laid to rest beneath a plain stone slab in the mother house in A.J.C. Bose Road, a centre of continual prayer, close to the people she had served.

In a message read out at her public funeral the Pope called upon others to continue the work Mother Teresa had begun, and from her valedictory address, in which she pledged that she would do so, it was clear that Sister Nirmala had the same unshakeable faith as the congregation's first "Mother", that God would provide whatever was needed. "None of us has what this world looks for," Mother Teresa once wrote. She also said "We must never think any one of us is indispensable. God has ways and means." She left behind her a sense of immeasurable loss but also a legacy of some 4,000 Sisters, over four hundred Brothers, and countless Missionary of Charity Fathers, Lay Missionaries of Charity, Co-Workers and other volunteers, in whose hearts her spirit would live on.

There were still those who from the vantage point of radio and television studios and newspaper offices thought that she might have done it better. Uncomfortable with goodness, sceptical of simplicity, they were unable to accept that for her funding was a question of Divine Providence. Nor could they accept that she treated dictators like friends just because she believed that every human being contained the divine life and that every human being should have the opportunity to do good. But this was a woman who at Christmas sang "Happy Birthday" to Jesus, who regarded sanctity as a "simple duty" for everyone, and for whom the moment most of us so dread was merely a matter of "going home to God".

APPENDIX A

List of Missionary of Charity Foundations outside India

Cocorote, Venezuela	26 July 1965
Rome, Italy	22 August 1968
Tabora, Tanzania	8 September 1968
Bourke, Australia	13 September 1968
Catia La Mar, Venezuela	19 March 1970
Melbourne, Australia	27 April 1970
Amman, Jordan	16 July 1970
Marin (Edo Yaracuy), Venezuela	21 November 1970
Southall, London, England	8 December 1970
Bravington Road, London W9, England	14 July 1971
Bronx, New York, USA	18 October 1971
Dhaka, Bangladesh	21 January 1972
Khulna, Bangladesh	11 February 1972
Port Luis, Mauritius	15 August 1972
Gaza, Israel	26 February 1973
Katherine, Australia	25 March 1973
Hodeidah, Yemen Arab Republic	22 August 1973
Lima, Peru	4 October 1973
Addis Ababa, Ethiopia	23 November 1973
Hanubade, Papua New Guinea	28 May 1974
Palermo, Sicily, Italy	9 June 1974
Port Morsby, Papua New Guinea	18 July 1974
Taiz, Yemen	13 August 1974
Mausaid, Dhaka, Bangladesh	25 October 1974
Naples, Italy	16 June 1975
Tokarara, Papua New Guinea	4 November 1975
San Felix, Venezuela	6 January 1976
Sanaa, Yemen Arab Republic	2 February 1976
Rome, Italy	23 February 1976
Santa Fe, Mexico	8 April 1976
Guatamala City, Guatamala	26 April 1976
Bronx, New York, USA (Contemplative)	25 June 1976
Dar-es-Salaam, Tanzania	14 July 1976
Tejgaon, Bangladesh	31 October 1976

Kerema, Papua New Guinea	3 February 1977
Binondo, Manila, Philippines	11 February 1977
Tabora, Tanzania (Noviciate)	9 March 1977
Haiti, West Indies	5 August 1977
Rotterdam, Netherlands	15 August 1977
Dire, Dawa, Ethiopia	28 August 1977
San Salvador, El Salvador	21 December 1977
Metro-Manila, Philippines	11 February 1978
Caracas, Venezuela	30 April 1978
Zarate, Argentina	24 May 1978
Syhlet, Bangladesh	16 July 1978
Liverpool, England	21 July 1978
Dodoma, Tabora, Tanzania	25 October 1978
El Dorado, Panama	15 September 1978
Tondo, Manila	2 February 1979
Beirut, Lebanon	10 March 1979
Reggio, Calabria, Italy	31 May 1979
Essen, Germany	22 June 1979
St Louis, Missouri,USA	22 June 1979
Bari, Italy	22 June 1979
Detroit, Michigan, USA	22 June 1979
Toluca, Mexico	16 July 1979
Salvador-Bahia, Brazil	16 July 1979
Chimbote, Peru	16 July 1979
Nairobi, Kenya	16 July 1979
Sanfil, Port au Prince, Haiti	6 August 1979
Kigali, Rwanda	29 September 1979
Vittoria, Sicily, Italy	19 December 1979
Cebu City, Philippines	30 December 1979
Berina, Papua New Guinea	7 January 1980
Via Casilina, Rome, Italy	6 June 1980
Ghent, Belgium	13 June 1980
Madrid, Spain	21 June 1980
Skopje, Macedonia	26 June 1980
Katmandu, Nepal	16 July 1980
Santiago, Chile	19 July 1980
Frontera, Argentina	15 August 1980
Miami, USA	8 September 1980
Marseille, France	4 October 1980
Primavalle, Rome, Italy	1 November 1980
Cairo, Egypt	7 March 1981
La Paz el Alto, Bolivia	25 March 1981
East Berlin, Germany	30 March 1981
Tokyo, Japan	24 May 1981
Cucuta, Colombia	27 May 1981

Alexandria, Egypt	1 June 1981
Batuco, Santiago, Chile	21 June 1981
Washington DC, USA (Contemplative)	25 June 1981
Newark, USA	26 June 1981
Macau, China	26 June 1981
Anyang, South Korea	6 July 1981
Belabo, Cameroon	18 July 1981
Harlem, New York, USA	1 August 1981
Jijiga, Ethiopia	12 August 1981
Santo Domingo, Dominican Republic	20 October 1981
Las Matas de Farfan, Dominican Republic	20 October 1981
Jacmel, Haiti	4 November 1981
Queanbeyan, Australia	8 January 1982
Setubal, Portugal	11 February 1982
Tampico, Mexico	13 April 1982
Jenkins, USA	30 April 1982
Giteranyi, Burundi	23 May 1982
Florence, Italy	25 May 1982
Sabadell, Spain	18 June 1982
Dublin, Eire	18 June 1982
Brooklyn, New York, USA (Contemplative)	27 July 1982
Jima, Ethiopia	15 August 1982
Bonsucesso, Rio de Janeiro	1 September 1982
Borasal, Bangladesh	11 January 1983
Kowloon, Hongkong	17 January 1983
San Francisco, USA (Noviciate)	17 January 1983
Jeremie, Haiti	20 January 1983
Tennant Creek, Australia	25 January 1983
West Berlin, Germany	2 February 1983
Ngaroma, Rwanda	9 March 1983
Chicago, USA	19 March 1983
Livingston, Scotland	10 June 1983
Davao City, Philippines	10 June 1983
Calbayog, Philippines	10 June 1983
Darwin, Australia	10 June 1983
Tegucigalpa, Honduras	16 July 1983
Mahe-Victoria, Seychelles	16 July 1983
Little Rock, Arkansas, USA	16 July 1983
Bujumbura, Burundi	17 August 1983
Zaborow, Poland	4 November 1983
Milan, Italy	13 November 1983
Chemnitz, Germany	18 December 1983
Pereira, Colombia	15 April 1984
Jenkins, Kentucky, USA	30 April 1984
Santa Rosa de Copan, Honduras	1 July 1984

Winnipeg, Canada	22 August 1984
Tainan, Taiwan	28 August 1984
Colombo, Sri Lanka	8 September 1984
Norristown, Pennsylvania, USA	20 October 1984
Alamata, Ethiopia	27 November 1984
San Francisco, USA	16 December 1984
Chicago, Illinois, USA (Contemplative)	23 December 1984
Villahermosa, Tabasco, Mexico	19 January 1985
Sukutha Marmar, Kenya	1 February 1985
Bogota, Colombia	2 February 1985
Las Piedras, Uruguay	24 February 1985
Damascus, Syria	10 March 1985
Salvador Bahia, Malvinas, Brazil	25 March 1985
La Paz, Bolivia	10 April 1985
Khartoum, Sudan	1 May 1985
Vienna, Austria	10 June 1985
Colon, Panama	13 June 1985
Lahore, Pakistan	14 June 1985
Inchon, South Korea	14 June 1985
Glasgow, Scotland	15 June 1985
Paris, France	15 June 1985
Toronto, Canada	24 June 1985
Baton Rouge, Louisiana, USA	27 June 1985
Gift of Love, Singapore City, Singapore	30 June 1985
Mannheim, Germany	30 June 1985
St George's, Grenada	1 July 1985
Dagupan City, Philippines	11 July 1985
Mek'ele, Ethiopia	13 July 1985
Warsaw, Poland	15 July 1985
Kingston, Jamaica	20 July 1985
Taipei, Taiwan	10 August 1985
Cali valle, Colombia	29 August 1985
Cotonou, Benin, W. Africa	2 September 1985
Assiout, Egypt	9 September 1985
Manhatten, New York, USA	24 December 1985
Lisbon, Portugal	2 February 1986
Beccar, Buenos Aires, Argentina	11 February 1986
Tanguieta, Gouande, W. Africa	19 February 1986
Kulaura, Bangladesh	24 February 1986
Ponce, Puerto Rico	25 March 1986
Cagliari, Italy	6 June 1986
Chorzow, Katowice, Poland	6 June 1986
Lafayette, Louisiana, USA	16 July 1986
Athens, Greece	16 July 1986
Gallup, New Mexico, USA	1 August 1986

Tondo 2, Manila, Philippines	15 August 1986
St Paul, Alberta, Canada	22 August 1986
New Amsterdam, Guyana, S. America	28 August 1986
Washington DC, USA	8 September 1986
Espirito Santo, Vitoria, Brazil	10 September 1986
Nagoya, Japan	1 October 1986
Havana, Cuba	2 November 1986
El Obeid, Sudan	18 November 1986
Managua, Nicaragua	8 December 1986
Chichiltah, New Mexico, USA	24 December 1986
Naga City, Philippines	28 December 1986
Davao City 2, Philippines	4 January 1987
Cebu City 2, Philippines	5 January 1987
Olangapo City, Philippines	6 January 1987
Aleppo, Syria	11 February 1987
Orange, NSW, Australia	15 March 1987
Nablus, Israel	25 March 1987
Colombo 2, Sri Lanka	11 April 1987
Boston, USA	7 June 1987
Szezecin, Poland	10 June 1987
Dallas, USA	22 June 1987
Kibera, Kenya	2 July 1987
Kisantu, Zaire	9 July 1987
Kanyinya, Burundi	9 July 1987
Goba, Ethiopia	16 July 1987
Mongkok, Kowloon, Hong Kong	16 July 1987
Ljubljana, Slovenia	16 July 1987
Mukkattam, Cairo, Egypt	15 August 1987
San Jose, Costa Rica	22 August 1987
Hinche, Haiti	8 September 1987
Yaounde, Cameroon	29 September 1987
Freetown, Sierra Leone	7 October 1987
Adowa, Ethiopia	7 October 1987
Guayaquil, Ecuador	27 February 1988
Abidjan, Ivory Coast	27 February 1988
Antsirabe, Madagascar	19 March 1988
Ouesso, Congo	6 April 1988
Santa Cruz, Bolivia	12 April 1988
Kumasi, Ghana	18 May 1988
Vatican City, Europe	22 May 1988
Vancouver, Canada	29 May 1988
Amsterdam, Holland	31 May 1988
San Francisco, USA (AIDS)	2 June 1988
Bayamo, Cuba	6 June 1988
Onitsha, Nigeria	10 June 1988

Pec, Korsova	27 June 1988
Tijuana, Mexico (Contemplative)	1 July 1988
San Salvador, El Salvador	4 July 1988
Montreal, Canada	1 September 1988
Memphis, Tenessee, USA	7 September 1988
Pokhara, Nepal (Contemplative)	7 October 1988
Georgetown, Guyana	21 October 1988
Maputo, Mozambique	3 November 1988
Cape Town, South Africa	8 November 1988
Aklan, Philippines	19 November 1988
Kampala, Uganda	26 November 1988
Nampula, Mozambique	8 December 1988
Plainfield, New Jersey, USA (Contemplative)	12 December 1988
Moscow, USSR	22 December 1988
Spitak, Armenia	25 December 1988
Ruseifa, Jordan	28 December 1988
Phoenix, Arizona, USA	2 February 1989
Conakry, Guinea, W. Africa	6 February 1989
Bormia, Malta	11 February 1989
Faro, Portugal	11 February 1989
Mantanzas, Cuba	17 February 1989
Monrovia, Liberia	24 February 1989
Port of Spain, Trinidad	1 March 1989
Addis Ababa, Ethiopia (AIDS)	4 March 1989
Montevideo, Uruguay	7 March 1989
Quito, Ecuador	31 March 1989
Rosslyn, Pretoria, South Africa	16 April 1989
Lusaka, Zambia	1 May 1989
Tananarive, Madagascar	31 May 1989
Borodol, Bangladesh	2 June 1989
El Florido, Tijuana, Mexico	7 June 1989
Vera Cruz, Mexico	10 June 1989
Lynwood, Los Angeles, USA	12 June 1989
Erd, Budapest, Hungary	18 June 1989
Tangier, Morocco	23 June 1989
Tbilisi, Georgia	29 June 1989
Moscow, USSR	19 August 1989
El Cobre, West Indies	7 October 1989
Cuba (Contemplative)	7 October 1989
Wewak, Papua New Guinea	21 October 1989
Kandy, Sri Lanka	22 October 1989
Makeni, Sierra Leone	28 October 1989
Denver, USA	12 December 1989
St Petersburg, USSR	21 December 1989
Torre Bella Monaca, Rome, Italy	6 January 1990

Bujumbura, Burundi	20 January 1990
Brazzaville, Congo	1 February 1990
Morete, Uganda	2 February 1990
Karachi, Pakistan	11 February 1990
Marinella, Naples, Italy	26 February 1990
Novosibirsk, Siberia	23 March 1990
Brussels, Belgium	1 May 1990
Milcov, Bucharest, Romania	5 May 1990
Cadca, Slovakia	16 May 1990
Prague, Czechoslovakia	29 May 1990
Hamburg, Germany	1 June 1990
St Gheorghe, Romania	9 June 1990
Vanimo, Papua New Guinea	14 June 1990
Budapest, Hungary	24 June 1990
Bacau, Romania	29 June 1990
Asuncion, Paraguay	29 June 1990
Bonio, Khartoum, Sudan	1 July 1990
Curriacou, Grenada	11 August 1990
Gambella, Ethiopia	22 August 1990
Phnom Penh, Cambodia	26 November 1990
Catania, Sicily, Italy	2 January 1991
Tirana 1, Albania	4 March 1991
Tirana 2, Albania	7 March 1991
Kretinga, Lithuania	19 March 1991
Tijuana, Mexico	19 March 1991
Skhodra, Albania	6 April 1991
Forsa, Sweden (Contemplative)	7 April 1991
Chittagong, Bangladesh	15 May 1991
l'Aquila, Italy	28 May 1991
Baghdad, Iraq	13 June 1991
Chitila, Bucharest, Romania	17 June 1991
Lahore, Pakistan	21 June 1991
Dushanbe, Tadzhikistan, USSR	21 June 1991
Tomsk, Siberia, USSR	26 June 1991
St Thomas, Virgin Islands	27 June 1991
Barcelona City, Spain	29 June 1991
Durres, Albania	12 July 1991
Diglipur, Andamans	16 July 1991
Peoria, Illinois, USA	16 July 1991
Elbasan, Albania	18 July 1991
Ciego de Avila, Cuba	15 August 1991
Las Tunas, Cuba	15 August 1991
Tlalnelnepantla, Mexico	22 August 1991
Kiev, Ukraine	14 September 1991
Munich, Germany	7 October 1991

Mahaney City, Pennsylvania, USA (Contemplative)	12 December 1991
Los Angeles, California, USA (Contemplative)	23 December 1991
Bangui, Central Africa	1 January 1992
San Pedro Sula, Honduras	1 January 1992
Chester, Pennsylvania, USA	6 January 1992
Piombino, Livorno, Italy (Contemplative)	11 February 1992
San Diego, California, USA (Contemplative)	1 March 1992
Aden, Yemen Republic	19 March 1992
Korce, Albania	25 March 1992
Baltimore, Maryland, USA	19 April 1992
Lilongwe, Malawi	1 May 1992
Escuintla, Guatemala	14 June 1992
Zurich, Switzerland	26 June 1992
Usulatan, El Salvador	3 July 1992
Bacalod City, Philippines	6 July 1992
Puke, Albania	16 July 1992
Tripoli, Libya	19 July 1992
Beppu Oitanken, Japan	15 August 1992
Las Cayes, Haiti	15 August 1992
Brasilia, Brazil	22 August 1992
Tallinn, Estonia	28 August 1992
Sao Paulo, Brazil	19 September 1992
Edinburgh, Scotland	8 December 1992
Granada, Nicaragua	12 December 1992
New Bedford, Massachusetts, USA	19 December 1992
Bethlehem, Bratislava, Slovakia	21 December 1992
Birmingham, England	1 January 1993
Atlanta, Georgia, USA	10 January 1993
Kinshasa, Zaire	27 January 1993
Trincomalee, Sri Lanka	26 February 1993
Durban, South Africa	25 March 1993
Bologna, Italy	31 May 1993
Southwark, England	8 June 1993
Tema, Ghana	18 June 1993
Ketu Lagos, Nigeria	3 July 1993
Tashkent, Uzbekistan	6 July 1993
Gomel, Belarus	4 August 1993
Rawalpindi, Pakistan	25 August 1993
Rio de Janeiro, Brazil (AIDS)	8 September 1993
Harare, Zimbabwe	7 October 1993
Varna, Bulgaria	9 November 1993
Vilnius, Lithuania	1 January 1994
Madhu, Sri Lanka	6 February 1994
Banjul, Gambia	17 March 1994
Warsaw, Poland (AIDS)	19 March 1994

Ralunge, Tanzania	19 March 1994
Stockholm, Sweden	24 May 1994
Genova, Italy	8 June 1994
Tunis, Tunisia	24 June 1994
Der-Ez-Zor, Syria	25 July 1994
Buenos Aires, Argentina	5 August 1994
Riga, Latvia	24 September 1994
Dona di amore, Rome, Italy (AIDS)	16 October 1994
Blarney, Eire	3 November 1994
Gondar, Ethiopia	17 November 1994
Niamey, Niger	6 December 1994
Juli, Peru	1 January 1995
Dareton, NSW, Australia	7 January 1995
Dwellah, Syria	25 January 1995
Tacloban, Philippines	2 February 1995
Esperanza, Ecuador	5 February 1995
Hosororo, Guyana	2 March 1955
Sydney, NSW, Australia	19 April 1995
Charlotte, North Carolina, USA	13 June 1995
Washington DC, USA	19 June 1995
Cartagena, Colombia	15 August 1995
Acilia, Italy (Contemplative)	5 December 1995
Aguadilla, Puerto Rico	25 January 1996
Galle, Sri Lanka	2 February 1996
Awasa, Ethiopia	5 February 1996
Copenhagen, Denmark	22 February 1996
Pinar del Rio, Cuba	19 March 1996
Castries, Santa Lucia	19 March 1996
Santos, Brazil	19 March 1996
Kaolack, Senegal	25 March 1996
Armagh, N. Ireland	14 June 1996
Swansea, Wales	18 June 1996
Mar del Plata, Argentina	29 June 1996
Nicaragua (Contemplative)	6 July 1996
Crete	21 July 1996
Johannesburg, South Africa	22 August 1996
Reykjavik, Iceland	1 January 1997
Nairobi, Kenya (Contemplative)	27 April 1997

APPENDIX B

Nobel Peace Prize Lecture

As we have gathered here together to thank God for the Nobel Peace Prize, I think it will be beautiful that we pray the prayer of St Francis of Assisi which always surprises me very much. We pray this prayer every day after Holy Communion, because it is very fitting for each one of us. And I always wonder that 400–500 years ago when St Francis of Assisi composed this prayer, they had the same difficulties that we have today as we compose this prayer that fits very nicely for us also. I think some of you already have got it – so we will pray together:

Let us thank God for the opportunity that we all have together today, for this gift of peace that reminds us that we have been created to live that peace, and that Jesus became man to bring that good news to the poor. He, being God, became man in all things like us except in sin, and he proclaimed very clearly that he had come to give the good news.

The news was peace to all of good will and this is something that we all want – the peace of heart. And God loved the world so much that he gave his son – it was a giving; it is as much as if to say it hurt God to give, because he loved the world so much that he gave his son. He gave him to the Virgin Mary, and what did she do with him?

As soon as he came in her life, immediately she went in haste to give that good news, and as she came into the house of her cousin, the child – the unborn child – the child in the womb of Elizabeth, leapt with joy. He was, that little unborn child was, the first messenger of peace. He recognized the Prince of Peace, he recognized that Christ had come to bring the good news for you and for me. And as if that was not enough – it was not enough to become a man – he died on the cross to show that greater love, and he died for you and for me and for that leper and for that man dying of hunger and that naked person lying in the street not only of Calcutta, but of Africa, and New York, and London, and Oslo – and insisted that we love one another as he loves each one of us. And we read that in the Gospel very clearly: "love as I have loved you; as I love you; as the Father has loved me, I love you." And the harder the Father loved him, he gave him to us, and how much we love one another, we too must give to each other until it hurts.

It is not enough for us to say: "I love God, but I do not love my neighbour." St John says that you are a liar if you say you love God and you don't love your neighbour. How can you love God whom you do not see, if you do not love your neighbour whom you see, whom you touch, with whom you live? And so this is very important for us to realize that love, to be true, has to hurt.

It hurt Jesus to love us. It hurt him. And to make sure we remember his great love, he made himself the bread of life to satisfy our hunger for his love – our hunger for God – because we have been created for that love. We have been created in his image. We have been created to love and be loved, and he has become man to make it possible for us to love as he loved us. He makes himself the hungry one, the naked one, the homeless one, the sick one, the one in prison, the lonely one, the unwanted one, and he says: "You did it to me." He is hungry for our love, and this is the hunger of our poor people. This is the hunger that you and I must find. It may be in our own home.

I never forget an opportunity I had in visiting a home where they had all these old parents of sons and daughters who had just put them in an institution and forgotten, maybe. And I went there, and I saw in that home they had everything, beautiful things, but everybody was looking toward the door. And I did not see a single one with a smile on their face. And I turned to the sister and I asked: How is that? How is it that these people who have everything here, why are they all looking toward the door? Why are they not smiling?

I am so used to see the smiles on our people, even the dying ones smile. And she said: "This is nearly every day. They are expecting, they are hoping that a son or daughter will come to visit them. They are hurt because they are forgotten." And see – this is where love comes. That poverty comes right there in our own home, even neglect to love. Maybe in our own family we have somebody who is feeling lonely, who is feeling sick, who is feeling worried, and these are difficult days for everybody. Are we there? Are we there to receive them? Is the mother there to receive the child?

I was surprised in the West to see so many young boys and girls given into drugs. And I tried to find out why. Why is it like that? And the

answer was: "Because there is no one in the family to receive them."
Father and mother are so busy they have no time. Young parents are in
some institution and the child goes back to the street and gets involved in
something. We are talking of peace. These are things that break peace.

But I feel the greatest destroyer of peace today is abortion, because it is
a direct war, a direct killing, direct murder by the mother herself. And we
read in the scripture, for God says very clearly: "Even if a mother could
forget her child, I will not forget you. I have carved you in the palm of my
hand." We are carved in the palm of his hand; so close to him, that
unborn child has been carved in the hand of God. And that is what strikes
me most, the beginning of that sentence, that even if a mother *could*
forget, something impossible – but even if she could forget – I will not
forget you.

And today the greatest means, the greatest destroyer of peace is abortion. And we who are standing here – our parents wanted us. We would
not be here if our parents would do that to us.

Our children, we want them, we love them. But what of the other
millions. Many people are very, very concerned with the children of India,
with the children of Africa where quite a number die, maybe of malnutrition, of hunger and so on, but millions are dying deliberately by the will of
the mother. And this is what is the greatest destroyer of peace today.
Because if a mother can kill her own child, what is left for me to kill you
and you to kill me? There is nothing between.

And this I appeal in India, I appeal everywhere – "Let us bring the child
back" – and this year being the child's year: What have we done for the
child? At the beginning of the year I told, I spoke everywhere and I said:
Let us ensure this year that we make every single child born, and unborn,
wanted. And today is the end of the year. Have we really made the children wanted?

I will tell you something terrifying. We are fighting abortion by adoption. We have saved thousands of lives. We have sent word to all the clinics, to the hospitals, police stations: "Please don't destroy the child; we
will take the child." So every hour of the day and night there is always
somebody – we have quite a number of unwedded mothers – tell them:
"Come, we will take care of you, we will take the child from you, and we
will get a home for the child." And we have a tremendous demand for
families who have no children, that is the blessing of God for us. And also,
we are doing another thing which is very beautiful. We are teaching our

beggars, our leprosy patients, our slum dwellers, our people of the street, natural family planning.

And in Calcutta alone in six years – it is all in Calcutta – we have had 61,273 babies less from the families who would have had them because they practise this natural way of abstaining, of self-control, out of love for each other. We teach them the temperature method which is very beautiful, very simple. And our poor people understand. And you know what they have told me? "Our family is healthy, our family is united, and we can have a baby whenever we want." So clear – those people in the street, those beggars – and I think that if our people can do like that how much more you and all the others who can know the ways and means without destroying the life that God has created in us.

The poor people are very great people. They can teach us so many beautiful things. The other day one of them came to thank us and said: "You people who have evolved chastity, you are the best people to teach us family planning because it is nothing more than self-control out of love for each other." And I think they said a beautiful sentence. And these are people who maybe have nothing to eat, maybe they have not a home where to live, but they are great people.

The poor are very wonderful people. One evening we went out and we picked up four people from the street. And one of them was in a most terrible condition. And I told the Sisters: "You take care of the other three; I will take care of this one that looks worse." So I did for her all that my love can do. I put her in bed, and there was such a beautiful smile on her face. She took hold of my hand, as she said one word only: "thank you" – and she died.

I could not help but examine my conscience before her. And I asked: "What would I say if I was in her place?" And my answer was very simple. I would have tried to draw a little attention to myself. I would have said: "I am hungry, I am dying, I am cold, I am in pain", or something. But she gave me much more – she gave me her grateful love. And she died with a smile on her face – like that man who we picked up from the drain, half-eaten with worms, and we brought him to the home – "I have lived like an animal in the street, but I am going to die like an angel, loved and cared for." And it was so wonderful to see the greatness of that man who could speak like that, who could die like that without blaming anybody, without cursing anybody, without comparing anything. Like an angel – this is the greatness of our people.

And that is why we believe what Jesus has said: "I was hungry, I was naked, I was homeless; I was unwanted, unloved, uncared for – and you did it to me."

I believe that we are not really social workers. We may be doing social work in the eyes of the people. But we are really contemplatives in the heart of the world. For we are touching the body of Christ twenty-four hours. We have twenty-four hours in his presence, and so you and I. You too must try to bring that presence of God into your family, for the family that prays together stays together. And I think that we in our family, we don't need bombs and guns, to destroy or to bring peace – just get together, love one another, bring that peace, that joy, that strength of presence of each other in the home. And we will be able to overcome all the evil that is in the world. There is so much suffering, so much hatred, so much misery, and we with our prayer, with our sacrifice are beginning at home. Love begins at home, and it is not how much we do, but how much love we put in the action that we do. It is to God almighty – how much we do does not matter, because he is infinite, but how much love we put in that action. How much we do to him in the person that we are serving.

Some time ago in Calcutta we had great difficulty in getting sugar. And I don't know how the word got around to the children, and a little boy of four years old, a Hindu boy, went home and told his parents: "I will not eat sugar for three days. I will give my sugar to Mother Teresa for her children." After three days his father and mother brought him to our house. I had never met them before, and this little one could scarcely pronounce my name. But he knew exactly what he had come to do. He knew that he wanted to share his love.

And this is why I have received such a lot of love from all. From the time that I have come here I have simply been surrounded with love, and with real, real understanding love. It could feel as if everyone in India, everyone in Africa is somebody very special to you. And I felt quite at home, I was telling Sister today. I feel in the convent with the Sisters as if I am in Calcutta with my own Sisters. So completely at home here, right here.

And so here I am talking with you. I want you to find the poor here, right in your own home first. And begin love there. Be that good news to your own people. And find out about your next-door neighbour. Do you know who they are?

I had the most extraordinary experience with a Hindu family who had eight children. A gentleman came to our house and said: "Mother Teresa, there is a family with eight children; they have not eaten for so long; do something." So I took some rice and I went there immediately. And I saw the children – their eyes shining with hunger. I don't know if you have ever seen hunger. But I have seen it very often. And she took the rice, she divided the rice, and she went out. When she came back I asked her: "Where did you go, what did you do?" And she gave me a very simple answer: "They are hungry also." What struck me most was that she knew – and who are they? a Muslim family – and she knew. I didn't bring more rice that evening because I wanted them to enjoy the joy of sharing.

But there were those children, radiating joy, sharing the joy with their mother because she had the love to give. And you see this is where love begins – at home. And I want you – and I am very grateful for what I have received. It has been a tremendous experience and I go back to India – I will be back by next week, the 15th I hope, and I will be able to bring your love.

And I know well that you have not given from your abundance, but you have given until it has hurt you. Today the little children, they gave – I was so surprised – there is so much joy for the children that are hungry. That the children like themselves will need love and get so much from their parents.

So let us thank God that we have had this opportunity to come to know each other, and that this knowledge of each other has brought us very close. And we will be able to help the children of the whole world, because as you know our Sisters are all over the world. And with this prize that I have received as a prize of peace, I am going to try to make the home for many people that have no home. Because I believe that love begins at home, and if we can create a home for the poor, I think that more and more love will spread. And we will be able through this understanding love to bring peace, be the good news to the poor. The poor in our own family first, in our country and in the world.

To be able to do this, our Sisters, our lives have to be woven with prayer. They have to be woven with Christ to be able to understand, to be able to share. Today there is so much suffering and I feel that the passion of Christ is being relived all over again. Are we there to share that passion, to share that suffering of people – around the world, not only in the poor countries. But I found the poverty of the West so much more difficult to remove.

When I pick up a person from the street, hungry, I give him a plate of rice, a piece of bread, I have satisfied. I have removed that hunger. But a person that is shut out, that feels unwanted, unloved, terrified, the person that has been thrown out from society – that poverty is so hurtful and so much, and I find that very difficult. Our Sisters are working amongst that kind of people in the West.

So you must pray for us that we may be able to be that good news. We cannot do that without you. You have to do that here in your country. You must come to know the poor. Maybe our people here have material things, everything, but I think that if we all look into our own homes, how difficult we find it sometimes to smile at each other, and that the smile is the beginning of love.

And so let us always meet each other with a smile, for the smile is the beginning of love, and once we begin to love each other, naturally we want to do something. So you pray for our Sisters and for me and for our Brothers, and for our Co-Workers that are around the world. Pray that we may remain faithful to the gift of God, to love him and serve him in the poor together with you. What we have done we would not have been able to do if you did not share with your prayers, with your gifts, this continual giving. But I don't want you to give me from your abundance. I want that you give me until it hurts.

The other day I received $15 from a man who has been on his back for twenty years and the only part that he can move is his right hand. And the only companion that he enjoys is smoking. And he said to me: "I do not smoke for one week, and I send you this money." It must have been a terrible sacrifice for him but see how beautiful, how he shared. And with that money I brought bread and I gave to those who are hungry with a joy on both sides. He was giving and the poor were receiving.

This is something that you and I can do – it is a gift of God to us to be able to share our love with others. And let it be able to share our love with others. And let it be as it was for Jesus. Let us love one another as he loved us. Let us love him with undivided love. And the joy of loving him and each other – let us give now that Christmas is coming so close.

Let us keep that joy of loving Jesus in our hearts, and share that joy with all that we come in touch with. That radiating joy is real, for we have no reason not to be happy because we have Christ with us. Christ in our hearts, Christ in the poor that we meet, Christ in the smile that we give and the smile that we receive. Let us make that one point – that no child will be unwanted, and also that we meet each other always with a smile, especially when it is difficult to smile.

I never forget some time ago about fourteen professors came from the United States from different universities. And they came to Calcutta to our house. Then we were talking about the fact that they had been to the home for the dying. (We have a home for the dying in Calcutta, where we have picked up more than 36,000 people only from the streets of Calcutta, and out of that big number more than 18,000 have died a beautiful death. They have just gone home to God.) And they came to our house and we talked of love, of compassion. And then one of them asked me: "Say, Mother, please tell us something that we will remember." And I said to them: "Smile at each other, make time for each other in your family. Smile at each other."

And then another one asked me: "Are you married?" And I said: "Yes, and I find it sometimes very difficult to smile at Jesus because he can be very demanding sometimes." This is really something true. And there is where love comes – when it is demanding, and yet we can give it to him with joy.

Just as I have said today, I have said that if I don't go to heaven for anything else I will be going to heaven for all the publicity because it has purified me and sacrificed me and made me really ready to go to heaven.

I think that this is something, that we must live life beautifully, we have Jesus with us and he loves us. If we could only remember that God loves us, and we have an opportunity to love others as he loves us, not in big things, but in small things with great love, then Norway becomes a nest of love. And how beautiful it will be that from here a centre for peace from war has been given. That from here the joy of life of the unborn child comes out. If you become a burning light of peace in the world, then really the Nobel Peace Prize is a gift of the Norwegian people. God bless you!

10 December 1979

INDEX